DRIVEN

DRIVEN

A LIFE IN PUBLIC SERVICE AND JOURNALISM FROM LBJ TO CNN

TOM JOHNSON

The University of Georgia Press *Athens*

Published by the University of Georgia Press
Athens, Georgia 30602
www.ugapress.org

Designed by Erin Kirk
Set in Miller Text
Printed and bound by Sheridan Books
The paper in this book meets the guidelines for permanence and durability of the Committee on Production Guidelines for Book Longevity of the Council on Library Resources.

Most University of Georgia Press titles are available from popular e-book vendors.

Printed in the United States of America
29 28 27 26 25 C 5 4 3 2

EU Authorized Representative
Easy Access System Europe—Mustamäe tee 50,
10621 Tallinn, Estonia, gpsr.requests@easproject.com

Library of Congress Cataloging-in-Publication Data

Names: Johnson, W. Thomas, 1941– author
Title: Driven : a life in public service and journalism from LBJ to CNN / Tom Johnson.
Description: Athens : The University of Georgia Press, 2025. | Includes index.
Identifiers: LCCN 2025013286 | ISBN 9780820374536 hardback | ISBN 9780820374543 epub | ISBN 9780820374550 pdf
Subjects: LCSH: Johnson, W. Thomas, 1941– | Journalists—United States—Biography | Newspaper editors—United States—Biography | Cable News Network—Biography | Presidents—United States—Staff—Biography | LCGFT: Autobiographies
Classification: LCC PN4874.J623 A3 2025 | DDC 070.92—dc23/eng/20250507
LC record available at https://lccn.loc.gov/2025013286

CONTENTS

FOREWORD

Tom Johnson was already a major figure in American public life when I met him in the 1980s. Former close aide to President Lyndon B. Johnson, former publisher of the *Dallas Times Herald* and then of the *Los Angeles Times*, he was a larger-than-life personality who stood at the intersection of politics and the news media. I would see him in California at meetings of a Stanford University journalism board. I remember always wanting to be prepared for a friendly Tom grilling on my life and my work in Washington, first for NBC, then for PBS's *MacNeil/Lehrer NewsHour*.

We didn't get to know each other well until a dinner Katharine Graham hosted in honor of president-elect Bill Clinton in December 1992. Then the chairman of the Washington Post Company and the grande dame of journalism in the nation's capital, she made everyone feel lucky to be included in this event to welcome the next president to town. The meal over, I was starting to move to the next room, still making mental notes about what Clinton had said sitting a few seats away from me, when six-foot-two-inch-tall Tom Johnson suddenly appeared and asked if I'd ever consider leaving the *NewsHour*.

It was a surprise, even a shock, but I knew right away what to say: no, I loved my job as chief Washington correspondent and had no thought of going anywhere. That didn't deter him; he said he wanted to hire me to be a top anchor for CNN, which he had joined two years earlier. It was the start of an almost four-month-long conversation with Tom, who repeatedly and forcefully explained how this would give me an unparalleled opportunity to grow as a journalist, to be part of a serious, 24/7, global news organization. I agonized, because I did love the work I was doing. But eventually I agreed, we became fast friends, and to this day I am a big fan of Tom Johnson.

I share this as full disclosure: I was biased before picking up *Driven* and, having read it, am even more so. This is a compelling memoir by a central figure in American government and politics, then the news media, for more than four decades. To borrow from Lin-Manuel Miranda and *Hamilton*, Tom Johnson was "in the room where it happened." Many rooms.

From humble beginnings in Macon, Georgia, where his father sold watermelons and wood from the back of his truck and his mother clerked at a grocery store, Tom fell in love with journalism. He developed a fierce work ethic that catapulted him to Harvard Business School and a fellowship in the Lyndon Johnson White House. Overcoming insecurities, he would spend almost three and a half years there, first at the elbow of the president's top advisor, Bill Moyers, and then of the president himself, during that most consequential time in American history. These were years that saw the buildup of the hugely divisive war in Vietnam, Cold War tensions with the Soviet Union, and, here at home, Johnson's ambitious antipoverty and pro-civil-rights agenda and the shocking assassinations of Dr. Martin Luther King Jr. and Robert F. Kennedy. Tom Johnson was an eyewitness to history as Vietnam War escalation plans were discussed, something that he views in retrospect as a colossal mistake, which he blames largely on bad information and advice from generals and others who wanted LBJ to keep the war going.

Tom writes of the personal toll the war took on the president, his decision not to run for reelection, and a secretive move by Richard Nixon operatives in 1968 to get the South Vietnamese to delay peace talks until Nixon could take office. This may have cost Democratic presidential nominee Hubert Humphrey the election, but Humphrey himself refused to make it public beforehand because he thought "the country . . . cannot take another traumatic shock."

Loyalty to LBJ pulled Tom Johnson to Texas with the former president, leading him back to journalism, the Johnson family's television business, and an introduction to the West Coast newspaper mogul Otis Chandler, whom Tom describes, along with LBJ and Ted Turner, as one of the three great influencers on his life. Tom explains how he impressed Chandler with his own "incredible memory" and an ability to remember the names and connections of scores of people. After a stint as publisher of the *Dallas Times Herald*, owned by the Chandler family's Times Mirror Company, in 1977 Tom moved even farther west. At Chandler's urging, and in the heyday of American journalism, he set off for California, where he became publisher of the *Los Angeles Times*, the start of another adventure.

There he led a sprawling news empire, a stressful job that would take a toll later, and he became a witness to and participant in growing churn in the news industry, and the Chandler family empire itself. Eventually he was pushed out, but that made him available for an offer from the brash but brilliant Ted Turner to head his upstart cable news operation CNN with total editorial independence.

So began the next chapter of Tom Johnson's professional career: running the first 24/7 global television news organization from 1990 until 2001. At CNN he oversaw coverage of the Gulf War, saying "no" to calls from President George H. W. Bush and Secretary of Defense Colin Powell to pull Bernard Shaw and the rest of his news staff out of Baghdad because the United States was about to launch an attack and American journalists could not be protected.

All that meant Tom Johnson was at the center of even more unrest in the news industry as CNN was sold to one buyer, then another, and, with the advent of cable competition, became one of the first victims of Rupert Murdoch's conservative news channel, Fox, launched in 1996. Tom describes their slogan, "Fair and Balanced," as anything but.

Tom left CNN twenty-four years ago, but instead of engaging in anything resembling retirement, he's been active ever since as an advisor to media moguls, volunteering for the Mayo Clinic and the MD Anderson Cancer Center, continuing to mentor younger colleagues, and much more. He's a great storyteller and uses the last chapters of the book to not only share tales of Fidel Castro, Mikhail Gorbachev, Boris Yeltsin, and Lee Harvey Oswald but also to discuss his long battle with depression, which he has spoken about publicly for years in an effort to help others. He acknowledges there were times when he considered suicide, and credits his wife Edwina with being there, always, as a pillar of support and, literally, a life saver.

It is Edwina to whom he devotes the most personal gratitude, with repeated references to how he didn't spend enough time with their two children when they were growing up, that she is the one who did most of the parenting. The book title might have been tweaked to read, "Driven, with Edwina's Help."

Ever the journalist, Tom Johnson ends the book with 8 best practices for journalists, all of which I share, alongside 37 wise "life lessons." It's exhausting to think of following all 37, but they are a glimpse, as is this book, into the full and consequential life of this man who has seen a lot, who wants to share it with us, and who keeps on trying to make a difference. After reading his story, I'm prouder than ever to call him my friend and mentor.

JUDY WOODRUFF

ACKNOWLEDGMENTS

There are so many people in my life that made this book possible, especially incredible friends who soothed my anxieties and advised on countless versions. You are my dearest confidants, and you know who you are.

The first individual that I must acknowledge is my loving and inspiring wife, Edwina, to whom the last chapter of this book is dedicated. Thank you for your patience along this journey. You, along with our children and grandchildren, are everything to me, and this story belongs equally to you.

Next, I must thank my incredible assistant of more than thirty years, Ashley Van Buren. She and I first began working together when I was CEO of CNN in the 1990s, and she continues to support my work to this day, while managing a full-time job and her sincerely wonderful family. She is faithful, dedicated, and competent, managing everything, including my lifelong engagement with Washington, my philanthropic endeavors, and even the most granular elements of my personal life, such as work on this book. I cannot guess how many hours she has spent with me during its creation, organizing page after page of edits, attending meetings, and helping me to keep my head. Beyond her abilities, I cannot offer enough praise for the kindness she carries with her. Anyone who knows me understands the joy and progress that she brings to everything she does. If Ashley is a part of something, it will simply be better. She has my lasting gratitude and will forever be a member of the Johnson family.

Major thanks go to Sam Corden and Evelyn M. Duffy of Open Boat Editing.

When I first sat down to write a memoir, my dear friend and mentor from our days in the LBJ White House, Bill Moyers, told me, "You better get yourself a good editor." As I searched for a good fit, legendary reporter Bob Woodward told me that I would find that excellence in his former assistant, Evelyn, and her right hand, Sam. He was right.

Together, they took the time to understand not just my story but who I am as a person. Through interviewing me, editing, organizing, and assisting with crafting new material, they have helped make my book feel like the tumultuous decades in American history that exist within it: honest and meaningful, fueled with history and momentum—but not without bumps along the way.

For more than three years, Sam has proven himself to be one of those rare young people who possesses what I call "uncommon promise," and I would recommend him to anyone. Through countless visits to our home in Atlanta, Sam has become a confidant and persevered through every high and low of this book with great professionalism, empathy, and loyalty—all the while keeping a sense of humor. His knowledge of history and politics is deep; he understands the power of photographs; and he has tremendous capacities as an interviewer and writer.

Last but far from least, I must thank Parrish McCall. Parrish and I have known one another for many years as neighbors and fellow humans who struggle with depression. He has been the technology brains behind the process and knows my file archive like the back of his hand. I would not have been able to include so many key details without him and his dedication to this project from the beginning.

Thanks to those who worked to make the book a reality once the manuscript was complete, including the entire staff at the University of Georgia Press, but especially Lisa Bayer, director and acquisitions editor; Melissa Buchanan, production coordinator; Jon Davies, project editor; Erin Kirk, designer and compositor; Candice Lawrence, publicist; and Rebecca Norton, ebook production coordinator. Thanks also to Ann Marlowe, copyeditor; to Catherine B. Krusberg, proofreader; Vickie Jacobs, indexer; and to Robin Sproul and the Javelin staff.

Special acknowledgment goes to those who have read the full *Driven* manuscript or who have fact-checked chapters where he or she has extensive experience:

Lou Boccardi, former CEO of the Associated Press
Gail Evans, former executive vice president of CNN
Jonathan Bailey, a nationally recognized prepublication plagiarism analyst
Bill Moyers, former press secretary to President Lyndon Johnson
Louann and Larry Temple, former special counsel to President Johnson
Neva and Don Rountree, my college roommate at the University of Georgia
Don Graham, former publisher, *Washington Post*
George Cotliar, former managing editor, *Los Angeles Times*
Shelby Coffey III, former editor, *Los Angeles Times*
Jane and Ron Olson. Jane: author and journalist; Ron: partner, Munger Tolles and Olson law firm
Beth and Wayne Gibbens, friends of sixty years who advised me on content of *Driven*
Cindy and Bill Fowler, friends of thirty-five years who advised me on content of *Driven*
Ervin Duggan, former assistant to President Lyndon Johnson
Eason Jordan, former chief news executive, CNN
Max Holland, author and expert on the Kennedy assassination
Dick Schlosberg, former publisher, *Los Angeles Times* and *Denver Post*
Jennifer Cuddeback, archivist, LBJ Presidential Library
Claudia Anderson, former archivist, LBJ Presidential Library
Landon Parvin, former presidential speechwriter
Harold Pachios, former White House assistant
Earl Casey, former managing editor, CNN
Carolyn Shields, former White House assistant
Connie Gerrard, former White House assistant

And more than seventy others who know who they are.

AUTHOR'S NOTE

There are lifetime goals that many of us establish for ourselves, some of which are more realistic than others. From the time I was young, my goal was to become a success. This book, while a story about some of the most historically important figures of the twentieth century, is equally a story about a boy from Georgia, his nearly fanatical drive to "make it," the good he did, and the price he paid to do it.

My mother Josie repeatedly told me: "Tommy, if you will work hard and do right, you can become anything you hope to become in life." Over the last sixty years I've progressed from a junior high school reporter for the *Macon Telegraph*, to a twenty-three-year-old White House Fellow in the Lyndon Johnson administration, to publisher of the *Dallas Times Herald* and the *Los Angeles Times*, to leader of a twenty-four-hour news network with Ted Turner at CNN. In many ways, that path accomplished my goal of becoming a success. I sure have worked hard.

My story begins in 1941 in Macon, Georgia. As a young boy helping my father sell watermelons and wood from the back of his red International pickup truck, I could never have imagined all of the dramatic changes that lay ahead, much less that I would find myself an active participant in many of them, both in media and in government.

It was journalism that first ignited my passion. As a high school intern for the *Macon Telegraph*, I was taught the importance of accuracy—"getting it right." The publisher of the *Macon Telegraph*, Peyton Anderson, became my first mentor, financing my studies at the University of Georgia Grady College of Journalism and then my MBA at Harvard Business School. Without Peyton, it is unimaginable that I would have been chosen in 1965 for the first class of White House Fellows, where I witnessed the awesome leadership that LBJ exercised to improve life in America—especially for civil rights and social justice. Sadly, that same power also resulted in the deaths of thousands of U.S. troops and millions of Vietnamese.

After the White House years, my career advanced through executive positions with LBJ family businesses in Austin, followed by roles as editor and publisher of the *Dallas Times Herald*. At that point Otis Chandler became an enormous influence in my life, overseeing my rise within the Times Mirror Company of Los Angeles. In 1980 Otis chose me as the first non-Chandler family member to become publisher and CEO of the *Los Angeles Times*, the largest division of Times Mirror.

In 1990 Ted Turner recruited me to become CEO of CNN Worldwide. Much like LBJ and Otis Chandler, Ted Turner was an outsized inspiration—a true genius. All three men passionately wanted to excel, to win, and to make the world a better place. Working with these three, I saw their accomplishments and their faults, as well as my own.

While I remain immensely proud of the exemplary journalism that often is recognized by Pulitzers and Peabody Awards, it is painful now to witness the reprehensible levels of misinformation and outright lies that are distributed both online and through cable channels. Even though Rupert Murdoch has made the *Wall Street Journal* a broader, deeper, and far better newspaper, he should be ashamed of what he and the late Roger Ailes did at Fox News to lower standards of modern journalism. However, we should never forget that William Randolph Hearst and the early generation of Chandlers also used their media power for raw political purposes.

Our national politics are guided today as much by lies as they are by truth. So many of our leaders—especially Donald Trump—and many of our institutions, including the United States Congress, are failing us. Political partisanship and growing inequality have divided us in unprecedented ways.

It wasn't until my wife Edwina, the most positive influence of my life, encouraged me to write my story for our grandchildren that I began to prepare this memoir. However, telling interesting stories—many never told before—was not a sufficient reason alone for me to undertake writing this book.

While my experiences in media and in government may add something of historical value to researchers and archivists, I hope that my sharing the story of my painful journey with chronic depression will help others deal with this mysterious illness. DEPRESSION IS A TREATABLE ILLNESS. Those suffering from it need to know there are medications and other treatments today that work. I devote a chapter of this book to that topic.

To be clear, I do not knowingly disclose any still-classified national security secrets that were shared with me while I held high-level government clearances. However, I do provide new revelations, especially about the war in Vietnam. So many matters of my time in the LBJ administration could not have been so accurately described without the support of Claudia Anderson, the archivist at the LBJ Library in Austin for more than forty years, as well as her successor, Jennifer Cuddeback. They have my lasting gratitude.

Additionally, I remain loyal to my friends and would never intentionally hurt them because of anything I write. Even after the deaths of President Johnson, Otis Chandler, and other people with whom I've worked, I will not knowingly betray their trust in me.

On the issue of plagiarism and historical accuracy, I have done my very best to bring the expertise of other historical voices, but only in the most proper of ways. This has been such a "must" for me that I was not satisfied until one of the nation's most esteemed independent plagiarism experts, Jonathan Bailey, signed off on the book. With that said, the burden for getting it right falls entirely on me.

While I've done my best to be honest and accurate, the book is not perfect—just like the rest of my life.

I hope you will enjoy reading it more than I have enjoyed writing it. This was hard work!

DRIVEN

CHAPTER 1

THE EARLY YEARS

Macon, Georgia, a town I still call home

My story began in Macon, Georgia, and it may very well end there. I have asked that my ashes be scattered by my son on a small tract of Macon land where I lived as a child.

I was born September 30, 1941, in Macon Hospital after my mother, Josie, had experienced several miscarriages. She was thirty-four and had been married to my father, Wyatt, for eighteen years. I am an only child. Family members have said that my birth was the happiest, most exciting moment in my mother's life. She so wanted a child. She absolutely adored me. She thought I could do no wrong. My aunt Sarah Foy told me my mother did not allow young "Tommy" even to crawl on the floor or in the yard for fear that germs might make me sick. Josie was a worrier.

Josephine Victoria Van Valkenberg Brown Johnson was the daughter of John F. Brown, a farmer from Lizella, Georgia. John did not provide funds for Josie to attend college, even though he had the money to do so. Instead, after graduating from high school at age sixteen, she married my dad, Wyatt Thomas Johnson Sr., who was twenty-three. Later her father did give her money to buy a small two-bedroom house on Columbus Road in Macon. For purely sentimental reasons, I still own that home and property.

My dad had only a third-grade education. He never was employed full-time for most of my life. In my opinion, that was more his personal choice than an inability to keep a job, poor health notwithstanding.

Old photos show that Wyatt Sr. was handsome, a dashing dresser in his early years, with a beautiful collection of ties. He was a free spirit who simply loved life and loved people.

During the summer months my dad would purchase watermelons at the local farmers market for ten cents each and sell them in the Black section of town called Unionville for twenty-five cents, or five for a dollar. Occasionally I'd ride along with two young Black men in the back of Dad's red International pickup truck, helping to deliver melons. Often he would pay me with a silver dollar, many of which I've kept all my life.

In the winter Dad would buy the rejects from a local wood factory that produced handles for brooms, shovels, and axes. In our backyard he'd cut those handles into twelve-inch pieces of wood that would fit into a #2 galvanized steel tub and sell the wood just as he would the melons—one tub for twenty-five cents, or five tubs for a dollar. Wood at that time was still used in many homes in fireplaces and in woodburning stoves. People cooked everything on those stoves—food, coffee, you name it.

Dad made close friends with his customers and was also popular with the farmers at the Macon Farmers Market, where he'd spend many late nights drinking black Maxwell House coffee and smoking Lucky Strike cigarettes. As far as I know, Dad was not an alcoholic or philanderer. But he was a big flirt. He would pick up and deliver laundry from the local Macon brothel on his route. I was told, "The girls loved your dad."

Growing up, I thought that he was the most irresponsible person I had ever known. But I also admired his fairness. If anybody's watermelon was too ripe, or not ripe enough, he would replace it immediately at no cost. His lesson of keeping the customer happy remained with me throughout my career. I regret not having established a better relationship with him. I do know that he was quite proud of me and would have been proud of my accomplishments that he did not live to see.

By comparison, Josie was the hard worker. Along with being a beautiful woman, my mother was very serious and a worrier. I always told her, "Mother, I'm glad you worry so much; because of that I sure

Tom's dad, Wyatt Sr., holding Sparky the family dog, with Edwina and Tom.

don't need to." Later in life, however, I also became a worrier, especially after chronic depression hit me in my mid-forties.

I didn't see my mother and father together very often. My mother was always working. They slept in separate bedrooms, likely due to my father's often coming home late and drinking coffee and smoking well into the night. My mother was not a smoker. I slept in a separate bed in the same room with my mother until I was a teenager.

Although I was embarrassed by my dad, my mother *never* criticized him. I couldn't believe that she carried so much of the load but never complained. More than anything, she worried about Dad and his health, especially in his later years when he grew very thin.

My childhood home was not an unhappy one. My parents were just very different people. My mother embodied hard work, and my father was a happy-go-lucky, very likeable guy.

I regret once saying that our family grew up "on the wrong side of the tracks." What I meant to say was that we were part of a hardworking blue-collar class, rather than living among doctors and lawyers in the upper-class section of Macon.

My mother worked six days a week as a clerk in a small Macon grocery store owned by Sarah and Henry Foy Sr., an aunt and uncle from my dad's side of the family. Foy's Grocery, then at the intersection of Columbus Road and Log Cabin Drive, was the center of much of my life during my elementary and high school years. When I wasn't working with Dad, I often worked afternoons and weekends sacking groceries and pumping gas at Foy's Grocery. One of my duties was as a stock boy, refilling the shelves, always making sure that the labels were clearly visible. I also learned to make change in a vintage cash register where I can't recall ever seeing a bill larger than a twenty.

Foy's Grocery had a small meat department where Uncle Henry served as the butcher. He bought very high-quality beef and pork. Many people drove several miles just to purchase those excellent cuts. The store had an aroma of fresh vegetables that had been purchased at the farmers market. Sales of cigarettes were brisk.

Uncle Henry Foy had been a World War I army medic. In his eighties he still had his battlefield medical kit. He was as fine a man as I've ever known. He was kind and thoughtful and often did not even collect for groceries bought by customers who were too poor to pay.

The store was somewhat of a family compound, where I saw my cousins often. Bobby Foy and I frequently built play forts behind the store near a drainage ditch that was filled with red wiggler worms we used for fishing. When called on, all of us worked in the store, especially when one of us was ill or had to look after other family responsibilities. Although large chain grocery stores were built later in the area, few customers would shop for their food anywhere but Foy's, especially for fresh meats and vegetables at moderate prices. Customers were more like good friends.

The store had two Sinclair gasoline pumps—one regular and one ethyl. Many customers asked me to fill their tanks, check their radiators' water levels, and check their tire pressures. I even learned how to repair rubber inner tubes on flat tires.

On one occasion an overheated radiator cap exploded on me. I was scalded badly and hospitalized. I'll never forget the alarmed look on the face of my then girlfriend Jann Bass when she saw me in the Macon Hospital emergency room. Thankfully, I made a full recovery. Never again have I opened an overheated radiator.

As with most places in the South at that time, Macon had two different worlds—Black and white. Those worlds were difficult to bridge even if you tried. It was a segregated community, both by race and by sex. There were separate high schools for white boys (Lanier) and white girls (Miller) and a different school (Ballard-Hudson) for Black students. Our sports teams were segregated the same way. Had our schools been fully integrated, the legendary Black musician Otis Redding would have been a classmate of mine.

While there were racists among us, there were enlightened, open-minded students as well. I once told our son, Wyatt, about the segregation policies of that time. He suggested to me that we plan a fiftieth reunion of the Macon Black and white classes. With a committee led by the class presidents of the three schools—Lanier Senior High, Miller Senior High, and Ballard-Hudson—we planned our first reunion in 2009. It was a big hit. More than two hundred classmates, at least half of whom were Black, attended. I received only one seriously racist letter from a classmate for being a "n—— lover." I can still remember how sad it made me that someone could have so much hate in his heart.

Fortunately, racism was not something that the people closest to me ever taught, or believed in. At some point in my youth, I learned that one of my uncles likely had been in the Ku Klux Klan. However, I never felt racism from any of my family, nor do I remember either of my parents ever being racist. Foy's Grocery reflected my family's views on race. The store was near where many Black residents of Macon lived, and they were all welcomed openly.

Beyond the two young Black men who worked with my dad on his wood and melon routes, my first really close friend in the Black community was Cora Robinson. Cora was the cook and housekeeper at the Foys' home next to the grocery store. While my mother was working, Cora would look after me. Despite their work ethics, neither my mother nor Cora ever made much money, but it didn't deter them from living each day as good, hardworking people. Over many years, Cora became almost as close to me as my own mother. She had one daughter, who lived in Ohio. Later in life, I never returned to Macon without going by Cora's house to check on her and make sure she had everything she needed.

In my younger years I spent a great deal of time with the Foys. My mother and father did too. My older cousins, Henry and Bob Foy, were almost like brothers to me. They taught me how to build and fly model airplanes, play baseball, and serve as an unpaid caddy for them on the golf course. The caddy role was one that I disliked, and possibly the reason for my never taking up golf.

On occasion, my mother and I would take a trip. Once we took a train—the Nancy Hanks—from Macon to Atlanta just so I could ride the newly installed escalators in Rich's, an Atlanta department store. "Moving stairs" they were called at that time. I must have ridden up and down those stairs twenty-five times in a single day.

During my grade school and high school years, I had several friends with whom I hunted, fished, and played. My closest friends, Jimmy and Karen Kennedy, Steve Doolittle, Ed Herren, and Billy Hartley, all lived within a half mile of my home. I drank my first Budweiser as a teenager with Jimmy Kennedy. I smoked one "rabbit tobacco" hand-rolled cigarette with Steve Doolittle. It was so terrible that I almost gagged on it.

Billy and Bobby Foy and their sister, Nancy Foy Batson, all the children of my older cousin Bob, were not only relatives but close friends. So were Steve and Donna Foy and Helen Marion Brown Scott.

Bobby and I often hunted and fished together. He was better at both. My prize fishing lure was a Cotton Cordell Silver Fin with which I caught many largemouth bass in neighborhood lakes. We also "shocked" a nearby river with a battery-powered army surplus unit that drove catfish crazily to the surface, where we netted dozens of them. I later learned that we were violating both state and federal fish and game laws with this electrical shock method of fishing. As they say, it was a different time.

Steve Doolittle, the son of a local Chrysler-Plymouth auto salesman, was my very best childhood friend. He and I played many sports together. He was a much stronger athlete and better than I was at every sport.

Once, as a means of getting Steve to come along to the Ebenezer Methodist Church Youth Fellowship meetings on Wednesday nights, I enlisted the help of Sandra Reeves—a cute girl in whom I had my own romantic interest. Sandra was a wonderful pianist and church organist, and Steve absolutely flipped out over her. As a result, I lost the best playmate I ever had. Steve eventually persuaded Sandra to marry him.

Unfortunately, Steve died in 2002, cutting short an incredibly close lifetime friendship. I still think of him every time I look at the scar on my forehead, which Steve inflicted with a toy cap pistol when we were about six years old. He always said that blow, which he called a "brain readjustment," was the key to my later success in life.

It was at Ebenezer Methodist Church—the place where I introduced Steve to Sandra—that my mother and I would spend our Sunday mornings. A young minister at that church, Ralph Porterfield, had a very positive influence on my early years. He made religion interesting for me, and made me realize the importance of becoming active personally in causes that mattered.

Ralph was perhaps the first genuinely liberal minister I knew, and his messages inspired me to do more than attend church services, understanding that regular church attendance does not necessarily mean that you must adhere strictly to the Ten Commandments. I felt terrible when the leaders of Ebenezer asked Ralph to leave the church after he had been seen having a cocktail in the bar of the local country club. My own uncle Henry Foy was one of the straitlaced church leaders who demanded Ralph's expulsion for that very minor infraction. To me, it was not fair.

In 1955, when I was in the ninth grade at Lanier Junior High School—an all-boys, all-white public school—it became clear to me that I needed a job. I wanted to help my mother with expenses. I also wanted to buy a car.

At the start of the ninth grade, my English teacher, Ed Cagle, asked if I would like to apply for a paying position as "sports stringer" at the *Macon Telegraph*. In the 1950s, Georgia labor laws permitted students under age sixteen to work at newspapers and in grocery stores. I had sacked enough groceries and stocked enough shelves at Foy's Grocery to know that I did not want to make a career of that line of work. The *Telegraph* offer sounded good.

Later I learned that the first two students to whom Mr. Cagle had recommended applying for the position had decided they would rather play sports than report on them, which made me the third choice. I didn't care. I was thrilled to be offered the job. It required that I attend Lanier High School football, basketball, baseball, and track events and then call in by landline phone or bring the results to the Macon newspaper that evening for publication the following day. Right from the start, I began to appreciate just how much I enjoyed journalism.

The *Macon Telegraph* was probably one of the most outstanding small papers around the country at that time. It had a publisher and editors who believed in good journalism—who did not give in to public officials or cave to the owners of local businesses. I was fortunate that it was not one of the many segregationist papers around the South in the 1950s. Rather, the *Macon Telegraph* was exceptionally enlightened and published truthful information for the community.

An example of its commitment to fairness was the way we covered DUIs, guided by a policy requiring that we print the name of anyone arrested for drunk driving. One afternoon, a reporter picked up the list of DUIs from the night before and the name of Katherine Anderson, the wife of our publisher, Peyton Anderson, was on the list. Peyton insisted that we print her name along with all the others. Such was the ethical quality of that paper.

Even though they were older, the *Macon Telegraph* reporters and editors showed a significant interest in me, sparking a lifetime love affair with journalism. I liked the staff, and they liked me. They were my mentors, my coaches, and my inspirations.

Sam Glassman, the cranky sports editor, taught me how to keep the official scorebooks and to write brief stories about the games. Sam was the dean of southern sportswriters at the time. His manner was gruff and straightforward. He admired hard workers and took a special liking to my work ethic.

Sam also taught me the hunt-and-peck method of typing. It was a primitive way of banging out a story by using three fingers on my right hand and two fingers on my left. I'm using that same typing technique to write this book more than sixty-five years later.

I was on the sports staff when Sam died. A new editor named Harley Bowers replaced him. Bowers would go on to select Lee "Mose" Walburn as his full-time assistant sports editor, but for a short time I became his top assistant.

For a few of the games that I covered, specifically for our Triple-A baseball team, the Macon Peaches, I was also the official scorekeeper. Glassman and Bowers accompanied me to several games, edited my copy closely, and introduced me to coaches and players. During the summers, I also was the official scorekeeper for the Macon Little League.

By the twelfth grade at Lanier High, I had developed a blazing fire inside of me to "make it"—to become successful. First, I wanted to better provide for my mother. Second, as an insecure child, I wanted to build a name for myself. And finally, because I saw how well people on the other side of town in Macon lived, I knew that one day I wanted to live that way too. I wasn't searching for fame or fortune. I only recall wanting to be able to afford a nice house and earn a good salary, enough to support a family.

I've had several people tell me, "Tom, you were so mature while you were still so young." They were right. I reached a level of maturity, especially in what would become my profession, at a young age. I can't explain it, but, like my mother, I was a serious person.

Perhaps the biggest turning point in my young life—the "wow" moment—was when I saw my first byline in the sports section of the Macon paper. It was a story about the Lanier High football team, and beneath the headline at the top it read, "By Tommy Johnson." The editors didn't give out bylines easily—you had to earn it with a really good story—so that was heady stuff for a fifteen-year-old.

As I look back, I still find it extraordinary that my mother, after working a full eight to ten hours at Foy's Grocery, would drive five miles to pick me up at the *Macon Telegraph*, sometimes as late as 11 p.m. I couldn't have done it without her. I am also indebted to my mother's half sister Annie Ruth Brown for driving me each day to Alexander II elementary school and for her strong interest in my getting a good education, as she had, at the University of Georgia.

While I loved newspaper work, the pay was modest. I received $7.50 for every game I covered, as well as fifteen cents for every column inch that the article ran in type. It wasn't much, but I managed to save enough to buy my first car, a Ford convertible, for six hundred dollars when I turned sixteen.

That time in my life was full of learning experiences, and not just at the newspaper. Buying that car taught me something else entirely: Don't trust every used car dealer. The Macon dealer had applied putty to temporarily cover rusted-out holes in the side of the car. Three months later the putty began falling out, and the dealer would not repair the car or take it back. It was my first time really getting screwed. After that, I watched more closely anytime I made a major purchase. I still do.

After several months of my reporting on Macon high school sports, people started complimenting me. I also was receiving praise from my family. Almost overnight, because of that job, I was indeed becoming somebody. It was an important time when I began to grow more confident and shed some, though not all, of my insecurities.

My relationship with the staff of the *Macon Telegraph* newsroom continued to grow, and they all took me under their wings. I found a love for writing news in addition to sports. I even learned to operate a boxlike Rolleiflex camera that I would take to different news events, including a breaking-news event when a small plane crashed near Macon.

Admittedly, I had trouble with that camera. A terrible time, in fact. It was too large and too complicated. The photos I took were often of poor quality. The shot that I took of the air crash was barely publishable. But the photo of the crash and the story both ran on the front page with credit to me. That was another high.

From then on, I have been addicted to journalism and to newspeople. They are interesting, unconventional, curious, smart, great storytellers, and at times very funny. I learned lessons from them that have stuck with me for my entire life. Most important was learning to be accurate, to always get the facts right. I have tried to do that in writing this book.

Learning to write brief stories during those early years was crucial for every part of my life that came after, from the White House to the fast-paced newsrooms in the world.

Most important of all, however, was that I had discovered my lifetime passion. More than sixty-five years later, I still love journalism, even though it has changed dramatically.

Developing alongside my love of journalism was my interest in public service. For three years, during the tenth, eleventh, and twelfth grades at Lanier High School for Boys, Army ROTC was mandatory. We wore uniforms, we had noncommissioned officers from the U.S. Army teaching us various skills, and we spent time at the rifle ranges with the weapons we would use. I rose to the rank of cadet captain in the twelfth grade (Jr ROTC) and to lieutenant colonel in my senior year at UGA (Sr ROTC).

My mother would press my ROTC uniform each night, and I would spit-shine my shoes. I often won best-dressed cadet in inspections.

I've tried to describe it to various people, but there seemed to be a stronger sense of commitment to military service in the South. Perhaps it was just one part of southern culture, but I was very much affected by that.

That same commitment to things greater than myself would define the next decade of my life, beginning with ROTC at the University of Georgia, then Harvard, and ultimately the White House.

Tom in front of the Macon Telegraph Building.

CHAPTER 2

THE COLLEGE YEARS

Georgia Bulldogs, more journalism, and love at first sight

During my senior year of high school, the managing editor of the paper, Jim Chapman, told me that Peyton Anderson, the owner of the *Macon Telegraph*, wanted to see me in his office. I had never met him, so I was somewhat apprehensive, but Anderson had a genuine warmth about him that I've never forgotten. I noticed that he wore a small diamond angel on the right shoulder of his coat. I also saw several small Buddhas in his office. I learned that he collected them and gave them away as presents.

"Tommy," he said, "almost everybody in the newsroom has told me about you, especially how hard you work. What are your plans for college?"

I told him I hoped to get a journalism degree, but I wasn't sure I could. I knew that one of the editors, Bill Ott, had attended UGA and had graduated Phi Beta Kappa from the Grady College of Journalism. I never mentioned that I did not have the money for college. But I suspect Anderson already knew that.

He said that his editors—Bill Ott, Jim Chapman, Harley Bowers, and Joe Parham—all felt that I should attend the University of Georgia to study journalism. Anderson concluded our meeting by telling me: "If you can get accepted to Georgia, I will pay your way."

There was one condition: that I continue to work full-time during summers and part-time on weekends. That would mean driving back to Macon from the UGA campus in Athens, Georgia, on Friday afternoon and then driving back to Athens on Sunday night—a round trip of about 180 miles in those days, before the four-lane highways that exist today.

I returned to my newsroom desk as exhilarated as I ever can recall. Peyton Anderson's financial aid wasn't only generous beyond imagination; it was a way for me to pursue my passion.

Anderson established a scholarship that paid for my tuition and books. I did not ask for reimbursement for the gas that it took for me to drive between Athens and Macon each weekend. However, I was paid competitive hourly rates for weekend work hours.

After graduating in 1959 from high school as an ROTC cadet captain, and having led Lanier's honor company, I decided to continue my commitment to ROTC at UGA as well.

While attending UGA, when most of my Sigma Nu fraternity friends were enjoying parties on the weekends, I happily made the trip home and back. I never felt any disappointment about missing what was taking place on campus; I simply had fallen in love with journalism.

My reporting and editing in Macon complemented very much what I was doing in class with my teachers and other students, particularly my roommate at UGA, Don Rountree. Don's family owned a newspaper in the small town of Dawson, Georgia, and he stayed with me at my home in Macon to work for two summers on the *Macon Telegraph*.

Don and I also were writing for the *Red and Black*, the UGA student newspaper. I wrote some of the best investigative pieces of my career there—all while simultaneously writing stories for the *Macon Telegraph*. One series reported on conditions in the campus married housing units, where there was a significant infestation of rodents. Another series focused on the potholes around the student housing areas, which were being neglected by the university while roads around the faculty areas were well maintained.

I also wrote many articles for the *Red and Black* and the *Macon Telegraph* about the desegregation of the university. In particular I remember Charlayne Hunter and Hamilton Holmes during their

Among press covering the desegregation of the University of Georgia, Tom as a young reporter for the *Red and Black* and the *Macon Telegraph* standing third from left in a black coat, while Charlayne Hunter stands third from right. Courtesy of the *Atlanta Journal-Constitution*.

Charlayne Hunter and Tom sitting for an interview for the *Red and Black*. Printed with permission from the *Red & Black*, an independent student media organization based in Athens, Georgia.

traumatic early days as the first Black students admitted to UGA in 1961. Standing amid the crowd on their first day of attendance, I heard some students shout, "N——, go home." I even saw one student try to spit on Charlayne. He missed, and ended up hitting a reporter's jacket. Later I was in front of Myers Hall when a student hurled a brick at Charlayne's dorm room window. Thankfully, it too missed.

Charlayne eventually came to work at the *Red and Black*. It saddened me that a few of the newspaper staff made her feel unwelcome. However, several staff members befriended her, especially Marcia Powell, and lifetime friendships developed.

Through it all, Charlayne showed uncommon courage, dignity, and composure. She walked quietly through the campus, excelled academically, and was a heroic pioneer in the civil rights movement. Later she became an outstanding journalist with media organizations such as the *New York Times*, PBS, and CNN.

Clippings from the *Red and Black* with a photo of Charlayne from a January 1961 issue. Printed with permission from the *Red & Black*, an independent student media organization based in Athens, Georgia.

She and I have remained friends throughout our lives.

Courageous, independent journalists like Charlayne are needed today as never before.

As I reflect on that time, and the lessons that experiences like Charlayne's taught me, there is no question that the stories I wrote at the *Red and Black*, and with Reg Murphy for the *Macon Telegraph* on the desegregation of Atlanta public schools, were the most important of my time in college.

While I loved my time at UGA, I suffered a badly broken heart when my girlfriend since the ninth grade, Jann Bass of Macon, told me in our freshman year at the UGA library that she wanted us to get married "now." I said I could not. I told her that I always thought we would marry after our graduation from UGA, but at that time I just didn't have the money to support a family.

She gave me an ultimatum. "Tommy, I want us to get married now. If you are not ready to get married, I want to date others." That news was a gigantic hurt. Still, as much as I loved Jann, she and I argued too often, particularly about her not wanting to complete college.

Jann dropped out of UGA, returned to Macon, began to date, and in a few months she married Wayne Busby, also of Macon. They had two children and lived happily until, sadly, Jann died at age fifty of colon cancer.

As for me, I found greater happiness with another UGA student—Edwina Chastain of Athens, Georgia.

When I saw Edwina walk into a UGA economics classroom, I was smitten almost at first glance. Little did I know, the young woman sitting directly in front of me would become my wife two years later.

Almost every day she was late to class. Her excuse was that she had to walk from the south campus to the Commerce-Journalism building on the north campus. Later I learned she was late as a result of talking with girlfriends or flirting with guys on the south campus.

Edwina could get away with anything. She still can.

Several days each week, she dressed in an Angel Flight Air Force ROTC drill team uniform. It was just tight enough to reveal a cute, athletic figure. Seeing her in that uniform, I'd think to myself, "Man, that is one woman I want to get to know."

Other classmates told me, "Oh, that's Edwina Chastain," as if everyone already knew her. She was a high school basketball star at Athens High. She also had been the girlfriend of Pat Dye, the captain of the University of Georgia football team, an All-American guard who went on to become the head football coach at Auburn University. The playing field at Auburn's football stadium is named after him.

Edwina herself had a reputation as an outstanding athlete from a family of outstanding athletes. After moving from Ellijay in the North Georgia mountains to Athens in the ninth grade, she made the varsity basketball team that year as a guard and starred at Athens High for four years.

I never got to see her play, but at some point I asked a friend, Nan (Mrs. Jody) Powell, "Tell me about Edwina. I know you played against her in high school." I'll never forget Nan's answer: "Hell yes, I played against Edwina in high school. She was all hips and elbows. Very competitive. She loved to steal the ball away from the other team. She was very, very fast. Exceptionally fast."

Of course, as a young sports reporter for the *Macon Telegraph*, I was impressed by that.

Edwina recalls that I did ask her once to study together for a test. She told me she had not read the chapters. I thought she was kidding. Later I learned that she actually had not read them, yet she did better on the multiple-choice tests than I did.

When I really got lucky was outside of economics class at a campus polling box while Edwina was running for secretary-treasurer of the sophomore class and I was running for secretary-treasurer of the junior class. We both campaigned around the sorority and fraternity houses and had posters up around campus. It was at the polling box that my Sigma Nu fraternity brother Dunbar Dykes and Edwina's friend Betty Busby, who would later marry each other, pulled up in Dunbar's car. They formally introduced us and convinced us to go on a double date.

A photo of Edwina and me at that first meeting hangs in my home office. It captures one of those historic personal moments in time, and it means more to me than all the photos that I have had taken with world leaders and industry titans over the years.

I won my campaign. Edwina lost hers. But she was unfazed. Even though she sure doesn't like to lose, she always does it with grace. I witnessed then just how determined she is to win. In every aspect of her life, she's always been a natural competitor. When she does win—which is often—she seems slightly embarrassed.

As I got to know Edwina better, I found her to be just the most positive of people, with an absolutely infectious personality.

Edwina Chastain and Tom while meeting for the first time at a UGA polling station. Printed with permission from the *Red & Black*, an independent student media organization based in Athens, Georgia.

Having fallen in love with her long before she fell in love with me, I felt so lucky that she had broken up with Pat Dye. It was a crushing heartbreak for her, not so different from my split with Jann Bass. Edwina's friends told me that the breakup left her exceptionally depressed. Both of us having experienced a significant heartbreak made us each understand something about the other at that young age.

When Edwina agreed to go out with me—a double date to a circus in Athens with Betty and Dunbar—I was excited. She was my dream girl. But it turned out not to be a good night for me.

As I recall, there was no chemistry, and Edwina showed absolutely no interest in me. She was talkative with Betty and spoke to a variety of UGA students that we saw at the circus, but I certainly didn't have her attention.

Edwina recalls that I mostly talked about myself, and she told her friends, "I thought he was real cocky." I don't recall it that way, but I guess she did.

Luckily, she agreed to see me again, but the second time didn't go much better. Her interests certainly were not mine. I had little concern with the social life at UGA. I never learned to dance well, except to slow dance. I was not an athlete. Not a "hunk" like Pat Dye. And while I was working happily as a journalist both at UGA and back in Macon, journalism was probably the furthest thing from Edwina's mind.

As I returned to my fraternity house after that second date, I resolved to end my overtures toward Edwina. I'd already had my heart broken by Jann Bass. I wasn't about to pursue another relationship that seemed to be a dead end.

For the next several months I continued my weekend trips to Macon, where I kept working at the *Macon Telegraph*. I maintained an active campus life as a member of Sigma Nu, an editor of the *Red and Black*, a leader in the Army ROTC program, and secretary-treasurer of the junior class.

In the spring quarter of 1964, Edwina's sorority came to my fraternity house for a "social." As I was walking out the back door, on my way home to my job at the *Macon Telegraph*, Edwina's sorority was coming

Tom escorting Edwina Chastain to a UGA ROTC military ball.

in. I gave her a very brief hello. She stopped me and said, “You’re on my blacklist.” I asked why. She said, “You never called me back.”

I can still remember the adrenalin that shot through me. Wow! Here was my dream girl—the one who had stiffed me on our first two dates—now flirting with me big-time.

I went ahead to Macon, thinking about Edwina the entire ride home. Sigma Nu’s big White Star black-tie gala was coming up, and she would be my first choice to invite to it. At the time, as it happened, she was dating another guy, whose Kappa Alpha fraternity had their annual ball the same night as Sigma Nu’s. Still, I had to try.

When I called her, she accepted. My spirits soared. She told her KA friend that she could not go to their Old South ball, that she had “other plans.”

Playing hard to get obviously worked for me. I recommend it to others.

Our relationship at UGA developed to a point where Edwina would occasionally ride with me on weekends to Macon to stay with my parents while I worked. She would also come into the campus office of the *Red and Black* to do her homework while I wrote and filed stories.

My continued weekend work at the Macon paper sometimes included serving as the acting managing editor or city editor in charge of directing a small staff. It was my first time making decisions about what stories were to be run and which stories would be placed on page one. The older reporters and editors were astounded that somebody so young had been given authority over them. However, they treated me with great respect and pride.

These were the early days of my learning just how important journalists are—that they can make just as great a difference on important issues as elected officials, without having to make the types of compromises that elected officials tend to make.

Inscribed "To Tom Johnson: My greatest pride is in your many outstanding accomplishments. Peyton Anderson. 1977."

Edwina "studying" at the *Red and Black*.

All of this I owed to Peyton Anderson. Without him, so much of what life had in store simply would not have been possible. I would not have had the money to attend college, and at other stages he enabled me to advance personally and professionally. After showing me such great generosity, and giving me more responsibility at the paper, Anderson became a lifetime mentor. Other than my mother and Edwina, he was by far the most important influence in my early years.

In many ways, because of my serious commitment to work, my campus newspaper offices were where Edwina and I fell in love. On one historic night, I proposed marriage to her in my office as business manager of the *Red and Black*.

"Isn't it time for us to get the ring?" I asked.

"What ring?" she replied.

Edwina says it was the worst proposal that she ever heard of in her life.

The next day, she and I went to Cohen's Jewelers in Athens to pick out a beautiful, but reasonably priced, engagement ring. Mr. Cohen suggested that rather than paying him in cash for the ring, I compensate him by providing ad space in the *Red and Black*. I declined, knowing that would have been unethical.

My engagement to Edwina was the most momentous thing that happened to me that year, but not the only one. Being admitted to Harvard Business School certainly was another.

CHAPTER 3

HARVARD BUSINESS SCHOOL

The best piece of bad luck I ever had

By the time I graduated from UGA, I had completed seven years of ROTC—three at Lanier High in Macon and four at UGA. Following ROTC summer camp in 1963 at Fort Benning, Georgia, I was scheduled to begin active-duty U.S. Army service as a second lieutenant.

Meanwhile, during the spring of my senior year at UGA, I had applied for, and been offered, an appointment as a research assistant through the School of Journalism at the University of North Carolina at Chapel Hill. The position afforded an opportunity both to pursue a master's degree in journalism and to work for the university. While I fully planned to comply with my commitments to the U.S. military, I wanted to keep as many options available as possible. I thought that additional journalism studies would be helpful to my career.

Before long, an alternative post-graduation path proved to be a good idea indeed.

Unfortunately, or fortunately, I was injured during camp while jumping from the Fort Benning jump towers, suffering a left inguinal hernia that could not be surgically repaired in time for me to deploy that fall. To my shock and distress, an army doctor told me that they would be medically discharging me. Moreover, he said the army could not pay for my surgery. Although I would have been commissioned as a second lieutenant only a few weeks later had I not been injured, technically I was still a civilian. Only Edwina knows the depths of my disappointment.

Incidentally, the army placed me in a closet in the barracks for a few days between my injury and my discharge. The heat was almost unbearable. I was assigned to clean the latrines with a toothbrush. I still identify with those who clean toilets at airports as I travel. Often I give a twenty-dollar bill to the attendant with the story that I cleaned toilets myself at Army ROTC camp.

As it turned out, that accident at Fort Benning at summer ROTC camp in 1963 was the best piece of bad luck I ever had. If I had not been injured and had been deployed to the war in Vietnam, my life could have been so very different. Many of my classmates lost their lives there, along with countless others.

With the prospect of a military career no longer immediately ahead of me, I met with *Macon Telegraph* publisher Peyton Anderson to advise him of my acceptance to graduate school at UNC Chapel Hill and to seek his advice on what to do next.

It was a meeting I'll never forget. He said: "Tommy, what is it you really hope to do?"

I replied, "Mr. Anderson, I would like one day to become a publisher just like you."

"In that case," he said, "you do not need more journalism studies. You have all the journalism you need from your years in our newsroom and at the University of Georgia. You need a business degree. If you can get accepted into Harvard Business School for its MBA program, I'll pay your way."

Once again, I was absolutely stunned by Peyton Anderson's generosity and his commitment to helping me succeed.

He told me how he always had wanted to attend Harvard Business School himself but was never able to do so because of family responsibilities.

Peyton also described a long-term development program for me at his two Macon newspapers, the morning *Macon Telegraph* and the afternoon *Macon News*. He said he wanted me to work in all of the departments: circulation, advertising, production, finance, and personnel.

Even though the fall of 1963 admissions deadline had closed for Harvard Business School, letters from Peyton, *Macon Telegraph* editor Bill Ott, and Dean John Drewry of UGA's Grady College of Journalism had such an impact that I was admitted to the incoming class anyway.

I was shocked in the most positive way possible, and my admission to Harvard Business School officially put my consideration of graduate studies at UNC to rest.

With that settled, Edwina and I began to plan for our wedding and our future together.

Surprisingly, Peyton Anderson opposed our getting married at that point, even though he loved Edwina. He was simply of the opinion that I should complete my two-year MBA at Harvard before our wedding, because of the rigorous academic program he knew I would encounter. He also felt that I should hold off on marriage until I was working full-time and could afford a family.

While I greatly valued Peyton's advice, I was afraid that I might lose Edwina to one of several other suitors who were hot on her heels, or to Delta Airlines, where she had started to think about becoming a flight attendant to see the world.

Despite Peyton's reservations, we went ahead with our wedding plans and selected December 29, 1963, as the date. By waiting until December, Edwina would have graduated from UGA with her bachelor's in education, having attended summer school all three years to be able to graduate ahead of schedule. During her final semester of college, Edwina lived in Athens with her parents, and I missed her enormously while I completed my first semester in Cambridge.

Marrying Edwina remains by far the best decision I've ever made.

Our wedding date fell during my winter holiday break from Harvard. I drove straight through from Massachusetts to Athens, Georgia, only stopping for gas and restroom breaks, with Riley Wilcox, a business school classmate from Dublin, Georgia, riding shotgun.

It was a traditional wedding, with our parents, grandparents, friends, and other family in attendance. We had friends from high school, UGA, and Harvard there. My best man was Don Rountree, my roommate from the UGA Sigma Nu house. The service took place at the First Baptist Church of Athens. Afterward we headed north, bound for Boston as newlyweds.

For the next three days we cruised along in our new white Ford, loaded with virtually all of our possessions. I had bought the car with money borrowed from C&S Bank. I was surprised they approved the loan, since I had absolutely no collateral.

We didn't have any plans, time, or money for our honeymoon except to drive all the way from Georgia to New England, through Washington, D.C., and New York City, nor any money for sightseeing. We just drove through the cities, enjoying the scenery as we went.

We also underestimated the cost of tollways, not calculating how expensive those fees would be. Between the two of us, we only had about $250 total for food and motels.

From New York to Boston there was seriously dangerous weather, with snow and ice on the highways almost the entire trip. The most dramatic moment came when the passenger-side windshield wiper flew off during a blinding snowstorm, leaving us able to see out only from the driver's side. That may have explained our taking a wrong turn that led us to Springfield, Massachusetts, rather than to Boston. (Of course, I blamed Edwina—one of many times in our marriage that I've found it more convenient to blame her for a mistake that was actually mine. She never has seen my humor in those episodes.) Fortunately, we arrived safely, still talking to one another. Our new life in Boston was waiting.

My two years at Harvard Business School were some of the most stressful of my life, perhaps second only to writing this book. After being without her during my first semester, it was absolutely wonderful to finally have Edwina there with me. She was proud of me for securing my MBA, but always in a way that kept me humble.

"I never doubted anything that you wanted to do," she once told me. She thought we were a good fit because I was "smart, but not controlling." She's always been supportive in that way.

That first semester alone at business school had been a particularly trying time, not just for me but for the entire country. Mere weeks before I returned to Georgia for our wedding, there came a terrible day that no one alive then will ever forget.

It was November 22, 1963, and as I was leaving class, students were shouting, "The president's been shot!" Everyone raced to the very few TVs in dorms and campus offices at that time. Most of us followed the CBS news reports delivered by Walter Cronkite.

There have not been many occasions in life when I've seen men weep. But it seemed that day that most did.

Knowing that President Kennedy had attended Harvard and that so many of the Kennedy roots were in Boston, I called the *Macon Telegraph* and volunteered to write about the public reaction in Boston to the shooting.

I rode the subway to the city's downtown. Black ribbons, drapes, and scarves were placed around photos of President Kennedy and in store windows everywhere. Stores were closing all over town. Flags were lowered to half-staff. People were crying in the streets.

It was a difficult note to finish the semester on. It left the country with feelings not only of sadness but of uncertainty. Finally having Edwina with me in my new home—*our* new home—helped to ease those feelings.

Our first temporary home was on Commonwealth Avenue in downtown Boston. There were multiple locks on the door—something that we found strange compared to Georgia, where neither of us knew anyone who ever locked their homes.

While I went to class, Edwina mostly stayed home in our apartment. The Boston Strangler had recently struck and killed a woman in an apartment not far from where we lived. Likely unrelated, but making an already tense situation worse, Edwina received a very mysterious call that scared her immensely.

Fortunately, we only stayed in that Commonwealth Avenue apartment for two weeks before moving into Harvard's new married housing unit in Cambridge, directly across the Charles River from Harvard Business School.

Even though our financial aid from the *Macon Telegraph* paid most of my tuition and living costs, Edwina needed to work so that we could cover all of our other meager expenses. She first worked in the Harvard Fund office, and the next year moved to the subscription office for the *Harvard Business Review*.

The biggest fight that Edwina and I had in our early marriage was over a quart of orange juice. I badly wanted to buy the juice in a supermarket. She told me that we did not have the money for it. I pouted for at least three days. Edwina is not so frugal about money anymore.

A fun time out during those years meant going to Elsie's in nearby Harvard Square for a vanilla frappe and a hot pastrami sandwich, or buying a large slice of pizza for a quarter.

Many of the courses that I enrolled in for my MBA were quantitative, ranging from Production and Accounting to MERC (Management of Economics Reporting and Control). Prior to my arrival on campus, Harvard Business School sent me two books—one on basic accounting, which I still have, and another on statistics. The HBS admissions staff were concerned that I did not have enough preparation in quantitative studies. Indeed, I had had very little quantitative education in high school or at UGA, so it was critical for me to catch up on those classes, which other students had taken as undergraduates.

The other major stressor was the Case Method that was pioneered at HBS.

Every day, I did not know if I would be called upon by the professor to start a case presentation. It was possible for it to happen multiple times a day, in different classes. At times I would go for several weeks not being called on to start any class, but you never knew. The pressure was on to be prepared every day.

WACs (Written Analyses of Cases) were due at the drop box—"the chute"—on the side of Baker Library by 5 p.m. sharp on Saturdays. If they were not down that slot by 5 p.m., it meant a 0 grade on that WAC and a reduction of up to 20 percent of your overall grade. If I had somehow finished my work early, Edwina and I, along with other friends, would sit and watch last-minute arrivals at the chute. Business students drove like madmen, jumping curbs and parking on the grass, to run as fast as they could to reach the drop box on time.

My roommate during my first four months at HBS, before I married Edwina, was Merv Roberts. He was an engineering major from the University of Michigan, as strong in quantitative experience as I was weak in math and accounting. Fortunately for me, Merv could not write as well as I could, so together we learned to work as a team. He helped me with quantitative work that I did not understand, and I assisted him in writing his WACs. Between the two of us, our grades were good.

Lifetime friendships were established while Edwina and I lived at Harvard. Three couples that became our very best friends were Deedie and Rusty Rose, Bobbie and John Harrell, and Carol and Bill Wyman.

One day, when Edwina and I were walking up a flight of stairs in the new Harvard married housing complex, we smelled smoke. I ran to get the building manager while Edwina kept watch over the smoking apartment. This was our introduction to Deedie and Rusty Rose. Deedie had been finishing a wooden table with linseed oil. A pile of cleaning cloths that she had thrown on the floor combusted.

Newlyweds from Dallas, the Roses had almost all of their possessions in the apartment. Everything was damaged by smoke. Deedie took all their clothes and many other items to the cleaners. That night the cleaners burned to the ground. Everything of theirs was destroyed.

Some misfortunes in life are so ironic that you couldn't dream them up if you tried.

Through all the years since, I've taken credit for "saving the Roses." That's an overstatement, but one I've enjoyed telling.

Not so different from Edwina and myself, Deedie was the income provider while Rusty was at Harvard Business School. She is a brilliant woman who worked as a programmer with IBM. Many years after Harvard Business School, Deedie and Edwina remain extremely close friends. They are in a group of eight women called Wilderness Warriors who have made annual wilderness trips for more than thirty years.

Harvard memories include one April Fools' Day when I picked Edwina up from work and told her I'd failed my courses so badly that

I had to leave Harvard. She handled the news with perfect grace. She was absolutely fine about our moving back to Georgia and so caring in that moment. When we got to our apartment, my new grades were sitting on the counter—all passing marks. To this day, Edwina tells me it was the worst thing I ever did to her. For years I have felt terrible guilt about pulling that bad joke.

During my time at Harvard Business School, second-year students were required to complete an elective research project. The traditional path offered by the school and selected by most of our classmates was to enroll in a course, form into groups of eight or so, and select, from a list, a situation to analyze and strategies to recommend.

Classmate Lee Moore and I had been discussing our shared interest in the management of innovation. My undergrad degree in journalism and Lee's in engineering steered us toward newspapers as an industry ripe for innovation. We were not interested in working with a group of eight.

We approached Professor Arch Dooley, who taught Production at HBS. He liked the idea and gave us the go-ahead to travel the path less traveled—to be our own team, define our own project, and meet the MBA requirements.

Our final grade, D for distinction, the highest that could be awarded, proved that our plan worked well, and our work went on to be published by Nimrod Press as a book titled *The Impact of Advanced Technology on the Composing Rooms of America's Newspapers* or, in paperback, *Automating Newspaper Composition*. We even earned $2,500 from book sales.

During that same year of 1965, with the help of classmates David Pulver, Ferdinand "Moose" Colloredo-Mansfeld, David Vione, and David Neuberger, we planned and designed a new paper, the *Collegian*.

What made the *Collegian* unique was our intention to distribute it on the twelve college campuses in the Boston area. It would feature events, concerts, speeches, and even protests on each of the campuses. Major Boston area advertisers loved the concept because it would enable them to reach all campuses. Students loved it because it would inform them of events happening at the other universities. Each campus editor of each school's newspaper—such as the *Crimson* at Harvard or the *Heights* at Boston College—would serve as an associate editor of the *Collegian* and would be paid by us.

All the university administrations, except for one, tentatively approved of our delivering it free of charge to dorms, campuses, restaurants, and newsstands. The Harvard University administration refused to give us permission to distribute, stating that it would harm their own campus newspaper, the *Crimson*.

So much for freedom of the press.

We appealed, but Harvard would not relent. In hindsight, we should have put up more of a fight. However, we did not have either the time or the funds to litigate in the courts. Sadly, the *Collegian* folded, because we felt that without Harvard students, we ultimately would not succeed.

Later, a newspaper was created called the *Phoenix*, which did serve all of the campuses as well as the city of Boston. How they did it without Harvard's approval is a question I still can't answer.

For all of us, the nation was changing rapidly. The death of President Kennedy was enormous, the conflict in Vietnam was escalating, civil rights struggles were becoming more contentious, and the Cold War was still burning. Sometimes it could be difficult to know whether it was a time for mourning, excitement, or concern.

During my second year, in 1964, I did get some sense of personal closure regarding JFK's passing. I saw Jacqueline Kennedy and a small contingent of Harvard representatives and Kennedy family members inspecting a possible site for a Kennedy presidential library on acreage that adjoined Harvard Business School. I didn't meet her in person at the time, but I was impressed that she came personally to inspect the location, and thought it would have just been wonderful to have his library on the campus for which he had such fondness. It was not chosen. A site on Columbia Point in Boston was selected.

Later that academic year, Edwina learned of a new government fellowship. Our friend Bill Wyman had brought her an article in the *New*

York Times announcing the establishment of the White House Fellows program. Bill was applying for it. Edwina thought I should too.

She said to me, "What a great opportunity." I felt my chances were so low that I should not even bother to apply. But Edwina persisted, as she often does. So I agreed.

A huge motivating factor for Edwina was that she absolutely was not fond of my hometown of Macon. We had lived there during the summers of 1964 and 1965. She found that the weather was too hot and that the Macon paper mill emitted an odor of sulfur.

Edwina was a North Georgia girl. She loved the mountains, the clean air, the wonderful lakes and rivers near her original home in Ellijay. Athens, which became Edwina's home from the ninth grade through her college graduation, was a dynamic college town. Most of Edwina's family lived there. They still do. It also was well on its way to becoming the home of a splendid university: the University of Georgia.

I felt differently about Macon then, as I do now. It was home. I had many close friends there. I loved my work at the *Macon Telegraph*. I had begun to gain a reputation for my reporting. I was excited to return. I was also looking forward to being near my mother again.

My father had passed away during my time at Harvard, but his funeral was another important lesson that came from my hometown. Seeing his friends from the Macon farmers market at his service made me realize what his personality meant to so many different people. Watching them made me understand that there was much more for me to learn from my dad about life, even though he was gone. His funeral connected me still more closely to the Macon community.

Despite my love for Macon, and my looking forward to returning home, my journey in parts farther north was not yet meant to end.

My application to the White House Fellows progressed better than I had anticipated. I was interviewed by an Atlanta regional panel and then by a national selection committee headed by David Rockefeller, at which point the more than 3,000 original applicants were reduced to 45 finalists, from which 15 were to be chosen.

After three days of interviews, each of the finalists was handed a sealed envelope. Inside was one of three possible messages: "You have been chosen as a White House Fellow"; "You have been selected as an alternate"; "You have not been chosen."

Standing next to me was Elizabeth Hanford, a graduate of Duke and Harvard Law School, a brilliant young woman who later became Elizabeth Hanford Dole, wife of the legendary Senator Robert Dole of Kansas, and who served in turn as secretary of transportation, secretary of labor, president of the American Red Cross, and a U.S. senator from North Carolina.

I opened my envelope first.

To my astonishment, I was chosen. Sadly, and just as surprising, Elizabeth was not.

I can still remember embracing her, absolutely crushed.

Not a single woman was selected in that first class of fellows, but there's no doubt that Elizabeth should have been.

After graduating from Harvard Business School, I spent the summer working at the *Macon Telegraph* before beginning at the White House in the fall of 1965. Nothing changed my life more positively than that program did.

Not returning to Macon meant that I would not begin working again with Peyton Anderson. Even though he had helped me so significantly with my education, he fully supported my decision. Peyton was able to see me complete Harvard Business School—a place he had always wanted to attend himself—and he was proud of the next opportunity Edwina and I had: the White House Fellowship.

CHAPTER 4

THE WHITE HOUSE

From "Tommy" to "Tom"

LBJ was the first president to welcome a class of White House Fellows, and my starting year, 1965, was the inaugural year.

Of the fifteen men selected, only one was Black: Army Major Ronald B. Lee, who would become a close lifetime friend.

The all-male composition was something that really upset Lady Bird Johnson. My class ended up being the first and only one in the program's history that didn't include women.

The woman finalist of 1965 that I knew well, Elizabeth Hanford, later Elizabeth Dole, many times over the years "stuck it to me" because I had been chosen and she had not.

On one occasion Elizabeth was the featured speaker at an annual American Newspaper Publishers Association meeting. With hundreds of VIPs looking on, she was introduced this way: "Ladies and gentlemen, I now would like to introduce the nation's secretary of labor. In 1965 she applied for a White House Fellowship. She was not chosen. Fifteen men were, not one of whom has been heard from since."

Few people would argue that Elizabeth wasn't as strong a candidate as any of us fifteen men who were selected. She blazed a remarkable path in government even without the connections and training of the White House Fellowship.

Having continued to actively support the White House Fellows program for many years, I can personally attest that Lady Bird's insistence that female applicants be given equal consideration is one of the

Young Tom Johnson stepping off Air Force One. Courtesy of the LBJ Presidential Library.

best things that has ever happened to the program. Since that time, 29 percent of total White House Fellows have been women, which has brought much more diversity into government at large.

As August of 1965 approached, I had high anxiety about the impending White House Fellow assignment, especially waiting to find out for whom I would be working. I was asked to provide my top three choices.

My first choice was Bill Moyers, press secretary to the president.

My second choice, because I saw major news potential in it, was Secretary of Defense Robert McNamara. With the war in Vietnam flaring, working at the Department of Defense would have been a spectacular assignment for a journalism major with seven years of Army ROTC experience. I had even written my ROTC senior paper in 1963 on Vietnam, with the help of Edwina's uncle Henry McCurley, who was an army colonel actively serving as an advisor in Vietnam. I received the highest grade in the class, in large part because of his help.

Third was Secretary of State Dean Rusk, a fellow Georgian I admired greatly. Rusk had been president of the Rockefeller Foundation.

I preferred Bill Moyers because he was a young journalist himself. He also had a champion mentor in his life, as I had. Bill had long worked with the *Marshall (Texas) News Messenger*'s publisher Millard Cope, who had been to Bill what Peyton Anderson had been to me. We were also close in age. At that time I was twenty-four and Bill was thirty-one.

The only other assignment I thought might be fascinating was at the CIA. For the news junkie that I have always been, to have access to all kinds of secret information would have made the CIA an especially exciting place to work.

In August 1965, I received a call at our home in Macon. I can remember it almost like yesterday. "Mr. Johnson, this is the White House. Mr. Moyers is calling." Bill came on the line and said, "Tom, after reviewing the resumes of the fifteen White House Fellows, I have chosen you to work with me this year." I told him how very pleased I was.

White House Fellows class of 1965. Courtesy of the White House Fellows.

Moyers choosing me was one of two historic things happening in our lives at that time. Edwina had given birth to our first child, our son Wyatt, so we would be moving to Washington as a family of three.

My White House Fellows assignment with Moyers was superb. He not only mentored me, but he also included me in some of the most important top-secret meetings. I never dreamed that it would lead to a role as notetaker at the most classified of all White House meetings, "the Tuesday Lunch."

Bill was both presidential press secretary and a very senior policy advisor to LBJ. He had worked with President Johnson in Congress as well as the vice presidency. He had also served as a deputy director of the Peace Corps. Bill had access and power that sometimes made him the envy of other White House aides. I don't think there was any other person in government at that time who could have provided me with the rare opportunities that Bill did.

My first day on the job, I drove to the White House and was directed by a Secret Service agent to the West Executive Avenue entrance, where I was asked to wait. Bill Moyers's executive secretary Carol Welch greeted me and took me to his office. It was one of the largest in the West Wing.

Bill could not have been more gracious. Almost immediately he said: "Tom, I would like to introduce you to some of the other people around here."

I was thinking we would meet other staff like Jack Valenti or Joe Califano. Instead he walked me past the presidential personal secretaries Juanita Roberts and Marie Fehmer and took me into the Oval Office and introduced me to this giant of a man, LBJ himself. First day!

Bill's close relationship with LBJ was built while he worked years before as an intern and staffer when LBJ was in the Senate. Their closeness made Bill an exceptionally wonderful mentor for me.

I'll never forget the enormous presence that LBJ had, particularly one-on-one or in small groups.

When we entered the Oval Office, President Johnson reached out to shake my hand and said, "Tom, since this is its first year, we haven't

Left to right: Bill Moyers, Tom, and Deputy Press Secretary Bob Fleming. Inscribed "To Tom, a friend for all seasons—Bill Moyers." White House Archives.

had much experience with a fellowship program like this one. So, we've decided to treat you just like a full-time member of our staff."

Standing in the Oval Office with LBJ and Bill Moyers was an awesome experience in itself. I can still recall LBJ's telephone console holding the names of every one of his top White House staffers. Two years later, my name was among those who had direct lines. I noticed another console containing the three network feeds: ABC, CBS, and NBC. LBJ could activate the sound on any of the three when breaking news occurred. He also had both the Associated Press and United Press International wire service machines providing twenty-four-hour reports on national and international topics. He clearly had an intense interest in news coverage.

From the first day, LBJ treated me as a full-time member of the staff. At no point did I feel I had been relegated to the role of an intern.

Years later, LBJ told me how he had been treated so wonderfully when he was working as a young assistant for Congressman Richard Kleberg of Texas. Kleberg didn't particularly care about running his office, so he turned much of the responsibility over to LBJ and Lady Bird. It was during that time that LBJ came to know many members of Congress at a very young age.

As president, LBJ identified with young people and had a young group working for him. It wasn't just me with whom he connected. There were other White House Fellows such as Charles Maguire, who became an indispensable speechwriter.

My desk was within ten yards of Bill Moyers's office, and Bill included me in virtually every Press Office meeting.

I was welcomed by other members of the White House Press Office, especially by Deputy Press Secretary Harold Pachios, Assistant Press Secretary Joe Laitin, and Executive Secretaries Carol Welch, Connie Gerrard, Ann Patton Garmon, Rosemary Peterson, Jean Hundley, Mary Catherine Curran, and Sammie Bear.

That same first day, Hal Pachios took me to dinner, just the two of us. That was the beginning of a friendship that has flourished all the way through the White House years and into the later years of our lives.

There may have been some backstabbing in other parts of the White House, but I never found that with Bill or Hal, and certainly not with any of the Press Office staff.

Within the Johnson White House, between September 1, 1965, and January 20, 1969, my roles would go on to include: assistant presidential press secretary, deputy press secretary, briefing officer, special assistant to the president, and executive secretary of the Tuesday Lunch.

Great advice came early from Helen Thomas of United Press International: "Tom, never lie. Always tell the truth." It was just that simple. "And if you can't provide the answer to a press question, just say: 'I can't answer that.' Do not say, 'I don't know,' when in fact you do know. That would be lying."

I simply used this response when necessary: "I cannot answer that." I didn't say I didn't know. I made a point not to say, "I don't know," unless I really didn't know. There were many times when I honestly didn't know the answer.

From that first day forward, I was assigned a mix of work ranging from incredibly important to downright unimportant. But to me, a twenty-four-year-old kid, it was a thrill to be there every single day.

Initially, most of my duties were as low-level as existed on the White House organization chart.

I escorted White House reporters and photographers from the West Wing over to events in the East Room or in the Rose Garden. I assisted in drafting press releases. I monitored the Associated Press and United Press International wire service tickers. I was asked to try to anticipate what questions reporters would ask at the two daily press briefings and to secure draft answers from different cabinet departments (especially the Department of Defense) ahead of the press briefings.

As time went on and my experience improved, Bill began to send me out to advance presidential trips, both within the United States and outside the country. That role entailed a tremendous amount of responsibility.

While I earned Bill's trust, and my tasks became increasingly important, he never stopped advising me on the little things. On one occasion he said, "Tom, stop running!" In my quest to get everything done as quickly as possible, I had begun running between the West and East Wings and on other occasions out to the South Lawn to oversee photo opportunities for the press corps. Bill said it made me look too much like a kid. I was.

Bill was also the one who shortened my name from "Tommy" to "Tom." His own formal name had been Billy Don Moyers, but he eventually shortened it to Bill. He thought shortening mine to Tom would show a more serious persona.

I thought that was a pretty brash thing for Bill to suggest. I'd been Tommy up until then, and I'd gotten along just fine. But I relented.

Now in my eighties, I know that anybody who calls asking for "Tommy" dates back to my childhood, or days at UGA and Harvard

Business School. Those asking for "Tom" knew me beginning with my White House years.

Bill had a tremendous amount of confidence, knowledge, and intellect. He also had quite a presence himself. He was able to articulate the positions of the president to reporters and to other staff members in a way that few others could, and he had a deep background in policy. During his early years in the White House, Bill was in charge of developing many of the task forces that created the Great Society programs that the LBJ administration is known for.

Bill emphasized the importance of integrity, staying well informed about current events, and handling assignments within tight deadlines. He assigned me to draft White House press releases, and he showed me that you don't have to be Hemingway to write concisely and clearly.

To this day, Bill is the hardest-working person that I ever have known. At times he even outworked LBJ.

Bill had become an ordained minister at the Southwestern Baptist Theological Seminary years before our time together. He had qualities of integrity, exceptional thoughtfulness, and an unwavering drive to always demand the best from himself that lived up to his ministerial training.

Bill would go on to excel at the highest levels of media throughout his career at CBS and PBS.

My relatively low-level role under Bill at the White House advanced even further near the end of my White House Fellowship year.

President Johnson wrote a two-page letter to *Macon Telegraph* publisher Peyton Anderson asking him to approve my remaining at the White House following my year as a White House Fellow.

Bowing to LBJ's powerful persuasion, Peyton reluctantly gave his approval for me to stay in Washington. This marked a third delay of my return to work at the *Macon Telegraph*—first to attend Harvard Business School, then to serve as a White House Fellow, and now to become a White House staffer.

As a thank-you to Peyton, LBJ invited Peyton and his wife Katherine to the Oval Office in April of 1968. They were also invited to a black-tie dinner that same evening, honoring the prime minister of Barbados.

THE WHITE HOUSE
WASHINGTON

July 28, 1966

Dear Peyton:

Last Saturday I had what I considered a very successful trip through three states of the Midwest. Your Tom Johnson set up the whole thing for the Press Office. I don't think one man has ever done so much work in such a short period of time. But it was a flawless effort and greatly impressed the press and me.

Before he left to advance that trip, I had Tom sitting in on my highly confidential meetings with the Congressional leadership and the National Security Council. His notes were lucid, thorough and accurate.

Mrs. Johnson asked Tom to help out with some of the press problems attached to the wedding. He has been of immense help, and Luci and Pat in particular have come to have a deep appreciation for what he has done.

I don't know of anyone who is held in higher esteem by the working members of the regular White House Press Corps than Tom. He has become an invaluable pillar of the Press Office and one of the most popular members of my staff.

All of which is to say: I need Tom Johnson. Can you spare him?

Tom feels a strong moral commitment to return to Macon because of everything you have done for him. His conscience won't let him just walk away from that commitment. I am proud of the way he feels and of his integrity, but I also believe that he has a great opportunity here to make a significant contribution and to continue to grow. This place has a way of stretching one's capacities, especially if he is young and eager like Tom.

- 2 -

I have told Tom that I would like for him to stay on if he could do so without breaching your confidence and faith in him. I know him well enough now to know that his sense of loyalty to you and his profound appreciation for your help in his life are overriding. He is torn between knowing that I need him and his desire to honor your confidence. I wanted you to know this, and also to say that if you feel you can spare Tom Johnson, his country and his President need him.

Sincerely,

Mr. Peyton Anderson
Publisher
The Macon Telegraph
The Macon News
Macon, Georgia

White House Archives.

As supporters of LBJ's 1964 election over Barry Goldwater, Peyton and Kat were thrilled by that day, but certainly not out of place. Peyton had been a major leader of the Southern Newspaper Publishers Association, American Newspaper Publishers Association, and various other national entities. Peyton and Kat were both power players in their own right. Still, being there at the personal request of the president was an event that they talked about for many years afterward.

Despite my eagerness to continue working in the White House, not everything was set to remain the same. For deeply personal reasons Bill Moyers resigned to become publisher of the Long Island (New York) tabloid *Newsday* in 1967.

LBJ did not agree with Bill's decision to leave. He felt he needed Bill then more than ever. His Great Society programs had begun to encounter fierce opposition, especially in the white-dominated South.

Peyton Anderson, LBJ, Katherine "Kat" Anderson, and Tom in the Oval Office. White House Archives.

Indeed, segregationists and Republicans had vigorously opposed the Civil Rights Act and the Voting Rights Act when those bills were introduced in 1964 and 1965.

Opposition to the Vietnam War was also building on college campuses and across the nation.

For me, Bill's departure meant the loss of both a friend and a mentor in the White House. However, we would remain very close. My relationship with Bill continued to be one of the most important of my life.

Later I would hire his son, William Cope Moyers, to work with me both at the *Dallas Times Herald* and at CNN. And when he was at CBS News, Bill helped our son, Wyatt, to get a job working for Dan Rather with the *CBS Evening News*. Everyone loved Wyatt and wanted him to stay. But Edwina recalls Wyatt saying, "I know this job makes Dad happy, but I really want to take the money I have earned and backpack around the world." So that's what he did.

Under the new White House press secretary, George Christian, I was elevated to deputy press secretary. My expanded role took me into morning meetings with George and LBJ in the president's bedroom. Soon after my promotion, President Johnson asked me to begin taking confidential notes of his most top-secret meetings, called the Tuesday Lunches. My new formal title was Executive Secretary to the Tuesday Lunch Group.

During LBJ's administration, this meeting was where the most important matters of U.S. foreign policy were discussed. Leaks were not tolerated. To allow my attendance at the meetings, I received security clearances even higher than Top Secret following extensive FBI full field investigations.

The meetings normally took place in the family dining room and included only LBJ's most trusted advisors.

LBJ thought it was the best team he could secure. Most had been key advisors to his predecessor, President Kennedy—men called by David Halberstam of the *New York Times* "the best and the brightest"—Secretary of Defense Robert McNamara, former president of the Ford Motor Company; Secretary of State Dean Rusk, former president of the Rockefeller Foundation; National Security Advisor Walt Rostow, a brilliant professor from MIT; Joint Chiefs of Staff chairman General Earle Wheeler, who was the most thoughtful military leader I ever met; and CIA director Richard Helms. Interestingly enough, the group also included the press secretaries Bill Moyers and George Christian, exemplifying LBJ's trust in those two, even though they were in close contact daily with the White House press corps.

An occasional participant in the Tuesday Lunches was General William Westmoreland, who was commander of Military Assistance Command, Vietnam (MACV). LBJ would summon him back from his headquarters in Saigon for special briefings. While remembered less positively today, General Westmoreland was always exceptionally crisp, well prepared, and persuasive in presenting his opinions.

Different and wiser decisions might have been made if more of the president's advisors had been involved, including skeptics such as Undersecretary of State George Ball.

One noteworthy person who often was not included was Vice President Hubert Humphrey. LBJ loved Hubert Humphrey, we all did—which is something historians often get wrong—but LBJ didn't trust him with secrets. (Nor was he the first president to keep his vice president in the dark about top secrets. Keep in mind, Franklin Roosevelt never told his vice president, Harry Truman, about the Manhattan Project that developed the nuclear bomb that Truman would later authorize to drop on Hiroshima and Nagasaki.)

LBJ believed that Humphrey simply could not resist talking with outsiders, which was true. Humphrey loved to talk. "The Hubert Humphrey disease" was something we occasionally laughed about, because while he didn't leak deliberately, he was so full of enthusiasm that conversations just happened.

Humphrey loyalist Walter Mondale—then a U.S. senator from Minnesota, later vice president—felt strongly about LBJ's treatment of his fellow Minnesotan Humphrey. Many years later, Mondale unloaded his feelings on me. To paraphrase, he said: "Tom, he treated Humphrey like shit. Why?"

I tried, without success, to explain.

After his retirement to Texas, LBJ told me why I'd been chosen as the Tuesday Lunch Group notetaker. He said, "I trusted you as much as I did Dick Russell." Senator Russell of Georgia was his closest confidant, despite their differences on civil rights.

Before Bill Moyers left for *Newsday*, he had taken notes at the Tuesday Lunches. His handwriting was so tiny that I barely could read them. I still cannot.

Vietnam was by far the most-discussed issue, but from ongoing tensions in the Middle East between Israel and its neighbors to the Glassboro Summit with Soviet premier Aleksei Kosygin, all important topics that demanded the highest levels of secrecy were on the table.

To ensure I was prepared for the Tuesday Lunch meetings, LBJ sent me to 7 a.m. classes in the Cabinet Room with White House executive secretary Phyllis Bonanno to learn Speedwriting, a version of shorthand.

I never mastered Speedwriting. I was simply overloaded and could read my own version of notes more accurately than I could decipher abbreviations that were a part of the Speedwriting process. This was long before the era of small audio recording devices.

I assembled dozens of notepads filled with my best efforts at transcribing the contents of these meetings. Most of my notes, hundreds of them, are now declassified and are stored at the LBJ Library in Austin. Many researchers, journalists, and authors already have used those notes in preparing their own books.

In the meetings, I was so focused on writing the notes, and so determined to make them as accurate as I could, that I often wasn't focused on the substance of the conversation. As soon as I left the meeting, I would type the notes in my hunt-and-peck style, because I knew that by the following day I wouldn't be able to understand them all. Connie Gerrard, one of the finest White House secretaries, retyped them in final form for the president's "nightly reading."

LBJ would read my notes each night, and they would always be returned to me the next morning. They never made their way to the

LBJ, Lady Bird, and Lynda Bird Johnson greeting Edwina and Tom at a White House event. White House Archives.

Pentagon or the State Department, nor were they included in the infamous Pentagon Papers.

Even when CIA director Dick Helms would call me to clarify something, I would check with the president before responding. The meeting notes were that closely guarded.

The trust that I gained with LBJ was gradual. I felt like I had a responsibility in my role. A duty. My goal was not to become secretary of state or secretary of defense. I was a junior briefing officer and a mid-level White House staffer. I did the job the best I could, but never treated it as a stepping stone to the next job. LBJ respected that, and we became closer over time.

My friendships also grew with Lady Bird Johnson as well as the Johnson daughters, Lynda and Luci.

As I earned more and more trust from the Johnsons, my positions continued to be elevated. In 1968 I reached the highest rank a White

Tom, mother Josie, and LBJ outside the White House.
Courtesy of the LBJ Presidential Library.

House aide could then attain—Special Assistant to the President at a salary of $30,000 per year.

From the time Edwina and I arrived in Washington as part of the White House Fellowship program in 1965 until now, the Johnsons have always treated us as family.

CHAPTER 5

LBJ PART 1

Lyndon Johnson: a man as big as the room

In the spirit of full disclosure, I admit that I can never be completely objective about Lyndon Baines Johnson, nor anyone in the LBJ and Lady Bird Johnson family.

While we share the same surname, we are not related. However, for more than fifty years our families have been closely connected. Some have characterized me as his surrogate son.

This book is my own story of a role I never imagined having and how it took me into LBJ's White House, to running his family business in Texas, and into lifelong connections with three generations of the Johnsons.

Several excellent biographies have been written about the life and times of Lyndon Johnson, including four volumes by Pulitzer Prize–winning author Robert Caro. I believe that Caro's LBJ books will be the most important collection of any presidential history, with the possible exception of those about Abraham Lincoln. While I disagree with certain elements of Caro's works, no author, writer, journalist, or historian has undertaken such detailed research and magnificent writing as he has. I predict he will most likely be selected for another Pulitzer.

The finest LBJ biography could have been written by Bill Moyers, considering Bill was not only close with LBJ but also a splendid writer. Bill chose not to write one. Only he can explain why. I so wish he had.

While Caro's work is more independent, my writings on LBJ are told through the eyes of someone who saw both his strengths and his weaknesses up close and personally on a near-daily basis. I also worked with the Johnson family for decades, including serving as chairman and CEO of the Lyndon Baines Johnson Foundation for thirty years.

Even though I consider myself a loyal "LBJ man," I do my best in this book to be honest about the fact that LBJ was flawed, as we all are.

He was perfect neither as president nor as a person. But he was—without question—a president who led during a time when a record number of landmark bills related to civil rights, education, health, immigration, consumer affairs, and the environment were passed. Inside the front cover of LBJ's book *The Vantage Point* is a list of 207 landmark laws, which represent only a fraction of the 1,931 public laws he signed in addition to 1,097 private laws.

Partisanship has always been a part of Washington, but LBJ was someone who brought people together, and it was a time when Congress and the presidency truly worked for the American people.

This chapter is based on firsthand notes and memories. It focuses primarily on my interactions with LBJ. Thankfully, my wife Edwina has helped furnish details in a way that only a partner of sixty-one years can.

Lyndon Baines Johnson was the most complex human being I ever had met. He would remain the most complex human being I knew until I began working for Ted Turner at CNN decades later. In terms of complexity, the two men were in a league of their own.

In my countless attempts to describe LBJ over the years, I've often compared him to a giant pizza containing dozens of slices. Ultimately, there were few people who saw all the slices of his life. His wife, Lady Bird, surely knew most of them, as would have his daughters, Lynda and Luci, and his closest political allies and aides, such as Walter Jenkins, Bill Moyers, Horace Busby, Liz Carpenter, Jack Valenti, Marie Fehmer, Marvin Watson, Jim Jones, Joe Califano, and Bess Abell. Over the years, I served with most of them.

At times LBJ could be yelling instructions to me from his high-pressure shower, swimming in the White House pool with Dr. Billy

Graham, or entertaining guests at white-tie events. At his ranch, I would occasionally be with him while he drove around in his Lincoln convertible.

Eventually, after LBJ retired as president in January of 1969 on the day of Nixon's inauguration, I moved with him back to Texas to become the executive assistant to the former president (1969–71) and then executive vice president of the Johnson family business, Texas Broadcasting Corporation (1971–73).

I mention all this simply to explain that for eight years LBJ had an enormous influence on me. In fact, he had an enormous influence on nearly everyone.

At six foot four, LBJ was a giant both in physical size and in overpowering personality. He could be warm and loving, but he could be equally intimidating, and he knew how to use both traits to his advantage.

He absolutely loved politics. It was a near obsession with him. If ever the political world had a workaholic, it was LBJ.

Even though he was able to relax while visiting his ranch in Texas, he was a full-time politician when he was in Washington. The most I ever saw him do to unwind around the White House was to take an hour at the pool, or stroll the White House grounds with his two beagles Him and Her (later succeeded by another beagle named J. Edgar, as well as the most famous LBJ dog, Yuki, known for "singing" with the president). Even during those walks, he would have a contingent of aides or members of the press around him.

From his earliest days in government when he was working as a young staff member for Texas congressman Richard Kleberg, he saw what it took to succeed. One of those qualities was hard work, almost around the clock. Throughout my eight years working with him, he drove his staff relentlessly. But he never asked more of those around him than he was willing to give himself.

Most of my workdays in the White House lasted fourteen hours, and I worked almost every Saturday as well as many Sundays.

Even though Edwina and I would sometimes take our two very young children Wyatt and Christa—both under five years old—out for family time, my White House work schedule was such that I was too much of an absentee father. My favorite memories were with them at Washington National Airport (now Reagan National) where we watched aircraft take off and land. Wyatt and I went fishing once at the nearby Occoquan Reservoir.

LBJ would start his mornings around 6 a.m. when a navy steward would deliver the morning newspapers and coffee to his bedroom. At that time Mrs. Johnson would go to her adjoining bedroom to begin her day.

Once LBJ had read the newspapers, one of his special assistants—Jack Valenti, Marvin Watson, Larry Temple, or Jim Jones—would arrive to deliver the day's schedule and other overnight reading, including a marked-up version of the *Congressional Record* that LBJ read first thing every morning.

The marked-up *Congressional Record* was prepared by White House aide William Blackburn to satisfy LBJ's incessant need to read what members of Congress were saying about him. (LBJ staff members actually drafted many of those statements about LBJ so members of Congress could insert them into the record to make sure there was plenty of positive coverage.)

LBJ's daily mood would vary depending on what was in the morning newspapers or on TV, or in the CIA's President's Daily Brief (PDB) that was delivered to him early each morning. He also received a "body count" of U.S. and North Vietnamese/Viet Cong military losses. In my opinion, this was a very bad practice, as the numbers were often incorrect.

Following LBJ's reading of the PDB, the presidential press secretary—first Bill Moyers, then George Christian—would arrive with his deputy to review questions we would likely face from the press at the morning briefing. It was always impressive how often our staff guessed right on the press's daily interests.

After breakfast LBJ would go to the Oval Office and work until about 1 p.m. before returning to the mansion—the White House's central section, the living quarters—for a working lunch and a brief nap. Then it was back to the Oval Office, where he'd often work until 9 p.m.

before dining at the mansion with Mrs. Johnson and staff members or guests. It seemed to me that he rarely slept. He made telephone calls late into the night and very early before breakfast each morning.

LBJ did not have a regular exercise routine. He was constantly dieting at the behest of Mrs. Johnson, although he relished eating bacon, tapioca pudding, or pralines from the plate of a staff member or guest sitting beside him at dinner if he could get away with it.

Following dinner he would retire to his bedroom for more work. An aide would bring his nightly reading, and he would go through dozens of memos while a navy corpsman gave him a massage.

Before going to sleep, he would read early editions of the *Washington Post*, *Washington Star*, and *New York Times* along with various clippings from Texas newspapers, and catch the late news on TV. He never watched anything else on television—just the news.

Running twenty-four hours a day in his office were two wire-service tickers printing continuous streams of information from the Associated Press and United Press International. LBJ monitored them incessantly, often opening the protective cabinet doors so he could read the copy as it flowed directly out of the printer rather than waiting for it to reach the viewing window only inches away.

His need for the most up-to-date information was insatiable, because he knew just how influential the press was. The high stakes of his tumultuous presidency—while the Vietnam War raged abroad and the civil rights movement was taking place at home—meant a love-hate relationship with the media. But he actually respected the press, at least most of them.

Some of his best friends were reporters—including Merriman Smith and Helen Thomas of United Press International, columnist Bill White of the *New York Times*, Hugh Sidey from *Time* magazine, Sid Davis of Westinghouse Broadcasting, Margaret Mayer of the *Dallas Times Herald*, and Frank Cormier and Fran Lewine of the Associated Press.

Occasionally he'd invite press members to lunch in the family dining room, to walk the South Lawn of the White House with him, or to take high-speed rides with him around his ranch in the Texas hill country.

Muriel Dobbin of the *Baltimore Sun* once was one of the reporters who rode with LBJ in his white Lincoln convertible on the ranch. It was one of Muriel's first assignments as part of the White House press corps. Marianne Means of Hearst Newspapers was one of the others.

Later that day, Muriel was at the Driskill Hotel bar in Austin, where she told the story about LBJ's wild driving, and how much fun the reporters had with him.

Muriel said she never intended for any of it to be reported publicly. However, Seth Cantor of Knight Newspapers wrote about the wild ride. It infuriated LBJ, and that reporting ended LBJ press rides at his ranch for a while.

Muriel temporarily was even taken off the White House beat by the *Baltimore Sun* editors.

Days later, when Muriel was reassigned back to the White House, she was spotted by LBJ in a press briefing. He went over to her and said, "You betrayed me."

LBJ never forgot when he felt someone betrayed him, but he occasionally forgave them. Muriel gradually recovered, and LBJ developed a wonderfully respectful relationship with her as a reporter.

The story with Muriel was not unique. LBJ was always a tough critic of the press. When he read or watched something that he felt was inaccurate or truly unfair, he might actually call the reporter who wrote the story. If he was really upset, he would call the president of the network. At that time, it was often Frank Stanton of CBS or Robert Kintner of NBC.

If an upcoming presidential appointment or trip leaked, LBJ might cancel it entirely. The only satisfactory option for LBJ was waiting until the day before a presidential trip to allow our press staff to inform the media. Our bags always had to be packed and ready, but even then, if news of a trip got out prematurely, he often would scrub it. We simply wouldn't go.

Over time I came to believe that LBJ's fear of advance word leaking about an upcoming trip was rooted in concern for his life. He had come to occupy the Oval Office only because President John F. Kennedy was shot during a motorcade in Dallas. That Kennedy trip, including the motorcade route, had been widely publicized ahead of time.

Despite LBJ's anger about leaks from others, he was the biggest leaker of them all.

He had a few favorite reporters to whom he would leak information—often without the Press Office staff knowing he had done so. These included William White of the *New York Times*, Hugh Sidey of *Time* magazine, Jack Horner of the *Washington Star*, Phil Potter of the *Baltimore Sun*, Margaret Myer of the *Dallas Times Herald*, Marianne Means of Hearst Newspapers, and two independent syndicated columnists, Jack Anderson and Drew Pearson.

Once, Phil Potter wrote an article for the Baltimore paper about how the president was set to announce a major food aid program that would provide millions of bushels of wheat to India. The *Sun*

Behind LBJ, Tom and George Christian overseeing an Oval Office press conference. White House Archives.

published Potter's article before LBJ was ready to announce it, and as a result LBJ abruptly canceled the entire program.

I investigated the leak for at least twenty-four hours before Potter confessed to me that LBJ was the one who had given him the information. LBJ did not expect that Potter would publish the story before any formal announcement from the White House, but Potter broke the embargo.

Thankfully, it was another case when LBJ put his personal anguish behind him, as he ultimately announced the program and opened the flow of critical support to India.

LBJ's relationship with the press was truly unique. He understood how much power they wielded, and how much a free press meant to the American people. To be sure, the same convictions that made him an incredible leader could also frustrate him. He would believe certain information to be true despite the press reporting facts that were much different. Yet LBJ respected the power of the free press so much that he signed the Freedom of Information Act in 1966, giving the public new access to information from all federal agencies. The next year, he doubled down by creating the Corporation for Public Broadcasting. He was a leader who appreciated that good information does not always coincide with the president's happiness.

One thing is certain: LBJ was simply an amazing consumer of information. He had a mind like a sponge and could retain almost every fact, name, or idea ever thrown at him.

LBJ would have absolutely loved, and been frustrated by, today's cell phones and the internet for their constant updates, and he would have been addicted to CNN, MSNBC, and twenty-four-hour breaking news. He would have also been astonished by the bias and lies that outlets like Fox News and other far right news organizations distribute so extensively.

Under his leadership in the White House, LBJ taught us that every phone call or piece of mail from a member of Congress should be answered the day that it arrived. It didn't matter if it came from a Republican or a Democrat.

Staying on top of information was crucial to LBJ's way of doing

LBJ reviewing a breaking news document with Tom and reporter Peter Lisagor of the *Chicago Daily News*. White House Archives.

business. He often reminded his staff and his family: "A man's judgment is only as good (or as bad) as his information."

While so much of LBJ's serious personality made him well suited to the presidency, his leadership was guided equally by his human side.

He connected with people and understood their emotions. He was a wonderful storyteller, and he had a terrific sense of humor. Sometimes this side of him would come through just for fun, while other times he'd tell stories and jokes to make a point.

He was so captivating to listen to when he told stories because he would be laughing along and enjoying himself as much as any members of his audience.

One he often told went like this:

> I heard a story the other day down in Houston about a fellow who was on death's door, and he rushed down to see one of the Houston transplant doctors. The doctor said, "Well, you are in luck. We have

three hearts in perfect condition that you can choose from. One belonged to a twenty-five-year-old ski champion who was killed in an avalanche. One belonged to a twenty-year-old Hollywood go-go dancer who was killed in an automobile accident. The third one belonged to a mean-spirited, spiteful, tight-fisted seventy-year-old Republican banker who died on the operating table just a few minutes ago. Now, you can take your choice."

Well, without a moment's hesitancy the man chose the banker's heart. The operation was successful, and the doctor sent the man home and said that he believed he could live a normal life. But just before he left, the doctor said to the patient, "I don't understand, when you had the choice of an active healthy young person's heart, why you chose that mean old Republican banker's heart."

The man said, "Because I wanted to be sure that I was getting a heart that had never been used."

He loved that one.

Another example:

A young boy sees a train coming at high speed from the left. And then he looks and sees another high-speed train coming down the same track from the right. He is asked: "Well, what are you going to do?"

He says, "I'm running home to get my brother."

And the other person says, "Why would you run home to get your brother?"

He says, "Because my brother's never seen a train wreck before."

LBJ would use that story anytime he saw two opposing sides heading toward a national disaster (such as a nationwide rail strike). He would gather the two sides in a room, often union representatives and management. He would say, "I hope that we can avoid a train wreck. Let's see what we can work out together."

He also used a favorite biblical passage from Isaiah 1:18: "Come now, and let us reason together."

One of my favorite LBJ jokes was about his least favorite types of people—consultants. Visitors meeting with LBJ at the White House would always want to bring their consultants with them, and LBJ would say:

> Let me tell you about consultants. Down in Johnson City, the town was just running wild with little puppies. And they had a meeting of the Ladies' Auxiliary in Johnson City about what to do about this. And a little lady raised her hand and said, "I know what we must do." She says, "It's that bulldog. That bulldog. And we've got to neuter that bulldog if we're going to stop all these puppies from being here every year just tearing up our gardens."
>
> So, they neutered the bulldog. And for a while there were no more puppies. Until the next year, there were again dozens of puppies running all over town. And so, they had another meeting of the Ladies' Auxiliary. They said, "What in the world are we going to do?"
>
> And the lady in the back said, "It's the same bulldog! Same bulldog!"
>
> And another lady said, "How could that be? We had him neutered."
>
> And the older lady said, "Yes, we did have him neutered. But now he's acting as a consultant."

I have a feeling that a lot of his jokes and stories originated decades earlier, when he was a young man playing dominoes with farmers and bankers down in Johnson City, Texas.

LBJ loved playing dominoes, but more specifically he loved cheating at dominoes. One of his favorite things was partnering up with someone like Congressman Jake Pickle of Austin, Texas, to cheat together.

They had names for all the different numbered tiles, and could just chat like old friends catching up:

"Hey Jake, have you heard from ol' Creight lately?" LBJ might ask.

"You know, I just heard from him not too long ago, as a matter of fact! He's doin' good. Real good," Pickle of Austin might say back.

Their casual back-and-forth would communicate that one of them had double-fives, or whatever the relevant code-talk might mean.

But LBJ's best qualities didn't stop at humor. He could also be amazingly generous and thoughtful.

During my first two years in the White House, I only made $7,500 a year, yet I had a wife and two children to support. In short, we were broke.

To buy milk for our son Wyatt, we once had to use old silver dollars given to me by my dad from our days selling melons and wood out of the back of his truck in Macon, Georgia.

When Edwina and I needed to cut our expenses, we moved from a $250-a-month apartment in Arlington, Virginia, to a $160-a-month apartment in Alexandria. It was such a small two-bedroom unit that our daughter, Christa, slept in a large closet.

With money so tight, we never even considered purchasing a second car, and the one we had I would sometimes leave for Edwina to get around town more easily while I was at work.

Early one morning, President Johnson had the White House telephone operator call our apartment in Alexandria looking for me. Edwina told the White House operator that I had taken the bus.

Not long after, LBJ called again, clearly upset that he could not reach me. Edwina repeated that I had taken the bus and was on my way.

When I arrived at the White House gate at roughly 8 a.m., the guard said, "The president wants you to come to his bedroom immediately," instructing me not to even stop by my office.

As soon as I reached the president's bedroom, he said: "Do you also bring a brown-bag lunch to work every day?" Not knowing really what he meant, I said, "No, sir, I usually eat in the White House mess."

Later that day, two things happened: LBJ doubled my salary from $7,500 to $15,000 a year, and he assigned me a White House car and driver for home-to-office service. At twenty-seven years old, I became the envy of other White House aides. White House cars were a privilege that LBJ had reduced dramatically since the Kennedy years.

On another occasion, Edwina decided to give me a small birthday party in our tiny apartment in Alexandria. Since we were new in town, and knew only a few people in Washington, she invited President and Mrs. Johnson.

Surprisingly, LBJ and Lady Bird accepted.

Edwina bought a new twenty-five-dollar casserole dish to bake shrimp casserole for dinner. She was not an accomplished cook, nor had she ever made shrimp casserole before, but she was always adventurous about everything. It was a lovely evening, and an introduction to just how gracious the Johnsons could be.

Tom, Wyatt, Christa, and Edwina in Alexandria, Virginia, 1968.

Many decades later, she still has that casserole dish, which brings back so many good memories!

On another occasion, I got to see that it was not only me who mattered to LBJ, but my family was important to him as well.

We were set to fly from Andrews Air Force Base near Washington to Austin, Texas. I was aboard Air Force One, while Edwina was on the accompanying commercial "press charter" with our two very young children, Wyatt and Christa, aged four and two.

As Air Force One began to taxi down the runway before going full power for takeoff, LBJ asked, "Where is Edwina?"

I told him she was on the press charter.

Immediately LBJ picked up the aircraft phone and ordered pilot Jim Cross to turn the plane around.

To my amazement and to the surprise of all the passengers on both planes, Air Force One came to a halt on the runway, turned around, and went back over alongside the press plane, where the crew had been ordered to "get Mrs. [Edwina] Johnson and their two children off and aboard Air Force One."

I can still remember how embarrassed Edwina was, but it was in those types of moments that you could not only see LBJ's care for others but really feel his warmth. Most presidents would be occupied by a million things on their mind, and it was a unique LBJ trait to look after everyone around him, while simultaneously looking after the nation.

I'll finish with one last example of LBJ's care and generosity.

During his post-presidency, LBJ had been working me night and day for several weeks, and he knew it had taken a toll on both me and my family. As a way of showing his appreciation, he took Edwina and me aboard his plane to Dallas to watch the Cotton Bowl between the University of Texas and Alabama.

Going to football games was one of LBJ's favorite things to do, especially if he was able to find a seat next to someone who loved politics as much as he did. He would talk about politics the entire game, but he also wanted to soak up the entire background of whoever he was speaking with. He wanted to know about their interests, their families, their grandchildren. Everything.

Incidentally, at the Cotton Bowl that we were attending, Edwina's old boyfriend from UGA, Pat Dye, was an assistant coach with Alabama under the legendary Bear Bryant. At halftime she wanted to go down to say hello, which meant I had to go along to protect my most prized catch—my wife.

Flying back from the game, LBJ said, "I want to take both of you to the ranch. I have a gift for Edwina. I want to see if it fits her rear."

Swapping looks of curiosity, Edwina and I both figured he was going to give her a saddle.

However, when we landed on the airstrip at the LBJ Ranch, a new Lincoln Continental with every imaginable option was waiting for Edwina. It did fit her rear just fine! This was LBJ's way of thanking me for having worked almost 24/7 in recent weeks.

Tom, baby Lyn, LBJ, and Luci at the Johnson Ranch pool.
Courtesy of the LBJ Presidential Library.

During my four years in the White House, LBJ became another mentor, after Peyton Anderson and Bill Moyers.

It was LBJ's political effectiveness—mainly his ability to manipulate situations to his advantage, to secure the needed vote of a congressman, for example—that was the most impressive thing to learn from up close.

Many people will refer to a person who has the charisma, intellect, and background to rise to the nation's highest office as a "statesman." That was not Lyndon Johnson. LBJ was a professional politician, and the best one I ever met. White House advisor Larry Temple often has said that politics and government were both his vocation and his avocation. They were all-consuming.

Media influence was only one of the ways that LBJ earned the reputation as a Texas wheeler-dealer. He knew how to make deals the gritty ways as well, finding compromise among groups that would otherwise see themselves as very different.

If LBJ really wanted something done, or was running out of time to whip votes, he would literally trap opposing sides in a conference room or his office, feeding them drinks and coffee with such efficiency that they never had a moment to get up to use the restroom. LBJ would continue talking and pushing them on an issue until they simply had to compromise with each other, in order to leave the room.

It was masterful to watch.

I can clearly remember one example, when we were trying to pass a very important yet controversial bill through Congress.

The Senate Republican leader, Everett Dirksen of Illinois—who was also a friend of LBJ's—held a news conference on a Friday to announce that he was absolutely opposed to the bill.

In response to his announcement, President Johnson invited Senator Dirksen to join him for a private meeting at the White House that evening. They met in a small room, just off the Oval Office—one that is often used for the most private presidential meetings. LBJ had his usual scotch and soda, as Senator Dirksen sipped bourbon and water.

As Dirksen explained his opposition to the bill, LBJ listened closely and calmly. He was so skilled at making someone feel like they were the center of the universe.

Then the meeting was briefly interrupted by White House aide Jim Jones, who brought in a small stack of documents.

LBJ took them from Jones, looked them over, and then turned to Senator Dirksen.

"Ev, totally separate from this bill I want you to help me pass, I need to let you know that my staff is recommending that the big Veterans Administration Center you want in your district back in Illinois actually should be built in Austin. They say that Austin is more centrally located, that it is closer to where most veterans live, and that it is much less expensive to build in Texas than in Illinois."

Dirksen said: "Now, Lyndon, don't treat me that way!"

After another drink or two, the meeting concluded with LBJ still needing Senator Dirksen's vote for his bill and Senator Dirksen still badly wanting that Veterans Administration Center to be built in his district in Illinois.

As I recall, that meeting took place on a Friday night. On the following Monday, Senator Dirksen called a surprise press conference.

He announced that he had changed his mind and was now very much in favor of LBJ's legislation—and urged his fellow Republicans to support it as well.

The press corps was astounded. One reporter asked the senator how he could have announced his opposition to the bill the prior week and now suddenly be announcing his support.

In his wonderfully melodious voice, Senator Dirksen addressed the crowd: "Ladies and gentlemen, I'm a wiser man today than I was on Friday."

Well, as you by now may have guessed, that historic bill that LBJ wanted was passed in Congress and became law.

And, I believe, though I do not know with certainty, a large Veterans Administration Center also was built in Senator Dirksen's district in Illinois.

In my opinion, this LBJ style of politicking was bipartisanship at its finest—horse-trading at the highest levels, where both sides won and the American people actually got results.

Half a century later, the country needs more of that same spirit of bipartisan cooperation. While not always the most transparent, it helped the nation find common ground, especially on fundamental public needs such as Medicare and civil rights.

Most of the people I've known over many years—Republicans and Democrats—want our leaders to focus on the immense issues facing our nation and planet, rather than catering to the narrow desires of special interest groups. These were ideals that LBJ lived by, even long after his departure from the White House.

Anytime I talk about my time working with LBJ in Washington, I do my best to make it clear that my primary role was as a junior aide and as a notetaker, even though I did have other responsibilities as a deputy press secretary and occasional briefing officer. However, there was one occasion when I was asked by President Johnson for my views on a major foreign policy decision, related to our Soviet communist adversaries.

It occurred in June of 1967 when Soviet premier Aleksei Kosygin was visiting the United Nations.

There were discussions between the White House, the State Department, and others about whether President Johnson should fly from Washington to New York to meet with Kosygin at the United Nations, or whether Kosygin should be invited to fly from New York to meet with LBJ at the White House.

The Soviets would not agree to meet in Washington, and as a result the American side held firm that LBJ would not meet with Kosygin in New York.

Finally President Johnson summoned his military aide, Air Force Colonel James U. Cross, to his bedroom with a local road map—no fancier than one from a local gas station—and a standard twelve-inch ruler. Sitting beside LBJ, Colonel Cross (soon to become General Cross) placed the ruler between New York City and Washington, D.C. Almost halfway between the two cities was the small town of Glassboro, New Jersey: a town that included Glassboro State College (now Rowan University).

A quick call to the president of the college, Dr. Thomas Robinson, confirmed that he would be "more than delighted" to offer his home as the site of a proposed summit between LBJ and Kosygin. However, the two sides still had not agreed.

On the morning of June 20 in his bedroom, President Johnson asked me, "What would you do, Tom?"

I told the president that I did not have the information or the foreign policy experience to answer that question.

However, by 5:30 p.m. I had organized enough thoughts well enough to send a memorandum (pictured) to the president.

MEMORANDUM FOR THE PRESIDENT

FROM: Tom Tom Johnson

DECLASSIFIED
Authority NLJ 83-40
By ics, NARS, Date 8-17-83

Mr. President:

Following up the morning conversation with the President on whether or not the President should visit with Kosygin in New York.

Realizing that I do not have the background information of your foreign policy experts, here is my opinion:

I recommend that the President meet with Kosygin at any location in the U.S., preferably outside New York but there if no alternative can be arranged.

Here are the reasons:

1. It would be "going the last mile" in the President's efforts to insure a durable peace in the world -- both in the Middle East and in Vietnam.

2. Even if it blew up into a propaganda device by the Russians, the American people would know that the President did take this step to seek peace for the world.

3. If we do not go, and Kosygin leaves the U.S. without seeing the President, there is a strong risk that any deterioration in U.S.-Russian relations that may develop, or any increased support by the Soviets to the Arab world or even to Hanoi, would be linked to the fact that no meeting between the President and Kosygin was held.

4. There could be a better understanding to follow. The President would learn something more about the nature of the Kremlin leadership, and their "face-to-face" personalities which may give the President new insights into how to deal with the Russians in the future.

In short, I believe that even a summit without concrete gains would be better than no summit at all.

White House Archives.

I strongly recommended that he go forward with the summit meeting "at any location" in the United States, including New York if it ended up being the only location Kosygin would agree to.

The president ultimately agreed, as did Kosygin.

On June 23, 1967, the two men met for five hours in the library at the Hollybush mansion on the Glassboro State campus, and they returned two days later for further talks.

Perhaps the most dramatic photo taken at the summit meeting was one of President Johnson literally grabbing me by my jacket lapels while Kosygin looked on in dismay. Also observing, with some confusion, are Secretary of State Dean Rusk, Secretary of Defense Robert McNamara, U.S. ambassador to the Soviet Union Averell Harriman, and White House press secretary George Christian.

The photo was circulated around the world by the wire services and other news organizations, with newspaper cutlines describing a scene in which President Johnson was conferring with a key aide: me. My mother was so proud to see that. But the real story was quite different.

LBJ had begun his remarks to the assembled press corps, diplomats, and university staffers and was quickly drowned out by the loud noises of 35mm film cameras, dozens of camera shutters snapping, and conversations among the press corps in the crowd.

He stopped the news conference and summoned me out of the press-only area and forcefully told me: "If you don't get the goddamned photographers to stop shooting, I am going to take him [Kosygin] back inside."

As quickly as I could, I ran over to the media area and asked all of those assembled to quiet down and to cease further photography. Fortunately, they did, and the summit meeting press conference concluded successfully.

In many ways, that was LBJ. Kind enough, and encouraging enough to trust a kid in his twenties for his advice on a meeting with the leader of the Soviet Union, yet brash enough to grab that same kid by the lapels in front of the press and a foreign dignitary in order to get his way.

LBJ reaching across the podium to grab Tom by the lapel.
Courtesy of the LBJ Presidential Library.

As monumental as LBJ was during those years, he was far from the only influence shaping me.

The world was in turmoil, and at times it was difficult for me to watch the struggles of the country as a young man stuck between two worlds.

On one hand, I saw a nation losing thousands of its young soldiers to war in Vietnam, and blood flowing in the streets amid demands for civil rights.

On the other hand, I saw a president who cared about human dignity and peace in Vietnam far more than the public understood.

So much of who LBJ was as a president, in my opinion, was shaped during his earliest professional life when he was teaching in Cotulla, Texas, at the age of twenty. The students were so poor, he'd often find them eating out of local garbage piles.

His experience in Cotulla immersed him in American poverty, minority struggles, and the challenges that held people back from pursuing a better life—an American ideal that he believed should be accessible to everyone.

Despite being the most powerful man in the world, LBJ was never immune to the pain and suffering happening around the globe, yet his decisions sent thousands of U.S. and Vietnamese troops (North and South) to their deaths in a war that he so wanted to end while he was president.

CHAPTER 6

VIETNAM: AN OVERVIEW

The commitment that became a catastrophe

In this chapter on Vietnam, my writing is based primarily on notes that I took in top-secret White House meetings between 1966 and 1969 and on previously classified documents that I obtained after they were declassified.

A great deal of what I will describe about Vietnam is very painful for me to recount. I know memories of the war are equally haunting—or even more so—to countless others who were injured, who lost husbands and wives, fathers and mothers, sons and daughters.

The LBJ administration of which I was a part sent tens of thousands of Americans to their deaths in a war that never should have been fought.

In the early days, I truly felt that what we were doing was preventing the North Vietnamese, the Russians, and the Chinese from expanding into other nations in the region. Our support of South Vietnam was especially important based on treaties we had signed.

Later, however, it would become clear to me that expanding beyond the borders of South Vietnam was not the intention of Ho Chi Minh.

No less important than the American lives lost, countless North Vietnamese and Viet Cong soldiers perished, along with millions of innocent Vietnamese noncombatants.

I was a junior press officer in an administration that conveyed information about the war that often was delivered far too positively to the American public.

It sounds inexplicable, but in those moments I did not reflect as seriously as I should have about the emerging differences between reports released by the White House and reporting done by the press.

I dislike the description "tunnel vision," but perhaps that best captures my situation at the time: Focus on the job. Don't become distracted. Take the notes. Set up the trip. Write the press release. Predict the questions. At times I erected walls around myself so that I didn't permit distractions to pull me off course.

Only later did I realize what a profound and truly unfortunate part of our administration's legacy that would be.

One of my best friends on the White House staff, Richard Moose of the National Security Council, had serious misgivings about the war and the conflict between the information that the president was receiving from government sources and the accounts he was reading from news reporters in the field.

Moose and I were in the same age range, unlike so many others around us who were quite a bit older. He was from Arkansas. I was from Georgia. His specialty was foreign policy, and I was a notetaker where foreign policy was discussed. We also had a chance to grow close by advancing many presidential trips together, sometimes even flying on cargo planes together.

We both had about the same rank in our respective positions. He was an assistant to McGeorge Bundy and then Walt Rostow.

Moose would sometimes question whether our strategy was working, especially when the casualties became so significant. He was a true student of history and of Southeast Asia in particular.

Moose was not an antiwar advocate, but I did know that he favored a negotiated peace plan.

Outside of Moose, I believe that most of the White House staff feared expressing themselves in ways that would be seen as disloyal by LBJ. He simply did not tolerate dissent.

At one point the then "acting" White House chief of staff, Marvin Watson, said to me: "You are the only loyal member of the Press Office staff." I've often wondered whether Watson had the FBI checking on other staffers such as Bill Moyers, but I do not know.

A meeting between Bill Gill of ABC News and LBJ, with Tom as the notetaker. White House Archives.

In my opinion, Bill was never disloyal to the president, but LBJ was stung when he left the White House to become publisher of *Newsday*. LBJ felt like Bill was leaving him during some of the hardest days. He was so upset that he replaced almost everyone that Moyers had hired in the Press Office, except for me.

It was one of the worst things that I ever saw him do.

Bill did not leave out of disloyalty. His only sibling, Jim, had died unexpectedly, which left Bill with members of his brother's family to support. The increased salary at *Newsday* was needed. I have never once felt anything other than admiration of Bill for making a such a hard decision so he could help care for his loved ones when they most needed him.

Bill's loss was so significant to LBJ's administration because our communication with the American public was in serious trouble, a situation that became known as the "credibility gap."

We were releasing reports such as body counts that were flawed, as information coming to us from the battlefields and the Pentagon was often incomplete or wrong. This is not an excuse. Instead, it is meant to be an acknowledgment of our failures as government spokesmen.

The most obvious example of the inaccurate information we gave to the American public was in 1968 when General William Westmoreland told President Johnson and Congress that there was "light at the end of the tunnel." Ultimately, Westmoreland said that victory in Vietnam was within sight.

Battlefield body counts comparing the loss of American lives with those of enemy lives always indicated that the United States was winning. We were not.

There was far too much emphasis placed on the numbers of enemy troops killed in action. It was very difficult to count Viet Cong and North Vietnamese bodies accurately, and it was not a reasonable way to determine winning or losing.

I do not think anyone in the administration ever actually ordered the questionable body counts. Instead, it was a way for a unit or field commander to claim success in an otherwise unwinnable situation.

Regardless of the lopsided numbers, by 1968 the United States was losing as many as four hundred soldiers a week. That certainly did not justify Westmoreland's quote that there was "light at the end of the tunnel." The actual numbers really shook the foundation of that optimistic assessment.

I'll never forget hearing that number—four hundred a week—and thinking, "Oh my God."

There were so many people I knew, especially from my Army ROTC days, who were in Vietnam getting killed or wounded, and I was certainly affected by it. But I just suited up every day, went out the door, and did my fourteen or sixteen hours of government service, although far from the field of battle.

It's my most sincere opinion that our nation owes great thanks to the courageous combat reporters such as Peter Arnett who were out there in war zones finding their own, more accurate, version of the truth. Who knows in what direction the conflict would have moved without them.

Among the best of the journalists were David Halberstam, Neil Sheehan, Peter Arnett, Bob Schieffer, Dan Rather, Morley Safer, Frances FitzGerald, Walter Cronkite, Joe Galloway, Malcolm Browne, and Don Oberdorfer, to name only a few. Their reporting was reliable, while our government briefings often were not. As a result, U.S. government credibility as a whole was damaged significantly.

In the early days of the conflict, especially in the late 1950s and early 1960s, the American media generally supported the United States' involvement in Vietnam. Certainly they were not critical of the war on their editorial pages. "Supporters" included major newspapers like the *Chicago Tribune*, the *Los Angeles Times*, the *New York Times*, and the *Washington Post*. However, as the war continued with little progress and more deaths, support from the media and the public began to shift.

With that opening, here is my personal report of the war in Vietnam:

President Johnson's demands for absolute trust and loyalty from his cabinet and White House staff were exceptionally rigid regarding Vietnam and issues of national security. An information leak could and did end careers.

Assisted by the infamous FBI director J. Edgar Hoover, LBJ learned who he could and could not trust.

I knew Hoover, and had respect for him, but he scared the absolute hell out of me.

On a few occasions I met with Hoover at his FBI office, where his private secretary of fifty years, Helen Gandy, kept dozens of rows of file cabinets. I was later told this was where he kept the most private files on virtually everybody in public life, including presidents, members of Congress, and journalists.

Hoover's behind-the-scenes methods ensured that he was feared by nearly anyone important in Washington. That also made him absolutely indispensable as an ally, or simply a non-enemy.

Luckily for me, I didn't attend social lunches or dinners around D.C. Every chance I could, I went home to my family directly from the White House, sometimes as late as 10 p.m. Because of my lack of interest in Washington social life, no one in the LBJ administration considered me a threat to leak.

I believe LBJ's decision not to include some of the roughly three dozen members of his full National Security Council in the highly classified Tuesday Lunch Group was in part because of Hoover's background investigations.

As I have written earlier, there were only seven full-time members. Included on rare occasions were a select few others such as General Westmoreland and Undersecretary of State George Ball.

As H. R. McMaster wrote in his 1997 book *Dereliction of Duty*, at the LBJ meetings "the only men present were those whose advice the President most wanted to hear."

Tom in the role of notetaker at secret meetings, with NSC Advisor Walt Rostow at left. Courtesy of the LBJ Presidential Library.

While there was capability for secret electronic taping of White House phones in a few select areas, LBJ made sure the Tuesday Lunch meetings were never held anywhere they might be recorded. For this purpose, the family dining room on the second floor of the White House was typically chosen.

Only my original notes were sent in for the president's nightly reading. A classification of TOP SECRET/EYES ONLY was placed on all of them, and no copies were made. Everything else went into special "burn bags."

Amazingly, there has never been a single example of my Tuesday Lunch notes having leaked.

It's taken more than fifty years for all of those Tuesday Lunch notes to be declassified. Even though I served in various media roles at the

Dallas Times Herald, the *Los Angeles Times*, and CNN between 1969 and today, I did not break the classification agreements that I had signed.

There still are sections of my notes that have been blacked out or "sanitized" by declassification teams, and some contents have never been published at all.

However, researchers and authors such as Robert Caro have discovered many of my notes, which were long filed at the LBJ Library and are now housed in a special National Archives facility for classified documents in Washington. I understand that Caro undertook a page-by-page reading of them, in preparation for the publication of his next book.

I predict that Caro's book will ask: Why didn't LBJ's cabinet, his staff, and his other advisors do more to persuade LBJ that he was on a disastrously wrong course in Vietnam? After all, Senator Russell had warned him. Former president Eisenhower had warned him. Two of his cabinet members had warned him.

An answer can be found in a January 27, 1965, memo written by McGeorge Bundy and Robert McNamara called "Fork in the Road." It showed that President Johnson *was* provided two very different paths: one that was quite hawkish and called for an intensification of the war, and another that was a peace path—a "dove" path that would accelerate diplomatic negotiations with Hanoi and the Viet Cong resulting in a peace treaty.

To quote the Bundy-McNamara memorandum directly:

"Both of us are now pretty well convinced that our current policy can lead only to disastrous defeat. . . . The future is without hope for anti-Communists. . . . The Viet Cong are gaining in the countryside. . . . The time has come for harder choices"—either to use massive military power or to "deploy all our resources along a track of negotiation."

The memo noted: "[Secretary of State] Dean Rusk does not agree with us. . . . What he does say is that the consequences of both escalation and withdrawal are so bad that we simply must find a way of making our present policy [the middle course] work."

In late 1968, president-elect Nixon looking at the president's telephone console, which was wired into a recording system. L–R: Herb Klein, Ron Ziegler, George Christian, LBJ, Richard Nixon, Tom Johnson. Courtesy of the LBJ Presidential Library.

The authors, however, saw no way to do so. Bundy concluded: "McNamara and I have reached the point where our obligations to you simply do not permit us to administer our present directives in silence and let you think we see real hope in them."

In short, President Johnson did have a few advisors such as Secretary McNamara, McGeorge Bundy, and Undersecretary of State George Ball trying to sway his thinking periodically. Unfortunately, he chose to stay with the middle course.

Sometimes he ordered fierce bombing campaigns; other times, he'd halt U.S. bombings for days in hopes of starting peace talks with Hanoi. Those were called "bombing pauses."

My notes quote LBJ saying: "I am damned if I do, and I am damned if I don't."

As much as LBJ wanted to find a path toward peace, he felt that the United States was obligated by the Southeast Asia Treaty Organization (SEATO) to protect South Vietnam from what then was described as "Communist aggression" from Hanoi, which was strongly supported by China and the USSR.

Because of the greater geopolitical risks, as well as humanitarian concerns, LBJ kept tight control over the bombing targets. In Tuesday Lunch meetings, there would often be a discussion with maps brought in by the chairman of the Joint Chiefs, General Earle "Buz" Wheeler, who reviewed the targets closely with the president.

Many military leaders have questioned LBJ becoming involved in selecting military targets and making detailed decisions on military tactics.

Wheeler knew that LBJ feared striking a Soviet or Chinese ship anchored in Haiphong or Hanoi Harbor, nor did he want U.S planes crossing into Chinese airspace to the north. LBJ was especially cautious not to strike the dikes located near civilian areas. He was always concerned some young fighter pilot from Johnson City, Texas, was going to accidentally drop a bomb down the smokestack of a Russian or Chinese ship and escalate the entire war. I heard him say that multiple times.

The threat of bringing China or Russia into the war, just as the Chinese poured into Korea to support Kim Il-Sung in the 1950s, was a lingering possibility that never left LBJ's mind.

Wheeler and the others who discussed targets with the president wanted him to know where the targets of military opportunity were. I had heard from several people that General Westmoreland and the chief of staff of the Air Force, General John McConnell, wanted to take more risks with target strikes, but LBJ never relinquished control.

Fortunately for the lives of so many innocent people, General Wheeler was not a warmonger at all. Unlike some of the other generals—such as McConnell's predecessor as Air Force chief of staff, Curtis LeMay, who wanted to bomb Vietnam back to the Stone Age and said so—Wheeler always seemed to be an exceptionally thoughtful man.

The only targets that had continuous approval were those that might disrupt the Ho Chi Minh Trail—the main North Vietnamese supply line. The North Vietnamese were immensely effective at moving supplies in trucks with no headlights at night along the route, and with bicycles during the day, enabling them to bring ammunition, provisions, and medicine down from the North into the South.

Enduring heavy air attacks, including B-52 bomber raids, the trail was constantly being repaired and rebuilt. Its continuous maintenance was a truly spectacular wartime achievement by the North Vietnamese and Viet Cong.

It wasn't until Nixon became president that the United States began secretly bombing sections of the trail that existed beyond the Vietnamese borders in Cambodia and Laos. There, enclaves existed where North Vietnamese troops were able to rest, regroup, and prepare for their next attack.

While there were occasional disagreements at the Tuesday Lunch meetings, I was never present for a confrontation between LBJ and senior military leaders about targets.

The only man who would ever debate LBJ in those Vietnam meetings was Undersecretary of State George Ball, but he was the exception, and he was not included in most Tuesday Lunch meetings.

There were times when I truly wondered if the president wasn't asking Ball to take him on, to get a view from the other side, and Ball would come loaded to meetings with LBJ ready to discuss contrary opinions. But between LBJ and Ball, it was never military targets, it was always about strategy, diplomacy, and the importance of peace talks. As far as I know, George Ball never leaked.

Ball was always raising questions. His positions were well thought out and often in contradiction with the policies that were being followed. The president was never angry or upset with him. At times LBJ really did seem to want to hear the other side. But not often.

Unknown to all of us in the Tuesday Lunch Group in 1968, Hanoi was preparing their massive 1968 nationwide attacks: Tet.

The strategy by Hanoi and the Viet Cong was an all-out campaign that would strike virtually every city in South Vietnam. Their goal was to totally overwhelm the South Vietnamese and American troops. It did just that.

The North Vietnamese's Tet Offensive became the defined turning point of the war, and there is no question that everyone in the LBJ administration was shaken by it.

In response to the highly coordinated surprise attack, General Westmoreland asked for 200,000 additional troops—which would have raised the level of U.S. in-country forces to 700,000. Westmoreland's request was denied.

Vietnam began a new era of warfare in many ways. It became America's first televised war.

Body bags and aluminum caskets with remains of American soldiers were stacked along South Vietnam runways waiting to be shipped home.

Wounded soldiers were shown being pulled by their comrades into bunkers for safety as mortars and grenades exploded around them.

Hellfire rained down from machine guns mounted on choppers. Injured civilians screamed, and blood ran in the streets. It was absolutely heart-wrenching to watch.

Even though it wasn't fed live from Vietnam to America, there is no doubt that TV broadcasts were directly influencing the American public's growing opposition to the war.

In his book *Tet!*, Don Oberdorfer of the *Washington Post* called the conflict "America's television super battle." Americans never had seen battlefield deaths and brutality like this in their living rooms at home.

Throughout the war, there were countless iconic antiwar moments happening across the United States and abroad: demonstrators placing flowers down gun barrels at the Pentagon, teach-ins at universities, black armbands worn with peace signs, John Lennon and Yoko Ono's two-week "bed in" for peace, the self-immolation of Vietnamese monks, the burning of draft cards, and protests happening in countless cities around the world.

As impactful as TV footage from the field was on public opinion, it was Walter Cronkite—regarded as "the nation's most trusted person"—who truly changed opinion about the war.

After reading flash teletype messages from the AP, UPI, and CBS correspondents in Saigon about the Tet Offensive, Walter Cronkite said: "What the hell is going on? I thought we were winning the war." That statement was repeated multiple times at the White House, especially by those who were not involved in foreign policy.

On February 27, 1968, Cronkite reported from Vietnam: "To say that we are mired in stalemate seems to be the only realistic, yet unsatisfactory, conclusion."

After hearing Cronkite on that fateful night, President Johnson told his press secretary, George Christian: "If I've lost Cronkite, I have lost the country."

Not long after, LBJ's approval ratings plunged to 35 percent: the lowest of his presidency.

President Johnson came to see that reporting from war correspondents was more accurate than what he was receiving from some of his own commanders in the field.

LBJ read daily dispatches from the combat correspondents of the Associated Press, UPI, the *Baltimore Sun*, the *New York Times*, the

Washington Post, and the *Washington Star*. When he wasn't reading the papers, he was watching the nightly news on the three networks.

Despite his awareness of the conflicting news, his credibility gap widened.

Over the course of 1968, reporters grew to no longer trust the military briefers in Saigon or in the Pentagon, nor at the White House. That was very humbling for me as deputy press secretary.

Having access to daily classified information, I would see reports coming back from General Westmoreland to the president, usually through the Department of Defense, the CIA, and NSC advisor Walt Rostow. But as a news junkie, I could understand that there was so much conflicting information. I appreciated that excellent combat journalists were doing their best to tell the story honestly to the public.

In one White House meeting at an earlier time, LBJ aide Jack Valenti said, "The reporting of Peter Arnett has been more damaging to the U.S. cause than a whole division of Viet Cong."

Jack was not lashing out at the press. It was simply a shorthand view of the impact that contrarian reporting was having on the war effort. On one hand, there was Westmoreland saying he could see a light at the end of the tunnel; on the other, there was AP correspondent Peter Arnett and a whole cluster of reporters who saw the war very differently.

Personally, I found Jack captured the essence of something very profound.

I refrained from making any judgments as to who was right and who was wrong until much later in my life.

I was at a very personal crossroads, both a young man with friends dying in the war and one who had firsthand knowledge of American leaders and how much they cared about securing "peace with honor." LBJ so wanted to find a way to end that devastating war.

Even though I sat in as notetaker for the secret Tuesday Lunch meetings, I didn't have any hidden personal feelings about the war in Vietnam, nor was I an antiwar advocate. However, I did understand there was different information about the war coming in to the president than what I was seeing and reading in the news.

Whatever the circumstances, President Johnson and his Tuesday Lunch Group always rejected proposals for press censorship such as those imposed during World War II.

In fact, the White House assisted the press corps in many ways. We authorized military field access, Pentagon access, and helicopters to get reporters to frontline outposts. We even facilitated the transport of press film from Saigon and Tokyo back to the United States for broadcast.

There is one time that stands out in my mind, however, when we did screw up badly with the press.

CBS White House correspondent Dan Rather came to us about an exclusive story. He had learned that a "McNamara electronic wall" was going to be deployed along the demilitarized zone and the Ho Chi Minh Trail. Small tracking devices, dropped from airplanes by the thousands, would sense any movement and alert the bombing crews.

Rather asked Press Secretary George Christian to confirm his scoop. Christian called the Pentagon, and was emphatically told that there was no validity to the story—information that Christian then passed on to Rather.

Days later, there was a big announcement from the Pentagon that the electronic wall *was* being deployed. We felt like absolute fools. We had just destroyed an already fragile reputation with an important member of the press. George Christian did call Dan to apologize, but the damage to our credibility was significant.

As the LBJ administration's relationship with the press became worse and worse, the public only became more and more restless—especially young people who were afraid of being drafted or losing their family members or friends in the war.

I'll never forget sitting in the backseat of the presidential limo next to LBJ when we drove by a group of students protesting and shouting one of the most infamous chants of the era: "Hey, hey, LBJ, how many kids did you kill today?"

He turned to me and said, "Tom, I wish they knew that I want peace as much as they do."

Every day LBJ would hear the loud chants from outside the White House. Seeing the youth of the country so upset by Vietnam—and knowing their anger was justified in so many ways—was a condemnation that hurt him to his core.

One particularly memorable event, which so exemplified LBJ's commitment to proving himself to the youth of our nation, came during my second year at the White House.

The third class of White House Fellows recently had been chosen, and part of that group was Doris Kearns (now Doris Kearns Goodwin), a whip-smart bleeding-heart liberal from Harvard who had been selected to work under Secretary of Labor W. Willard Wintz. During a trip aboard Air Force One, our staff was struggling with a dilemma. Kearns had recently published an article in the *New Republic* titled "How to Remove LBJ in 1968." We knew someone had to show the president, which unfortunately meant *I* had to do it.

I was very uneasy walking up to LBJ with a copy of the article, because I felt like it might make him so angry it could even lead to the end of the White House Fellows program.

Instead of anger or disgust, after looking at the article, LBJ simply said, "Tom, I want her to be assigned to me." He *knew* that he would be able to prove to her just how challenging the situation was that he had inherited.

Not long after they began working together, Kearns became another one of LBJ's closest confidants and allies. Their relationship evolved exceptionally. Both during and after his presidency, he found Kearns to be a terrific way to stay in touch with the moods of young people and what they felt was worth fighting for.

Unfortunately for LBJ, he was not able to convince the rest of the nation just how difficult the situation in Vietnam had become. People were so impassioned that he was unable to go anywhere except for military bases, Camp David, or his ranch in Texas without huge, sometimes violent protests.

Even as far away as a motorcade in Melbourne, Australia, where we were attending the 1967 funeral of Australian prime minister Harold Holt, LBJ's lead Secret Service agent Rufus Youngblood (of my hometown Macon) and other Secret Service agents were splattered in red paint, which we first thought was blood, during a protest. The paint was intended for LBJ, but he was in the enclosed security of his armored presidential limo.

It was hard to watch. I had a front-row seat to the tremendous anguish over Vietnam that wracked LBJ every single day.

He felt extreme emotional pain as he called the White House Situation Room in the middle of the night to get reports of aircraft that did not return from their missions.

He visited military hospitals where he saw soldiers missing arms, legs, eyes—some burned almost beyond recognition—as he visited the Fort Sam Houston Burn Center in San Antonio.

And he would read and respond to countless letters from parents who had lost their children.

Here is an excerpt of a February 9, 1966, letter from UPI White House reporter Merriman Smith about his son, a helicopter pilot who was killed:

"My boy did not die for an empty cause nor was he a war-maker. His hope was yours, Mr. President—peace and at least a chance at a better life for others."

On one occasion I received a personal note from a Georgia friend who was serving as a pilot in Vietnam. We had gotten to know each other during our time serving in Army ROTC. He mentioned that, while he was not aboard, his plane had been shot down and his entire crew had perished. He also told me how the South Vietnamese were not carrying their share of the load, not fighting well, and that many of them were often strung out on drugs.

For some particular reason, I had the courage to send that very personal note in to the president.

Unique to my relationship with Bill Moyers, my notes to the president did not have to be cleared with Bill. Things were very different for the aides who worked for Joe Califano or Walt Rostow, who couldn't send a note to the Oval Office saying "good morning" without a cover note from their superior.

Almost everything I ever sent to LBJ had three little slots at the bottom—“Yes,” “No,” and “See me.” The note that I sent in to him about Vietnam came back with nothing other than a little check on the side that indicated he had read it.

Of the friends I had from ROTC at Lanier High in Macon and from UGA, many went to Vietnam. Bibb County, where Macon is located, lost 51 soldiers in Vietnam, and the state of Georgia lost 1,581.

I suppose the reason I sent that letter from my friend in for LBJ to read was because, even then, there was no doubt in my mind that the credibility gap was a huge problem. It was my personal opportunity to offer the president a firsthand account.

I also knew it would have an impact, because he really felt the loss of people.

Beyond the four hundred Americans who were being killed many weeks, LBJ was also anything but insensitive to the immense loss of Vietnamese lives.

On a personal level, LBJ even had family members at risk. Both of his sons-in-law, Marine Captain Charles “Chuck” Robb and Airman Patrick Nugent (service: April 1968–April 1969) were actively serving in dangerous combat areas of Vietnam. Both men insisted that LBJ have absolutely nothing to do with their assignments, or have them protected in any way. LBJ felt a great deal of the war through their eyes.

One of the most widely distributed images of LBJ shows him in the Cabinet Room listening to a tape that his daughter Lynda Robb received from her husband. In the recording, taped in the field, Chuck can be heard describing the heavy losses endured by his unit, and LBJ can be seen stooped next to the audio playback unit on the table, with his head in his hands.

By far the most painful part of this chapter for me is the conclusion.

For more than fifty years I have thought about, but never before expressed publicly, my personal views about Vietnam. After all, I was only a notetaker: a junior White House aide.

Loyalty to President Johnson and to those who sat around that lunch table each Tuesday has long influenced my silence. I was awed

LBJ, in agony, listening to a recording sent from Vietnam by his son-in-law, Marine Captain Chuck Robb. White House Archives.

by all of those men. I thought then, and still do now, that they were "the best and the brightest." I can never bring myself to be disloyal. Not then. Not now.

With that said, neither they nor their judgments were anywhere close to perfect. Their failures guaranteed they did not leave Washington as glowing as when they arrived.

In particular, Defense Secretary McNamara left government a truly broken man. He was the leader who orchestrated so much of the Vietnam War. He ordered the helicopters, the aircraft, the ships, the napalm, and supported General Westmoreland's request for troops up to the 500,000 in-country level. In many ways it was "McNamara's war."

With each passing year, he sank lower and lower into a situation that he could not figure out how to resolve.

Unlike General Westmoreland, McNamara also knew Tet had been a total failure. Westmoreland, McNamara said, "interpreted Tet as a great victory for the United States. I always felt this was a preposterous claim."

By the end of 1967, McNamara was totally exhausted. LBJ even worried that he might kill himself, just as former secretary of defense James Forrestal had done in 1949.

LBJ knew that as brilliant as McNamara was, his leadership had failed, and everyone knew that it was time for him to move on. He had grown thin and weary. The war had taken a serious toll on him.

After Secretary McNamara left office in February 1968 to become head of the World Bank, he called and asked me: "Tom, was I fired?"

The story of how McNamara came to leave the White House for the World Bank has been retold in a variety of ways, but that phone call is something I will never forget.

I told him that LBJ felt he had served two presidents with distinction and that the World Bank job was a reward for a job well done.

I can remember so clearly that at times McNamara was an emotional wreck. Sometimes I would actually see tears on his cheek after he reported at the Tuesday Lunch meeting.

I don't think he—or others in the lunch group—adequately understood Vietnam and Southeast Asia. They did not understand that it was primarily a war to reunite North and South Vietnam, just as the United States had reunited after the civil war a hundred years earlier.

In his final years, McNamara said that the war was a mistake, and that he had been wrong about a great number of things.

As my close friend, retired Marine Lieutenant Colonel Jerry Lindauer, later asked McNamara in public at the LBJ Library: "What do I tell the men in my company who died in support of your policies?"

McNamara was silent. He gave no answer.

As described in the "Fork in the Road" memorandum written by McGeorge Bundy and Robert McNamara in 1965, LBJ perhaps could have taken the "dove" path earlier and left Vietnam after signing an agreement with Hanoi—much like the one Henry Kissinger ended up negotiating in 1972. However, South Vietnam likely would have fallen to North Vietnamese military forces, just as it did after Hanoi violated its agreement with Kissinger and Nixon in 1974.

President Johnson went to his grave believing that he had no choice but to pursue the course that he followed—that he was "caught in the middle." He ultimately agreed with Singapore prime minister Lee about the domino theory of countries throughout the region falling to communism unless North Vietnam was stopped from overtaking the South. (It was President Eisenhower who actually coined the expression "domino theory," based on the belief that the USSR and China would try to support the spread of communism from one nation to the next, growing their spheres of influence as far as possible.)

The American far left did not accept the domino theory. They simply wanted the United States OUT of Vietnam. NOW!

LBJ repeatedly said, "I do not want to be the first president in American history to lose a war." He said he could not "cut and run." He faced a strong right wing in Congress and in the military: people like General Curtis LeMay who were much more warlike. He also feared a more hawkish course might invite more involvement from the Russians and Chinese.

LBJ did not want to bomb the dikes and cities, destroy the rice paddies, or invade the North with an action like General Douglas MacArthur's in Korea.

He did not want to bomb Laos and Cambodia, as President Nixon would do later.

Most important: He certainly did not want to use nuclear weapons and start World War Three.

Had the United States really gone all out militarily as General Curtis LeMay, Senator John Stennis, and others recommended, America could have crushed North Vietnam with massive destructive force, but the ripple effects would have surely been catastrophic. China could have entered the war in support of Hanoi. So could the Soviet Union.

It wasn't until much later—after I had researched and studied documents from the war era more closely, and after Secretary McNamara admitted we were wrong in his historic book *In Retrospect: The Tragedy and Lessons of Vietnam*—that I began to see the war in a new light.

To me, it is now clear: Our Vietnam policies were wrong. Disastrously wrong.

Had the United States withdrawn earlier, as McNamara and Bundy proposed as one path in the "Fork in the Road" memorandum in 1965, more than twenty thousand Americans and perhaps two to three million Vietnamese might not have died.

The failure that I was a part of has been hard for me to reconcile. It was an enormous loss of human life, billions of dollars were wasted, and America retreated from the war defeated despite our massive military power.

One of my good friends, Army Captain Max Cleland, a paratrooper from Georgia, remains a personal reminder of the human toll.

Cleland had volunteered to go on a mission, code-named Pegasus, to rescue five thousand Marines who had been trapped at Khe Sanh. Cleland had just left a chopper when he saw a grenade lying nearby on the ground. Thinking it had fallen off his own web gear, he reached over to pick it up. A massive explosion ripped through his body. His legs and one arm were blown off.

How Max survived is a testimonial to field medics. How he has lived is a testimonial to his courage, his inner strength, and his faith.

Max received the Bronze Star and the Silver Star and went on to a career in Democratic politics.

During Max's 2002 reelection campaign for U.S. Senate, Republicans ran an infamous ad attacking his honesty and his record on national security. It was the single worst example of savaging a candidate I have seen in my lifetime. Senator John McCain said of his own party's campaign ad, "Putting pictures of Saddam Hussein and Osama bin Laden next to a picture of a man who left three limbs on the battlefield—it's worse than disgraceful, it's reprehensible."

The lessons of Vietnam stayed with Max.

Although he initially supported President George Bush's Iraq War resolution, he later said, "Now wait a minute. Let me run this back: We have a war. A bunch of Americans die. After the war, we try to figure out why we were there. There's a commitment of 240,000 ground troops with no exit strategy. You know what that's called? Vietnam! Hey, I've been there, done that, got a few holes in my T-shirt."

It's taken me a long time to accept that LBJ and his group of "the best and the brightest" could be so wrong. They were men I considered absolutely brilliant.

The "middle ground" strategy sure did not work. Building up our in-country U.S. military strength to above 500,000 did not work. Dropping thousands of tons of bombs did not work.

Nothing worked. America lost that war!

In 1967 there were secret letters exchanged between LBJ and North Vietnamese president Ho Chi Minh. I believe they are worth reflecting on.

LBJ wrote to President Ho on February 8, 1967, and I quote from his letter:

> I am writing to you in the hope that the conflict in Vietnam can be brought to an end. That conflict has already taken a heavy toll—in the

> lives lost, in the wounds inflicted, in property destroyed, and in simple human misery. If we fail to find a just and peaceful solution history will judge us harshly. Therefore, I believe that we both have a heavy obligation to seek earnestly the path to peace.

Seven days later, President Ho Chi Minh replied with an absolutely blistering letter:

> Your Excellency, here is my reply. . . . The U.S. Government has committed war crimes and crimes against peace and against humanity. . . . You have used the most inhumane and barbaric methods of warfare such as napalm, chemicals and toxic gases to massacre our people, destroy our crops and level our villages.
>
> You have rained down hundreds of thousands of tons of bombs, destroying towns, villages, factories, roads, dikes, dams and even churches, pagodas, hospitals and schools. . . . The Vietnamese people deeply love independence, liberty, and peace.
>
> Our cause is just and supported by all the peoples of the world including large segments of the American people. . . . The Vietnamese people never will yield to force nor agree to talks under the menace of bombs. Our cause is entirely just.
>
> It is our hope that the government of the United States acts with reason. Sincerely yours, Ho Chi Minh.

The question for us now is: Did we learn the lessons of Vietnam as we confront modern dangers—Russia, China, North Korea, Iran? Or, do those lessons of Vietnam even apply today in a new and different world? Russia's 2022 invasion of Ukraine has been devastating, including Putin's return to nuclear saber-rattling. The war between Hamas and Israel has been equally devastating. Both conflicts are reminiscent of Vietnam in their seemingly intractable nature and the huge number of innocent lives lost and portrayed as collateral damage. The thirst for what one group feels to be justified aggression so often overrides our ability to see each other as fellow human beings.

Ho Chi Minh, his followers, and fellow leaders—such as the legendary strategist General Vo Nguyen Giap—had a will to win that far exceeded our tolerance and our patience for a longer war with even more casualties.

Much has changed since the war in Vietnam ended: Stealth technology and precision weapons have replaced carpet bombing and dumb bombs. Drones have replaced manned aircraft in many situations. Our Special Operations teams expertly carry out successful covert missions that once required larger forces operating in the open.

But our experience in Vietnam teaches the enduring lesson that it is dangerous and costly to go to war—any war—especially when we don't understand the history, the culture, and the risks of the situation we are entering.

Many years later in 1997—when I was serving as CEO of CNN, roughly three decades after I served in the LBJ administration—I had a chance to sit down with General Giap to discuss the history we had shared from two different continents. The *New York Times* would later call Giap "the relentless and charismatic North Vietnamese general whose campaigns drove both France and the United States out of Vietnam."

I had reached out to the North Vietnamese in an attempt to establish a meeting with a North Vietnamese notetaker for Ho Chi Minh. It would have been a meeting with someone who had a similar role to mine during my years at the White House—notetaker for their nation's leader. I thought this would be a fascinating meeting.

Upon my arrival in Hanoi, along with a small team headed by CNN international editor Eason Jordan, we were informed that the Ho Chi Minh notetaker was unavailable to meet with me, because he was being "reeducated"—something that individuals would go through if they had been found to be sympathetic to the South. Reeducation meant being retrained in communist beliefs and the teachings of Ho Chi Minh.

Instead, my meeting was with General Giap himself. What a coup!

We sat down together in a beautiful Hanoi government house. Giap reached across the table to shake my hand, which I very much interpreted as a gesture that meant far more than "hello." Rather, it seemed to signify how far our two countries had come. Giap knew that I had been an assistant to President Johnson.

Tom with General Giap in Hanoi. Courtesy of CNN.

"Vietnam and America never should have gone to war," Giap told me. "You Americans never understood that this was a civil war. President Ho was committed to reuniting Vietnam—reuniting North and South Vietnam—just as your President Lincoln reunited America in your civil war."

It was a sad reminder of just how out of touch international conflicts can become. Great minds in Washington were trying to prevent the spread of communism. Great minds in Hanoi were trying to reunite their nation. Somehow, we should have been able to accomplish our goals without the loss of so many lives.

I certainly don't know how the conflict should have been handled, but what I did know, speaking with General Giap that day, was that he was a leader—the same as President Lyndon Johnson and his team of great generals—with a family and a love for his nation. And that had the White House leadership and the North Vietnamese leadership spent enough time together in the same room during those dark days in the late 1960s, far fewer people would have lost their lives.

To bring the same feelings I shared with Giap to the public, I tried to arrange a joint interview on CNN including Giap and General Westmoreland, moderated by anchor Bernard Shaw.

The idea was a Hail Mary, but both generals were retired by that point, and I always have enjoyed successful Hail Marys throughout my life.

General Giap did not firmly agree to the interview, but he indicated he was open to the idea. He told me, "We must not miss any opportunities between us. Vietnam is a peace-loving country. . . . We should accelerate all we can to compensate for what we missed fifty years ago. That is the task for both of us. It also is time for global and regional cooperation between Vietnam and the Asia Pacific region. The United States can give us a hand to heal the wounds of this war. It will serve the interests of both our countries.

"CNN can be very important in helping with that. CNN has been a good friend of Vietnam. Let's not let the dark clouds hover over our skies again. Let's care about the humanity. The Domino Theory was wrong. We were told we could not fight the Americans and win. But we fought and we won. Some told us it would take one hundred years to liberate South Vietnam, but most of the predictions about Vietnam were wrong. We love our country. We love our people. We love mankind. We founded our country so much along the lines of your president Jefferson."

General Westmoreland did not agree to a joint interview with General Giap. The interview never occurred. It was a major opportunity lost for America to reflect on the war.

It's impossible for me to say what the American or Vietnamese people would have learned from it, other than that General Giap was so certain that the war could have, and should have, been avoided altogether. Especially the horrors of 1968.

CHAPTER 7

THE SIX-DAY WAR OF 1967

"Truth is the first casualty of war."

The Six-Day War of 1967 between Israel and a number of Arab states began on June 5.

Tensions in the region had been high, and two Arab-Israeli wars had already occurred. Leading up to the third conflict, Egypt had moved military forces into place to prevent Israeli ships from using the Straits of Tiran, and Israel took it as a preemptive act of war.

During overnights, I was often the White House Press Office's duty officer. For that role, a secure White House phone had been installed in our Alexandria apartment by the White House Communications Agency, alongside our conventional phone.

At 2:38 a.m. on June 5, the conventional line rang. I was awakened by Helen Thomas of United Press International. She said, "Tom, war is breaking out in the Middle East between Israel, Syria, Egypt, and Jordan. Can you confirm that and secure a comment from President Johnson?"

I immediately picked up the secure White House line and asked for the Situation Room. To my surprise, the duty officer, Ray Wotring, said, "Mr. Johnson, we have absolutely nothing on that."

But before I could even relay that information back to Helen Thomas who was still on the other line, the duty officer said, "No . . . hold it. We're now receiving flashes from our embassies. I need to jump off to call Mr. Rostow."

Immediately I said, "Helen, UPI is ahead of us on this. It's unclear exactly what is happening. I'll try to provide a White House comment as quickly as we become better informed."

It wasn't the first time that journalists were ahead of the White House, nor would it be the last, but it was the first time in my career that the LBJ White House had been behind a news agency on something so major.

While on the phone with Helen Thomas, I realized that Edwina had fallen asleep with a cake in the oven. It was a lucky wake-up call for everyone in our house, except for the guests who were coming over the next evening for dinner.

As the situation developed, a White House car was sent for me, and I left Edwina with our two small children, Wyatt and Christa.

If any serious national emergency called for it, I knew that I would be included on the Marine One presidential fleet helicopter to be airlifted from the White House South Lawn to a classified secure location.

Fearing I might be traveling somewhere with the president rather than being available to take care of my family, I reminded Edwina that there was a plastic card in the glove compartment of our car that would give her instructions on where to go in the event that this was a situation that required evacuation of the White House staff and their families.

Edwina says she does not recall my telling her this, but my memory is that she was too preoccupied with frustration that her cake had been ruined. What she does recall is a series of loud sirens a few hours after I left for the White House.

Only having overheard enough of my conversations with Helen and the White House Situation Room, she knew there was something going on with "a war" but nothing more. When the sirens went off, she thought, "Well, I guess they've arrived . . . the Russians, the Iranians, someone . . ."

Fortunately, the sirens in Washington had nothing to do with the war.

For the next forty-eight hours there were nonstop communications between the White House, the Pentagon, the State Department, the CIA, and U.S. embassies in the region. This was a major crisis.

The Situation Room log prepared by duty officer Ray Wotring shows a FLASH was received from our embassy in Tel Aviv at 2:55 a.m. confirming an attack on Israel. By 5:00 a.m. the Situation Room log stated: "ALL HELL BROKE LOOSE."

However, the initial reports of an attack against Israel were false. It was Israel that had launched what was described as a preemptive strike against Egypt. Along with destroying almost all of Egypt's airpower, Israeli forces quickly captured the Sinai Peninsula, the West Bank of the Jordan River, the old city of Jerusalem, the Golan Heights, and the Gaza Strip.

The situation was tense, and in just five days, more than 15,000 Arabs were killed, while fewer than 1,000 Israelis died.

Throughout that week, U.S. and Soviet ships were ready to face off in the Mediterranean Sea, each of us there to protect our own interests and allies—the Soviets behind the Arab nations, and the United States behind Israel.

The situation with Russia was one of the tensest periods of all my time in the White House.

The most controversial moment that concerned the United States that week occurred on June 8—three days before the war's end—and, unexpectedly, was not due to the Soviets.

Israeli air forces attacked the *Liberty*, a U.S. Navy technical research ship that was later confirmed as a spy vessel. Thirty-four U.S. Navy officers and seamen were killed, along with one National Security Agency (NSA) employee. An additional 171 were wounded, and the ship was badly damaged.

U.S. authorities maintained that the *Liberty* was in international waters. Israel later apologized for the attack and stated that the ship had been attacked in error after being misidentified as an Egyptian enemy ship.

My closest friends on the National Security Council and at the CIA believed that the attack was deliberate. Sailors aboard the ship also were convinced the Israelis attacked the *Liberty* to prevent it from gathering and transmitting information about the war.

As I've heard for years, "Truth is the first casualty of war."

Israel made significant payments to the families of those killed and wounded. In 2023 a final payment of $22.3 million was made for damage to the ship.

Enormous numbers of people were displaced from the territories that Israel occupied, creating tensions that would last for years.

CHAPTER 8

1968

A nightmare year

There never has been a year in my lifetime quite as catastrophic as 1968. I so hope there never will be another one like it again.

In his book *1968*, author Mark Kurlansky called it "the year that rocked the world."

Nationally syndicated columnist Jules Witcover titled his book about 1968 *The Year the Dream Died.*

Tom Brokaw called it one of the most divisive years in American history.

President Johnson said it was "one of the most agonizing years that any president ever spent in the White House. I sometimes felt that I was living in a continuous nightmare."

Presidential historians labeled it the most consequential year of the twentieth century.

For many my age—twenty-seven at the time—1968 was a year of sex, drugs, and rock 'n' roll. Not for me.

Revolution was in the media, on the streets, and in the air.

Of course, the anti–Vietnam War music of the '60s was everywhere and very much a part of life then—no matter who you were, or where you worked.

I enjoyed some of the '60s and '70s music: Simon and Garfunkel, Crosby Stills and Nash, James Taylor. I sure loved Otis Redding, from my hometown of Macon, Georgia. (LBJ loved "Raindrops Keep Fallin' on My Head" by Burt Bacharach—he played it all the time!)

LBJ and Tom reviewing wire service reports at the White House. White House Archives.

However, I guess I was too straight to identify with much of the counterculture at the time. I avoided drugs, and I simply was not a part of the rock-'n'-roll scene. I never felt like I was missing out, but I was not what you might call a fun-loving person. Even at such a young age, I loved work and took my job seriously. I knew even then that I was incredibly fortunate to have a job that I loved doing.

So, while 1968 was traumatic for me—as it was for many—it would also prove to be an especially historic year, both personally and professionally. Working with some of the most important decision makers of the time could be as troubling as it was awe inspiring. The magnitude of the issues was almost incomprehensible, as the solutions to them often were.

After three years in the White House, my confidence and abilities as a young assistant to the president had grown dramatically. Fortunately, by 1968 I had found my footing.

So much of my time then was spent directly with the president—sitting in meetings, flying on Air Force One and Marine One, sometimes just the two of us, especially on days spent at his Texas ranch—often it felt like anywhere LBJ went, I was nearby.

Simply being in the presence of the president of the United States teaches you an immense amount not just about leadership and judgment but also about global issues. Beyond that, LBJ placed enormous responsibilities on me and on other young members of his White House staff.

This is another chapter based on my personal notes, White House recordings, photographs, presidential daily diaries, transcripts of telephone calls, and confidential materials that have been declassified, some of them recently.

Readers may find it quite surprising, but there are a number of disclosures in this chapter that never before have been published, even more than fifty years after the events occurred.

I have done my best to fact-check every element of this book. Where there is no documented backup information, I have attempted to compare my version of events with those who also were present.

Clockwise from left: General John McConnell, Air Force chief of staff; James R. Jones, appointments secretary to the president; Tom; and LBJ on Air Force One. White House Archives.

Now in my eighties, I simply do not trust my memory as much as I once did.

To the best of my knowledge, I do not break a single confidential agreement—either signed under oath or understood. I continue to take very seriously the lifetime agreements that I signed while in government.

Here is 1968 as I saw it:

January 1: A Fleeting Moment of Peace

The beginning was relatively quiet—at least for the first few minutes. Pope Paul VI had persuaded the governments of South Vietnam and the United States to declare January 1, 1968, as "a day of peace." The

North Vietnamese and their Viet Cong allies in South Vietnam also announced a thirty-six-hour cease-fire.

Despite the agreement, my notes show that only ten minutes after midnight, sixty miles from Saigon, the Viet Cong caught the South Vietnamese and the U.S. 2nd Marine Battalion by surprise in a rice paddy, killing 23 Marines and wounding 153 of the combined U.S.–South Vietnamese troops.

At that moment, the fighting resumed with the same violence and ruthlessness as before the cease-fire.

January 20: Khe Sanh under Threat

General William Westmoreland had heavily fortified the base at Khe Sanh, in hill country near the Laotian border, as a future staging point for U.S. and South Vietnamese attacks on the Ho Chi Minh Trail. The base had been under sporadic shelling since its establishment. Now, intelligence confirmed, attack was imminent—a massive, all-out attack by the North Vietnamese directed by the legendary General Giap—which would become one of the most controversial battles of the war.

President Johnson and his advisors saw in Khe Sanh the potential for a catastrophic military defeat that could change the course of the war—similar to the French defeat at Dien Bien Phu, a French base that the North Vietnamese overran in May 1954 after almost two months of intense battles as France was trying to retain control of its Southeast Asian colony.

The Dien Bien Phu attack was such a decisive victory for the communist-backed Viet Minh that it led to the termination of French involvement in Southeast Asia and ended with the historic signing of the Geneva Accords in 1954 that divided Vietnam at the 17th Parallel.

The French retreat from Vietnam allowed Chinese and Soviet influence to grow in the region.

Fourteen years later, with Khe Sanh in 1968, the stage was set for an equivalent event, and once again Western leadership was worried that an American loss would allow the influence of Chinese and Soviet communism to continue to grow. Further, the psychological impact of losing that U.S. base could result in an enormous loss of confidence within the ranks of the U.S. military, and in disastrous political consequences for LBJ.

The stakes were astoundingly high.

LBJ was determined that Khe Sanh not be lost, and he told Secretary of Defense Robert McNamara, Joint Chiefs chairman Wheeler, and General Westmoreland: "I do not want any damn Dien Bien Phu!"

During those days when concerns about an attack on Khe Sanh were highest, the president demanded the Joint Chiefs do "whatever it takes" to keep Khe Sanh from being overrun. He even demanded a written letter of assurance signed by all members of the Joint Chiefs of Staff.

January 21: Khe Sanh under Siege

Led by General Giap, massive artillery and ground troops surrounded Khe Sanh, launching devastating around-the-clock ground and mortar attacks against American and allied troops. It was apparent that Hanoi was prepared to lose vast numbers of troops in its determination to take Khe Sanh by sheer force.

Over the course of multiple months, the overrunning of Khe Sanh was prevented only by massive B-52 bombing all around the base, and countless U.S. Air Force and U.S. Navy air strikes with napalm and heavy munitions.

Recorded from my White House notes, there were 24,000 fighter-bomber sorties, 2,700 B-52 bomber runs, and 110,000 tons of bombs dropped during what would become a seventy-seven-day siege. The best estimates were that the North Vietnamese lost up to 15,000 women and men. America lost 205 soldiers, and hundreds more were wounded.

Following the end of the siege in April, the base at Khe Sanh was abandoned just three months later, in July 1968. I never learned why.

Had we lost the base during the period of the attack, it would have been one of the most important propaganda victories of the war for the North.

For me, the battle of Khe Sanh showed the incredible resolve of Hanoi to win the war at all costs.

January 21: B-52 Crashes with Nukes Aboard

Incidentally, within only a few hours of the siege beginning at Khe Sanh, the U.S. military lost a B-52 bomber, call sign HOBO 28, in Greenland with four live hydrogen bombs aboard.

Fire had erupted in the B-52's navigation compartment, and the plane plummeted to the ice about seven miles short of the runway. There were ruptures in the nuclear warheads, but although the conventional nonnuclear weapons did explode, there were no nuclear explosions—most fortunately, as the four hydrogen bombs aboard had one hundred times the power of the nuclear weapons that were dropped on Hiroshima during World War II.

The day we lost that bomber, President Johnson decided that no more live nuclear weapons were to be carried aloft at any time.

Despite the resulting military doctrine, on August 30, 2007, a B-52 mistakenly flew with six live nuclear-armed cruise missiles from Minot, North Dakota, to Barksdale Air Force Base in Louisiana. Thankfully, it landed safely.

At the end of his presidency, LBJ conveyed to me the relief he felt at not being the president who "pushed the button" and triggered a nuclear war.

January 23: The *Pueblo*

It is very rare that three junior White House staffers find themselves as the only three duty officers surrounding the president when an epic crisis breaks. Such was the case on January 23, 1968, for Richard Moose of the National Security Council and Art McCafferty, the head of the White House's Situation Room, and me.

Left to right: Tom, LBJ, Dick Moose, and Situation Room head Art McCafferty reviewing the *Pueblo* seizure by North Korea. Courtesy of the LBJ Presidential Library.

During those dark morning hours, we learned that North Korean ships had attacked and captured an American spy ship, the *Pueblo*, which was collecting electronic data off the coast of North Korea.

In the moments following the first FLASH message, the three of us assisted President Johnson, joining him in Press Secretary George Christian's office in the West Wing until more senior officials could arrive.

By the time LBJ learned of the capture, it was too late to scramble the two on-alert U.S. fighter jets in South Korea to try to intercept the North Koreans before they forced the *Pueblo* into a North Korean port.

LBJ could not understand why our on-alert jets could not get to the scene sooner.

The NSC staffer said, "Mr. President, we had to download the nuclear weapons that were aboard the alert jets before reloading them with conventional munitions."

There was never a time when I saw LBJ at such careful, thoughtful, and deliberate use of his judgment as that night. Decisions were made in those moments that could have resulted in the release of nuclear weapons, massive troop mobilization on the Korean Peninsula, and the deaths of all U.S. sailors aboard the *Pueblo*.

The *Pueblo* crew ultimately were held captive until December 23, 1968—eleven long months. North Korea still has the ship on display in their capital, Pyongyang. It is the only U.S. naval ship "still held in captivity."

January 30–31: Tet

In his book *As I Saw It*, Georgia native and former U.S. secretary of state Dean Rusk writes: "Most wars have a turning point, a key battle or series of engagements that are decisive. North Vietnam's Tet Offensive of 1968 was the turning point of the American involvement in Vietnam."

Ten days after the assault on Khe Sanh began, the massive 1968 Tet Offensive was launched on the Vietnamese lunar New Year. A highly coordinated nationwide offensive staged by the North Vietnamese and Viet Cong, it is still considered by many to be one of the greatest intelligence failures in American military history. The assault was a gigantic surprise for U.S. and South Vietnamese forces. The South Vietnamese army was particularly unprepared. Many South Vietnamese soldiers had gone home to be with their families for the Tet holiday.

However, I do want to praise director Dick Helms and the CIA. The CIA had in fact warned that the Viet Cong and the North Vietnamese were preparing a major assault, although they did not know exactly when, where, or how large it would be. They also did not know the attacks would focus on all the cities. But they were aware that something big was coming.

On January 28 my Tuesday Lunch notes show that Joint Chiefs chairman General Wheeler reported: "General Westmoreland faces a very serious situation. . . . He is about to have the most vicious battle of the Vietnam War."

Still, the timing and the awesome strength of the Tet Offensive did—and I emphasize *did*—surprise everybody in Washington, including President Johnson.

White House press secretary George Christian later said: "The Tet Offensive came as a brutal surprise to President Johnson and to all of his advisers. We had been led to believe that the Viet Cong were pretty well defanged." They had not been.

General Westmoreland was the only leader who maintained until his death that he was *not* surprised.

While I was an admirer and, later, a personal friend of General Westmoreland, I know that the president and his key advisors in Washington were shocked by the magnitude of the Tet Offensive.

More than 70,000 North Vietnamese and Viet Cong fighters attacked over a hundred cities, villages, towns, and military bases, hitting virtually every major city and military outpost in South Vietnam, causing significant losses. There are varying figures, but according to my firsthand notes, thirty-six of the country's forty-four provincial capitals, as well as five of the six autonomous cities, were assaulted.

In Saigon alone, the American Embassy, the Vietnamese Joint General Staff compound, Independence Palace, Tan Son Nhut Air Base, and the radio station were all struck. General Westmoreland was pinned down in his personal residence in Saigon, unable to get to his headquarters until morning. Once he did get there, he was isolated with more danger, and cut off from returning to his residence.

Rockets and mortars hit the major U.S. base at Da Nang. Several hundred fighters attacked the U.S. air base at Pleiku.

Walt Rostow took an urgent call in the Tuesday Lunch meeting at the White House on January 30. My notes show that he reported: "We have just been informed that we are being heavily mortared in Saigon. The Presidential Palace, our Bachelor Office Quarters, our embassy and the city of Saigon itself have been hit."

Severe battles took place throughout the country.

"Until Tet, our military kept the North from overrunning the South. Although support for U.S. policies was eroding, politically we still had the support of the Congress and the country," according to Secretary Rusk. "But, after Tet, things changed."

Rusk continued: "Even though U.S. and South Vietnamese forces dealt the North Vietnamese and Viet Cong a shattering military blow, the Tet Offensive unleashed a tidal change in American opinion about the war." It was more of a public relations and perception loss than an actual military loss.

In the White House, there was a sense of deep concern.

Casualties on the battlefield were mounting. Protests, especially on college campuses, were becoming more serious. Reports coming back from press correspondents in the field were alarming. The war had clearly taken a turn, and citizens back home were demanding accountability.

The battles raged for two weeks—except in the city of Hue, where the communists fought for a month against everything the United States and the South Vietnamese could throw at them. News footage of the Battle of Hue was shipped back to the three U.S. networks and into the homes of Americans. Dan Rather of CBS News saw that battle firsthand and reported it.

President Johnson reached General Westmoreland on the phone and tore into him. I remember clearly LBJ's words:

"Westy, what the hell is going on out there? You just told Congress there is light at the end of the tunnel and all that!"

Westmoreland's deputy, Brigadier General Zeb Bradford—my friend from Atlanta—recalled Westmoreland saying: "Everything that I have worked for is lost. It's all been a failure."

Westy was a soldier's general. I attended many meetings with him in the White House, in Hawaii, at Cam Ranh Bay Air Base in Vietnam, and elsewhere. He looked like a general and spoke with confidence. He continued throughout his lifetime to attend Vietnam Veterans parades dressed in the same uniform with a chest full of combat medals that he had won during the war.

Unfortunately, he was fighting a very different type of war than those he had been trained to fight at West Point. This was jungle warfare.

I actually do not think that Westmoreland intended to mislead LBJ, but there is no question that he was far too optimistic about the war. And as a result of his optimism, countless lives were lost.

For me, Tet was the turning point when I began to grasp how little those of us in Washington understood the situation in Asia.

Even in my later years, I still don't know when LBJ began to realize that news reports from Vietnam often were much more accurate than the government reports coming back from his own military commanders.

General Westmoreland addressing Secretary of Defense Robert McNamara, Vietnamese vice president Nguyen Cao Ky, and LBJ, while Tom takes notes. White House Archives.

Not long after the Tet Offensive began, General Westmoreland requested another 200,000 troops. Westmoreland believed very strongly in a search-and-destroy strategy that relied on highly trained U.S. ground troops supported by overwhelming airpower. His request would have taken our troop levels from 500,000 to over 700,000 in-country. To do that would have required a call-up of reserves and a huge increase in funding.

A new secretary of defense, Clark Clifford, made a thorough analysis of the war and recommended a major change of strategy, which greatly differed from Westmoreland's. Secretary Clifford recommended that more of the war fighting be shifted to the South Vietnamese. This program was called Vietnamization. Clifford also felt that we should pursue an all-out attempt for a negotiated peace with Hanoi, as the United States was shouldering too much expense for the prolonged war, with far too many lives already lost, and Westmoreland's request for 200,000 additional troops would only prolong the conflict.

Ultimately, Westmoreland's request was rejected.

More important, the president and his advisors concluded that Tet, the siege on Khe Sanh, and our extraordinary loss of American lives had made it clear that the war was just not winnable Westmoreland's way.

Some members of the leadership became so alarmed that they secretly discussed the use of tactical nuclear weapons (TAC/NUCS).

On January 31, Robert Ginsburgh, National Security Council staff member and assistant to the chairman of the Joint Chiefs of Staff, wrote: "If, despite General Westmoreland's best efforts, the situation should become desperate, the issue of TAC/NUCS will be raised." His memo went on to ask: "Would contingency target analysis be in order?"

He then wrote by hand: "Caution that plans should be very, very, very closely held."

February 2–16: Fracture Jaw

On February 2, National Security Advisor Walt Rostow wrote to President Johnson: "One reason for my particular concern for the battle of Khe Sanh is to avoid a situation of battlefield crisis in which General Westmoreland and the Joint Chiefs would ask you to release tactical nuclear weapons."

Protecting Khe Sanh was so important that Westmoreland even established a super-secret group to study the use of TAC/NUCS, code-named Fracture Jaw. In a cable, he wrote: "If Washington officials are so intent on 'sending a message to Hanoi,' surely small tactical nuclear weapons would be a way to tell Hanoi something."

On that same day, February 2, 1968, Joint Chiefs of Staff chairman General Wheeler told the president that the contingency of using nuclear weapons was "most remote, although planning IS going forward."

Admiral Sharp, Commander in Chief, Pacific (CINCPAC), later messaged General Wheeler with a copy to General Westmoreland:

"Military prudence alone requires that we do detailed planning regarding units to be deployed, delivery vehicles, weapon availability, preferred weapons by type and yield, constraints, preferred delivery means, tactics and other operational details. . . . We are accomplishing the planning under strictest security in Okinawa with a special planning team. The planning currently is well underway. . . . I forwarded to Westy on 29 January a message describing step by step procedures. . . . Air delivered tactical nuclear weapons provide the immediate capability. . . . I believe we are prepared for this eventuality."

On February 3, a sequence of events began that I describe as "plausible deniability" conversations.

Walt Rostow wrote this message to LBJ: "I thought you would not wish me to discuss the nuclear weapons matter in a [Tuesday Lunch] meeting. . . . I did discuss it with Clark Clifford. . . . He confined his advice in saying that I had the duty to share my anxiety with you verbally. . . . I told him that he could *explore* the question . . . with

General Wheeler . . . provided it was understood that this in no way was a White House request and the matter had never even been raised WITH the President, let alone BY the President. . . . I did not envision that any formal staff work would be set in train by that conversation. The fault for the JCS planning proceeding, therefore, is mine."

To clarify, Rostow did tell Secretary Clifford that formal nuclear contingency planning could begin. It was not President Johnson who personally authorized that step, as far as I know.

However, word of the secret nuclear contingency planning began to spread around the very highest levels in the Pentagon, as well as within the senior military chain of command in Vietnam.

I personally found the discussions terrifying.

On February 3, General Westmoreland wrote JCS chairman Wheeler and CINCPAC Admiral Sharp:

"Our situation at Khe Sanh as compared with the French at Dien Bien Phu is different in three significant aspects. We have [greater] supporting air[power] for all weather attack. We have reinforcing heavy artillery within range of Khe Sanh. We have multiple techniques of aerial supply, and we are within helicopter support range for troop reinforcement, logistic support, and Medivac."

He emphasized that the United States could reinforce Khe Sanh in all weather conditions including the use of massive B-52 bombings, and concluded:

"The use of tactical nuclear weapons should not be required in the present situation.

"However, should the situation in the DMZ area change dramatically, we should be prepared to introduce weapons of greater effectiveness against massed forces. Under such circumstances, I visualize that either tactical nuclear weapons or chemical agents would be active candidates for employment."

The use of cluster bombs or "controlled fragmentation munitions" *was* authorized. These bombs killed countless civilians. Around the world, these terrible weapons are still being used.

On February 7, CINCPAC Admiral Sharp sent a message to all generals and admirals under his command saying that the nuclear contingency plan "appears conceptually sound and contains the details necessary for implementation."

On February 9, everything hit the fan. Secretary of State Dean Rusk testified before the Senate Armed Services Committee, headed by Senator William Fulbright, who was a major critic of the Vietnam War.

Based on an anonymous tip, Senator Fulbright asked Secretary Rusk about the possible use of nuclear weapons in Vietnam. (I always have wondered if my friend Dick Moose secretly advised Senator Fulbright or his friends on the Fulbright staff. Dick had worked for Senator Fulbright, he was from Arkansas, and he strongly opposed U.S. strategy in Vietnam.)

Rusk denied the existence of any plans for nuclear use or stockpiling of nuclear weapons in Vietnam.

On the same day as Rusk's testimony, White House press secretary George Christian said that there hadn't been any recommendations received for the use of nuclear weapons. (Technically, that statement *was* true.)

On February 10, Rostow wrote to the president: "There are no nuclear weapons [currently] in South Vietnam. Presidential authority would be required to put them there."

They were, however, ready to be deployed on B-52s from nearby Guam, in case a nuclear confrontation with China or with the Soviet Union were ever to arise. They could be delivered by B-52s, specialized naval guns, specialized artillery, and a number of other means.

To the best of my knowledge, no nuclear weapons were ever stored inside Vietnam.

On February 12, Admiral Sharp sent this TOP SECRET/SENSITIVE cable: "Discontinue all planning for Fracture Jaw. . . . There can be no disclosure of the content of the plan or knowledge that such planning was either underway or suspended."

Declassification of my Tuesday Lunch notes and copies of classified cables now provide the facts. The truth cannot be erased.

On February 16, President Johnson said he never had been given a recommendation about deploying nuclear weapons. His quote: "No recommendation has been made to me." (Technically, that was also true.) In his most emphatic voice, he told reporters: "Beyond that, I think we ought to put an end to that discussion."

Thankfully, tactical nukes were never used. Even now, I hate to think of the possible consequences if they had been.

It's an understatement to say this put my greatest fear to rest.

March 31: The President Decides Not to Seek a Second Term

President Johnson had been considering not running for reelection in 1968 for some time.

He had shared those thoughts only with family members, especially Lady Bird, and a very few trusted friends and staffers, including his press secretary, George Christian. White House legal counsel Larry Temple told me that LBJ had been speaking with Texas governor John Connally since 1967 about the possibility of not seeking a second full term.

On January 14, 1968, former LBJ aide Horace Busby had written a two-page ending for LBJ's State of the Union address that was to be delivered on January 17. I was personally asked by George Christian to type the conclusion to the State of the Union in which LBJ would have announced, that night, that he would not seek another term as president.

On the night of the State of the Union, LBJ carried that ending in the inside pocket of his suit coat. But he did not use it. He had decided on the drive to the Capitol that he wouldn't make the announcement that evening.

Later he said that it would have been premature, explaining that he could not ask Congress to enact legislation in the speech and then say that he was leaving. It would make him a lame duck for almost a year. Yet the thought of not running for reelection was never far from his mind.

He had various reasons, but three dominated the discussion.

First was his health. LBJ had experienced a serious heart attack in 1955.

Dr. J. Willis Hurst of Atlanta, who as a young navy doctor had met the ambulance at Bethesda Naval Hospital in 1955, would be LBJ's physician for life, as well as chief of cardiology at Bethesda Naval, and later chairman of the Department of Medicine at Emory University in Atlanta. Dr. Hurst said heart bypass surgery was not an option. To cope with his pain, LBJ frequently took nitroglycerin tablets.

In 1968, after five years in the Oval Office, LBJ was not sure he would live four more years. His father had died at age sixty, and LBJ predicted he too would die young. He once told White House legal counsel Larry Temple, "All the Johnson boys die young."

The second reason not to seek another term, LBJ said, was that he wanted to devote the maximum amount of time to bringing about a peace in Vietnam. He said that he did not want to spend a single hour of a single day focused on the election when he could be spending his time focusing on peace. He was far more determined to end the war than to keep his political power.

"I can't get peace in Vietnam and be president too," he told longtime aide and advisor Horace Busby.

I always found this to be a very noble position for a politician to take. In my eyes even now, it shows the true LBJ.

With his focus solely on the task of ending the war, President Johnson authorized multiple peace missions to other nations. He so wanted to convince Ho Chi Minh to come to a conference table to negotiate "an honorable peace."

Several of these missions were conducted through the French and through North Vietnamese diplomats based in France. Dr. Henry Kissinger, then still a professor at Harvard, led one of these top-secret "channels" with a fellow academic in Paris.

My first contact with Kissinger was as a notetaker. Although he would become a polarizing figure in American history, Kissinger was well connected in both domestic and international circles, and there was enormous respect for him within the Johnson White House.

While some thought of him as a warmonger, it's my view that Kissinger wanted peace, and it was ultimately his connections with

China that helped the United States achieve "peace with honor" during the Nixon administration.

The third, and possibly most important, reason for LBJ's decision not to run again was that his wife, Lady Bird, did not want him to do so. Press Secretary George Christian and Texas governor John Connally, two of LBJ's closest political allies and advisors, felt the same way.

Only a handful of friends, family members, and aides knew in early 1968 how serious his thoughts were about not running for reelection. Neither Lynda nor Luci supported the president announcing his decision not to seek a second term. They both wanted him to run again.

During that time I had mixed feelings about LBJ's dilemma. I certainly could understand why he would want to move on, but I also thought he could win a second term if we secured the peace treaty with Hanoi that he so badly wanted.

On March 30, in a handwritten note to LBJ, I expressed my thoughts:

> Mr. President,
>
> You must consider the consequences of the decision and how it will be interpreted:
>
> 1. It will turn the country over to Bobby Kennedy—He and his legion will ruthlessly erase so much of what you have accomplished.
> 2. So much of this country and so much of the Communist world—including Hanoi—will interpret this as the President "running out."
>   a. Because he is afraid of defeat in the election.
>   b. Because he is no longer able to lead the nation.
>   c. Because we cannot reach our objectives in Vietnam.
>   d. Because Hanoi's will is stronger than America's.
> 3. Many men—many thousand boys the age of Pat [Nugent] and Chuck [Robb] and myself—have died supporting the President's will and objectives. They will feel, and their parents will feel they have died in vain—and if Bobby wins—will see this country having "lost" its first war.
>
> I say all this because I love my President and believe him to be right. We can win—we can persevere.

I admit now I was wrong. He did the right thing by deciding not to run again.

It was a tremendously challenging time to make such major decisions. The country was extremely divided. Shouts of "Hey, Hey, LBJ, how many kids did you kill today" continued to rack him with pain nearly every time he went out to public functions.

At 9 p.m. on March 31, 1968, LBJ went on television. Delivering his message with what the *New York Times* called a "funereal voice" and "solemn expression," he told the nation, "I shall not seek and I will not accept the nomination of my party as your president."

He later told reporters that his decision was "completely irrevocable."

April 3: A Chance at Peace

Hanoi Radio broadcast a report that North Vietnam was ready to meet American representatives to consider an end to the fighting. I handed the president this Reuters news service flash.

By this point, LBJ had announced he would be stepping down, and the United States would place a pause on bombing. It appeared—very briefly—that it was a message to Hanoi that had worked.

April 4: Trouble at Home

With so much attention going to the war in Vietnam, sometimes it's hard to remember how fragile things were on U.S. soil. It wasn't just opposition to the war; it was the height of the civil rights movement—one of the most important and tumultuous phases in American history.

At approximately 7:23 p.m. the Associated Press teleprinter in the Press Office erupted with a loud, continuous bell ringing as a FLASH came in. The first words to come across the teletype: "Dr. Martin Luther King has been shot in Memphis."

I ripped the alert from the machine and ran through the president's secretarial office into the Oval Office.

Sitting with the president were Robert Woodruff, chairman of the Coca-Cola Company, and former Georgia governor Carl Sanders, there on a personal courtesy call, a no-agenda meeting of a sort that the president occasionally held with old political friends and business leaders.

I greeted my fellow Georgians as LBJ read the alert. The President's Daily Diary shows I handed him the message at 7:24 p.m.

LBJ called Attorney General Ramsey Clark, FBI director J. Edgar Hoover, Governor Buford Ellington of Tennessee, Defense Secretary Clark Clifford, Coretta Scott King, Atlanta mayor Ivan Allen Jr., and others. All the while, he kept a close watch on live coverage shown on the three TV sets in his office.

He was incredibly steady during the crisis, as he always was when chaos circled.

Robert Woodruff and Governor Sanders stayed in the Oval Office as eyewitnesses to history until 7:45 p.m.

I thought that President Johnson's decision to invite Mr. Woodruff and Governor Sanders to remain in the Oval Office for a short time was a very good one. It enabled Woodruff to call Atlanta mayor Ivan Allen to alert him that there likely would be riots in all American cities that night and that Mayor Allen should take the necessary steps in Atlanta to maintain peace, including additional fire and police support, if needed.

Woodruff told Allen not to worry about the additional costs—conveying a commitment that he would personally cover the expenditures. That was classic Robert Woodruff, who for years was Mr. Anonymous in Atlanta, giving away large amounts of money to various causes, especially Emory University, and never looking for credit.

As the evening progressed, we sat and waited for more news, but had no real hope that Dr. King would pull through. At 8:20 p.m. the Justice Department confirmed that Dr. King had died.

There were demonstrations in Atlanta, but no violent riots occurred there as they did in many other American cities the night of Dr. King's assassination.

Tom greeting fellow Georgians, Coca-Cola CEO Robert Woodruff (*left*) and former Georgia governor Carl Sanders (*right*), as LBJ reads the MLK flash. Courtesy of the LBJ Presidential Library.

Over the next three days, all hell broke loose across the country: rioting in Washington, Chicago, Los Angeles, and Detroit.

Demonstrations that turned into riots in some areas spread throughout the District of Columbia, and the city could not handle the violent situation. Mayor Walter Washington asked LBJ for help. The next day, the president signed an executive order calling units of the 82nd Airborne in to restore law and order and to protect the White House and other government buildings across D.C.

In those moments, LBJ placed a great deal of faith in the team of legal advisors who were preparing that executive order—Larry Temple, Supreme Court Justice Abe Fortas, and Deputy Attorney General Warren Christopher.

Temple recalls LBJ telling them: "Boys, don't get me in unless you know how to get me out." Larry Temple knew exactly what he meant. It was quintessential LBJ behavior—always looking past the issue at hand and anticipating how it could backfire.

Meetings were held on April 5 with civil rights leaders Roy Wilkins, Whitney Young, Bayard Rustin, Walter Fauntroy, Dorothy Height, Leon Sullivan, Walter Washington, and Thurgood Marshall. The group constituted the most important Black leaders of the time.

Whitney Young made their position clear to LBJ: "We need more than patience and nonviolence. We need funds for the cities."

President Johnson pledged comprehensive action on a variety of bills such as open-housing reform.

After productive talks, all parties agreed that they would speak out and support his calls for nonviolence.

I never saw a finer hour of this president, his cabinet, and the Black leaders of America resolving to unite around nonviolence and to work together in Dr. King's honor to make America a better place for our minorities, our poor, our disenfranchised.

On that same day, LBJ accompanied the leaders to Dr. King's memorial service at the National Cathedral.

Even though LBJ attended more funerals than anyone I've ever known, the one time that he didn't attend an important funeral—and

I thought he should have—was Dr. King's in Atlanta on April 9. Instead, he sent Vice President Humphrey.

The Secret Service had reported potential threats to the president in Atlanta—particularly from white fanatics who opposed LBJ's passion for civil rights—and they recommended that he not attend. However, we received threats almost everywhere we traveled in the late 1960s. The only places that were truly safe from threats and protestors were military bases.

I thought then, and still believe now, there was a more personal reason LBJ did not attend Dr. King's funeral.

While the two men had once been close allies united on civil rights, they had become adversaries over the Vietnam War. The open opposition of one of America's most famous moral leaders forever changed the nation's outlook on the war, as well as their personal relationship.

I will always be so thankful that it was Dr. King who led Black America in that era through peaceful nonviolence, with other leaders like John Lewis, Jesse Jackson, Vernon Jordan, and Andrew Young. I hate to think what would have happened to the country if militant leaders who openly embraced violence, such as H. Rap Brown or Stokely Carmichael, had become the dominant voices in the civil rights movement instead of Dr. King.

Ultimately, Dr. King was morally correct in his opposition to the war as well.

April 7: The Aftermath

Three days after Martin Luther King had been killed, the District of Columbia and the Washington area were still in turmoil.

LBJ took a secret helicopter tour over the city as smoke still rose from fires below. I was with him in the chopper, along with a small group of other advisors. He was almost totally silent for the entire ride. The only sound was the noise of the helicopter rotors. He just sat and looked out the window, taking it in with an appearance of sadness and despair. He was soaking up the images of the flames and smoke

LBJ in profile, on Marine One flight over D.C. as the city burned. Courtesy of the LBJ Presidential Library.

rising from areas of downtown Washington not far from the White House itself.

In my later years, I sometimes wonder why I didn't think to myself during particular moments, "Tom, can you imagine that you're sitting up here in a helicopter, with the president of the United States, flying over the nation's capital and seeing Washington burning?"

I've thought about many of those historic moments, particularly those where I was the only person present with the president except the Secret Service. At the time, I was just too focused on the job at hand to reflect on the historic nature of what I was witnessing, and who I was witnessing it with.

When we did finally talk about the burning and rioting, I remember there being a sense of gloom because of Dr. King's steadfast message for nonviolent change.

The president designated Sunday April 7 as a National Day of Mourning in honor of Dr. King.

June 5: More Carnage

Just two months after the tragic killing of Dr. King, President Johnson retired to bed at 12:50 a.m. At 3:31 he was awakened by National Security Advisor Walt Rostow with a FLASH from the Situation Room that confirmed Senator Robert Kennedy had been shot at the Ambassador Hotel in Los Angeles while campaigning for president.

Between that call at 3:31 and daybreak, LBJ called Attorney General Ramsey Clark, Secret Service director James Rowley, FBI director J. Edgar Hoover, Secretary of Defense Clark Clifford, and the twenty-seven-year-old deputy press secretary who was the overnight press duty officer—me.

This was another moment of quintessential LBJ behavior in a moment of crisis. He wanted to make certain that his most important advisors provided him with all the information he might need to know.

He often told us, "A man's judgment is no better than his information."

LBJ and Mrs. Johnson dispatched messages to Senator Kennedy's mother, Rose, and to his wife, Ethel.

At 5:01 a.m. Walt Rostow called to advise the president that Senator Robert Kennedy was dead.

The president asked that I act as one of the White House liaisons to the Kennedy family, along with Appointments Secretary James R. Jones and Colonel Haywood Smith of the White House Military Office.

My personal view was that Senator Robert Kennedy never accepted LBJ as president. LBJ felt that Bobby did everything he could to undercut him during his presidency. It was visceral.

But hard feelings didn't prevent LBJ from treating Robert Kennedy's death as anything less than a national tragedy. Every request made by the Kennedy family was approved by President Johnson.

The White House provided Air Force C-140s (Lockheed JetStars), Boeing 707s, Secret Service personnel, special phone lines, and White House vehicles. Kennedy family members were transported from Boston and Hyannis in Massachusetts, and from New Hampshire.

Colonel Haywood Smith of the U.S. Marine Corps informed me that Air Force One's crew knocked out a section of the aircraft so that Senator Kennedy's casket could be brought aboard the plane in Los Angeles.

LBJ also assigned Secret Service protection to Senator Edward Kennedy, as well as all 1968 presidential candidates.

Despite the well-known hostility between Senator Robert Kennedy and President Johnson, the staffs of the two men worked together to do everything possible to support the Kennedy family.

August 20: Another Shock

Quite unexpectedly, the Red Army invaded Czechoslovakia.

This Soviet aggression surprised LBJ, Secretary Rusk, Secretary Clifford, Walt Rostow, and most of the intelligence community.

I did not see the intelligence reports—the President's Daily Briefs—in the days leading up to the Soviet invasion, so I cannot evaluate the quality of the information President Johnson received immediately prior to the event. But I believe, though I do not know, that it was a total surprise, just as the Tet attacks had been in Vietnam.

The Soviet ambassador to the United States, Anatoly Dobrynin, called and asked to meet with the president. They met in the Cabinet Room late in the evening of August 20. Dobrynin said that Soviet troops were moving into Czechoslovakia "because the Czechs asked us to do so."

General Earle Wheeler, chairman of the Joint Chiefs of Staff, later told the president there was no military action that the United States could take. "We do not have the forces to do it." Almost all of our military focus was on Vietnam and Southeast Asia, and there was no adequate way for the United States military to confront the Soviets in Czechoslovakia.

LBJ knew how thin our military capacities were already stretched. But he was devastated about his lack of ability to support Czechoslovakia.

August 27: Not a Happy Birthday

LBJ's sixtieth birthday was held at the LBJ Ranch in Texas with the people he loved most: his family. Even though the event was set up for rest and relaxation, it was a somber, sad occasion.

Much of this time at the ranch was spent watching the divisive 1968 Democratic National Convention in Chicago.

Aides Larry Temple and Jim Jones were manning the phones at the LBJ Ranch. Communicating with them from the convention in Chicago were Texas governor John Connally and former "acting" White House chief of staff Marvin Watson. (LBJ never had an official chief of staff: he wanted everyone reporting to him to hold equal access and authority. LBJ was the center of the wheel, with all of his advisors as spokes.)

Supplementing the information coming over the phone, LBJ monitored his three TV sets. He was aware of almost every aspect of the convention.

Larry Temple later told me he thought that LBJ wanted to be invited to the convention on his August 27 birthday. Others thought he was looking for approbation from the Democratic National Committee members in the form of being drafted as the nominee, even though he would have likely turned it down.

Air Force One had been placed on standby at nearby Bergstrom Air Force Base in Austin to take LBJ to Chicago if he decided to go.

After countless hard years—especially 1968—LBJ badly wanted the applause and the gratitude of his party. Sadly, it never came.

The Democratic convention ultimately proved to be a disaster for the party and for the nominee, Vice President Hubert Humphrey.

October 14: Furtherance

The "Furtherance" meeting took place on October 14, 1968, in the Cabinet Room of the White House. Of all the top-secret meetings I ever attended on issues of national security, Furtherance was the most chilling.

It began at 1:40 p.m. and lasted less than a half hour. I was the only notetaker in the meeting.

All of the Joint Chiefs of Staff were in attendance: General Earle Wheeler, chairman; Admiral Thomas Moorer, U.S. Navy; General Leonard Chapman, U.S. Marines; General John McConnell, U.S. Air Force; and General Bruce Palmer, U.S. Army. In addition, General Westmoreland had been called back from Vietnam.

Secretary of State Dean Rusk and Secretary of Defense Clark Clifford were the two cabinet officers present, as well as National Security Advisor Walt Rostow; the head of the National Security Council, Bromley Smith; Press Secretary George Christian; and myself.

Senator Richard Russell of Georgia was there as chairman of the U.S. Senate Armed Services Committee. He was representing the entire House of Representatives *and* the U.S. Senate.

I find it absolutely unimaginable today that a single member would be delegated the power to speak for the entire United States Congress. However, Senator Russell was so respected by his colleagues, by the Joint Chiefs of Staff, and by President Johnson that he had earned that role in this meeting. There is no other time I know of when such power was vested in a single elected official.

The Furtherance meeting began with Secretary Clifford describing how nuclear weapons can be released, emphasizing that only the president has the authority to make that release decision. I have chosen not to include those specific details out of my own personal concern for once-classified material being disclosed even now.

Clifford said the existing instructions—established prior to this meeting—stipulated that if the United States were attacked and if the president were killed or could not be found, a full-fledged nuclear response was to be ordered against *both* the Soviet Union and China.

Clifford said: "We recommend three major changes. The [United States'] response could go to either country—not both. There could be a small-scale or accidental attack. We do not recommend full attack [in all situations]. This [change in policy] would permit a limited response. . . . Instructions on the response to a conventional attack would be conventional, not a nuclear one, as is now in the plan. . . .

[Before today] there was only one document of [nuclear release] instructions. . . . Now there would be two documents." (That is, separate instructions for a nuclear weapons attack on the United States and for an attack on the United States with conventional nonnuclear weapons.)

Clifford concluded his remarks by saying, "We all recommend this."

National Security Advisor Walt Rostow said: "We think it is an essential change. This [existing nuclear release policy] was dangerous. We recommend going forward with this recommendation."

Joint Chiefs chairman Wheeler agreed. "All the Joint Chiefs of Staff and commanders have been consulted on this. We recommend approval."

At that point each member of the JCS—Admiral Moorer, General Chapman, General McConnell, General Palmer—said, "I concur, sir."

LBJ's lifelong mentor, Senator Richard Russell, said he was also in full agreement.

My notes of this meeting carried the highest classification of all the conversations that I transcribed by hand. A typed copy was declassified by the National Archives and Records Administration on December 18, 2012. (My records do not show when the notes were declassified by other intelligence agencies.)

A copy of the declassified, typed one-page "EYES ONLY FOR THE PRESIDENT" document is pictured.

October–November: The Anna Chennault Episode

What I will describe next is a story that was very tightly kept for more than fifty years.

Some documents, tape recordings, and intercepts became available only within recent years at the LBJ Library in Austin and at the Nixon Presidential Library. It is my understanding that additional files remain sealed at both the LBJ and Nixon libraries.

To be clear, there have been some press accounts, as well as a few official government attempts to release accurate information on the issue, based on limited knowledge of a few participants.

EYES ONLY FOR THE PRESIDENT

25

NOTES OF THE PRESIDENT'S MEETING WITH:

SECRETARY OF DEFENSE CLARK CLIFFORD
SECRETARY OF STATE DEAN RUSK
GENERAL EARLE WHEELER
ADMIRAL THOMAS MOORER
GENERAL LEONARD CHAPMAN
GENERAL JOHN McCONNELL
GENERAL BRUCE PALMER
BROMLEY SMITH

WALT ROSTOW
GEORGE CHRISTIAN
TOM JOHNSON

JOINING THE MEETING:

SENATOR RICHARD RUSSELL
GENERAL WILLIAM WESTMORE-LAND

OCTOBER 14, 1968
Cabinet Room
1:40 pm

SECRETARY CLIFFORD: There have been instructions issued on authority to release nuclear weapons in the event the President has been killed or cannot be found. This is to prevent a breakdown in the chain of command.

The project's code-name is "Futherance."

We recommend three major changes:

(1) Under the former orders, a full nuclear response against both the Soviet Union and China was ordered if we were attacked. Under the change, the response could go to either country -- not both. There could be a small-scale or accidental attack. We do not recommend full attack at all times. This would permit a limited response.

(2) Instructions on the response to a conventional attack would be conventional, not nuclear as is now in the plan.

(3) There was only one document of instructions beforehand. Now there would be two documents.

We all recommend this.

WALT ROSTOW: We think it is an essential change. This was dangerous. We recommend going forward.

GENERAL WHEELER: All the Joint Chiefs of Staff and commanders have been consulted. We recommend approval.

GENERAL McCONNELL: I concur, Sir.

GENERAL CHAPMAN: I concur.

ADMIRAL MOORER: I concur.

# # #

EYES ONLY FOR THE PRESIDENT

White House Archives.

Having been on the LBJ staff at the time, here is my version:

After years of war that resulted in catastrophic losses of life on both sides, in late 1968 Hanoi and the Viet Cong were on the cusp of agreeing to peace negotiations with the United States and South Vietnam.

Paris had been chosen as the site of the peace talks. Ambassador Averell Harriman had been chosen as the lead negotiator for the U.S. side.

LBJ had decided he would announce a halt in the massive bombing in return for immediate negotiations and a cease-fire.

On October 16, LBJ briefed former vice president Richard Nixon, Vice President Hubert Humphrey, and Governor George Wallace of Alabama—the three contenders for the presidency—in a conference call. All three pledged to support the bombing halt and the peace talks.

LBJ often talked about how Vice President Harry Truman had become president upon the death of President Roosevelt without Truman even knowing about the Manhattan Project. LBJ felt that peace talks were so critical to the future that he wanted to fully inform the three candidates of their status.

However, on October 27 the South Vietnamese president, Nguyen Van Thieu, suddenly reneged and backed off.

Over the next two weeks, actions were taken by the Nixon campaign to undermine the start of the Paris peace talks between the United States and South Vietnam on one side and Hanoi and the Viet Cong on the other side.

Key to this effort was Anna Chennault, a fixture of the Republican political scene in Washington and widow of the legendary General Claire "Old Leatherface" Chennault, who had fought with the Republic of China Air Force and U.S. Army Air Force and led the Flying Tigers against the Japanese in World War II.

With the Chinese-born Anna Chennault serving as an intermediary, Nixon's campaign operatives attempted to get the South Vietnamese to delay participating in the Paris peace talks until Nixon could be elected president. Nixon feared that a successful Paris peace agreement would strengthen the possibility of Vice President Hubert

Humphrey being elected in 1968. The Nixon strategists conveyed to the South Vietnamese through Madame Chennault that they should hold out for "a better deal" when and if Nixon was elected. The South Vietnamese complied, and withdrew from the Paris talks.

Around October 29, LBJ learned through intercepts and FBI tape recordings that Anna Chennault was communicating, through the South Vietnamese ambassador in Washington to President Thieu in Saigon, that South Vietnam should abort or cripple the deal by refusing to participate.

On October 30, LBJ briefed his mentor Senator Richard Russell on the Nixon campaign contacts with the South Vietnamese.

LBJ: Well, I've got one this morning that is pretty rough for you. We have found that our friend the Republican nominee, our California friend, has been playing on the outskirts with our enemies and our friends, both—our allies and the others. He has been doing it through rather subterranean sources here. And he has been saying to the allies that you are going to get sold out. Watch Yalta and Potsdam and two Berlins and everything. They're going to recognize the NLF, and I don't have to do that. You better not give away your liberty just a few hours before I can preserve it for you. One or two of his business friends have divulged it first a couple of days ago about the time he made the statement that he heard rumors that the staff was selling out, but he did not include me in it.

. . .

LBJ: The next thing that we got our teeth in was one of his associates, fella named Mitchell who's running his campaign, who's the real Sherman Adams of the operation, in effect said to a businessman, "We're going to handle this like we handled the Fortas matter. We're going to frustrate the President by saying to the South Vietnamese and the Koreans and the Thailanders, 'Beware of Johnson.' At the same time, we are going to say to Hanoi, 'I can make a better deal than he has because I am fresh and new and I don't have to demand as much as he does in the light of past position.'" Now when we got that purely by accident as a result of some of our Wall Street connections, that caused me to look a little deeper.

Russell: I guess so.

LBJ: And I have means of doing that, as you may well imagine.

Russell: Yes.

LBJ: Mrs. Chennault is contacting their ambassador from time to time. Seems to be kind of the go-between, the Chiang Kai-shek deal. In addition, their ambassador is saying to them that Johnson is desperate and is just moving heaven and earth to elect Humphrey, so don't you get sucked in on that. He is kind of these folks' agent here, this little South Vietnamese ambassador. Now, this is not guesswork.

. . .

LBJ: Mrs. Chennault—you know, of the Flying Tigers—she's young and attractive, I mean she is a pretty good-looking girl. She's around town, and she is warning them to not get pulled in on this Johnson move. Then he in turn is warning his government; then we in turn know pretty well what he's saying out there. So he is saying that, well, that he has got to play it for time and get it by the next few days.

[Johnson summarizes the state of the negotiations.]

LBJ: Meantime Nixon gets scared to death so he gets into the thing, and it gets off the track at the other place. . . . And then Nixon gets on and says there is no use in selling out now, just wait a few days, and you can't trust Johnson. Really, he's going to pat North Vietnamese, the NLF, on the back just like Roosevelt did the Russians. And that scares them.

A few days later, on November 2, LBJ briefed Senator Everett Dirksen.

LBJ: Now, I'm reading their hand, Everett. I don't want to get this in the campaign.

Dirksen: That's right.

LBJ: And they oughtn't to be doing this. This is treason.
Dirksen: I know.

. . .

LBJ: I'm looking at his [Nixon's] hole card. Now, I don't want to get in a fight with him there; I think Nixon is going to be elected. I think we ought to have peace, and I'm going to work with him.

. . .

LBJ: I know this, that they're contacting a foreign power in the middle of a war.
Dirksen: It's a mistake.
LBJ: And it's a damn bad mistake.
Dirksen: Sure, it is.
LBJ: Now, I don't want to say so, and you're the only man that I have enough confidence in to tell them. But you better tell them they better quit playing with it. And the day after the election, I'll sit down with all of you and try to work it out and be helpful. But they oughtn't to knock out this conference.
Dirksen: Wherever they are, I'll try to get hold of them tonight.

It was my personal view then, and it is my even stronger personal view now, that a public announcement of the Chennault episode before the election would have changed the course of history. It would have so damaged the Nixon campaign that Hubert Humphrey would have been elected president in 1968.

In researching this event, I asked the late LBJ Library director Harry Middleton why President Johnson, Vice President Humphrey, or the Johnson White House staff did not release to the public the information about the Chennault saga.

Middleton wrote me that former defense secretary Clark Clifford and former Supreme Court justice Abe Fortas—two of the most intimate friends of LBJ—had invited him and Lady Bird Johnson to Washington in the early 1980s to explain what had actually happened in the Chennault saga.

Middleton's letter said that he and Mrs. Johnson were told by Clifford and Fortas that the "Information about Anna Chennault's role had indeed been acquired and made known to Clifford and Fortas," who both thought the actions by Madame Chennault and the Nixon team were "tantamount to treason by Nixon." Senator Russell shared this sentiment.

Together, they said they had told President Johnson about the saga.

Clifford and Fortas said LBJ agreed with them that "it was indeed treason. . . . But, LBJ said it was not for him to reveal the information. It should be given to Humphrey, for him to decide."

So, together, Clifford and Fortas told Humphrey.

They said Humphrey responded that he would not release the event to the public. "The country has been through too much this year, and it cannot take another traumatic shock," Humphrey told them. "Even if it costs me the election, I will not use it." True to his word, he did not.

George Christian said he thought Hubert Humphrey's decision not to disclose the Chennault "treason" was made in part because Humphrey thought that he would win anyway.

I strongly felt that we should have gone public with the Nixon attempts to get the South Vietnamese to withdraw from the Paris peace talks. I feel even more strongly about that today.

Middleton says he never will forget Lady Bird Johnson's reaction: "Poor Hubert. Poor Hubert."

Unscathed by his actions, Nixon was elected president of the United States on November 5, 1968.

The peace that LBJ so wanted eluded him.

Until 2017, no "smoking gun" had ever been found that linked Nixon directly to Thieu's decision to delay coming to the Paris peace talks. Author John A. Farrell discovered the notes at the Richard Nixon Presidential Library while researching his 2017 biography *Richard Nixon: The Life*.

Farrell writes that Nixon told assistant H. R. Haldeman to find a way to secretly "monkey wrench" the peace talks in the final days of 1968. This secret directive demonstrated that Nixon himself was directly involved in interfering with peace negotiations that were under way in Paris.

As a result of the prolonging of the war, tens of thousands more Americans died in Vietnam, as well as Vietnamese estimated at more than a million, before Henry Kissinger finally negotiated an agreement in 1973.

As we now know, Ho Chi Minh and the North Vietnamese violated virtually every element of the Paris peace agreement and would go on to conquer South Vietnam.

Sometimes overlooked is the greater significance of the millions of Vietnamese lives that were lost. They paid a heavy price for their years of struggle to reunite their country. They lost more than a generation of their best youth to lift the burden of colonialism. That is, and will remain, one of mankind's darkest stains.

So there you have it—1968 was a terrible year.

We experienced assassinations, riots exploding in the cities, fierce antiwar protests, the loss of thousands of lives on the battlefield, capture of the *Pueblo*, a president stepping down, and so much more.

However, our nation came through it. And there was a happy note at year's end: *Apollo 8* circled the moon—the first time an American had orbited another world. Our astronauts Bill Anders, Jim Lovell, and Frank Borman broadcast a reading from Genesis to the American public on Christmas Eve.

BILL ANDERS:

We are now approaching lunar sunrise, and for all the people back on Earth, the crew of *Apollo 8* has a message that we would like to send to you.

"In the beginning God created the heaven and the earth.

"And the earth was without form, and void; and darkness was upon the face of the deep. And the Spirit of God moved upon the face of the waters.

"And God said, 'Let there be light: and there was light.'

"And God saw the light, that it was good: and God divided the light from the darkness."

JIM LOVELL:

"And God called the light Day, and the darkness he called Night. And the evening and the morning were the first day.

"And God said, 'Let there be a firmament in the midst of the waters, and let it divide the waters from the waters.'

"And God made the firmament, and divided the waters which were under the firmament from the waters which were above the firmament: and it was so.

"And God called the firmament Heaven. And the evening and the morning were the second day."

FRANK BORMAN:

"And God said, 'Let the waters under the heaven be gathered together unto one place, and let the dry land appear': and it was so.

"And God called the dry land Earth; and the gathering together of the waters he called Seas: and God saw that it was good."

And from the crew of *Apollo 8*, we close with good night, good luck, a Merry Christmas—and God bless all of you, all of you on the good Earth.

CHAPTER 9

LBJ PART 2

Peace above party, peace above self

One of the reasons that LBJ consumed so much information, and often took things so personally, was that he was a deeply sensitive man who wanted to be loved by everybody.

That has always seemed rather strange for me to say about him in either a speech or an article, but it's true. I think it was rooted in the fact that LBJ also loved people—most of them! When the mood struck him, bringing happiness to others was truly one of his greatest qualities.

Even though it may not be standard practice now, when important visitors came to the Oval Office, they would walk away with a pen, cuff links, or even a watch that was specifically meant for them. Yes, this was good politics, but he genuinely loved to see people happy.

One caveat is that he disliked being asked for things. LBJ felt that he had worked hard in his life to obtain what he had, and that it was his to give away.

He also loved things that others had. If I ever walked into his office with a tie on that he liked, he'd want one just like it; or if I were wearing a pair of shoes he liked, he'd want me to find him a pair. He was funny that way.

There were a number of times his generosity showed through—ranging from the Lincoln he gave Edwina, to gifts he would often give me or other members of his staff, to the time he bought fifteen cars for all the families that worked at his LBJ Ranch—but one time will always stand out to me.

LBJ was affiliated with a ranch in Mexico, owned by former president Miguel Alemán Valdés. With Texas bordering Mexico, he grew to love the country, and he had learned enough Spanish to have simple conversations with the locals.

On one trip down to Mexico, he had Edwina, me, and other members of his staff load a plane full of gifts to take to the families of Mexican ranch hands.

Between massive purchases in Austin at JC Penney and Dillard's, we took an enormous quantity of shoes and clothes, as well as toys, vitamins, and contraceptives. LBJ paid the bill himself, but there were tremendous discounts from JC Penney and Dillard's. We brought clothes for men, women, and children alike, but it was really the children and poor women that stole LBJ's heart the most.

This was not even the first time that I had heard of LBJ doing something like this, but it was incredible to see firsthand.

As the leader of a nation in turmoil, he digested hurt, anguish, and disappointment in ways that were more intense than anyone I've ever known. The triumphs were awesome—especially fostering greater equality and social programs—but the troubling major losses, deaths of friends, and personal defeats never left his mind.

I can so clearly remember moments when the nightly U.S. casualty reports from Vietnam would arrive from the White House's Situation Room. LBJ often stayed up late to await reports on how many U.S. aircraft had returned to their carriers and bases from their combat missions over North Vietnam. He always wanted to know exactly how many aircraft and pilots had been lost. After he read the reports, he would then retire to a restless sleep, racked with agony over the casualties.

Because of his own experience in the White House, LBJ felt empathy for anyone who had to endure the weight of the Oval Office—including president-elect Richard Nixon.

Following his presidency, LBJ never once criticized Nixon, despite having very good reason to distrust him personally.

LBJ once said, "America is like a fully loaded 707 airplane. We are all passengers aboard it. Nixon is the pilot. Spiro Agnew is the copilot. On the flight we are likely to encounter clear skies at times and very stormy weather at other times. Nixon and Agnew do not need passengers rushing the cockpit trying to knock them in the heads to get them to change course. If they can navigate the plane through the stormy weather, we will all land safely. But if somebody gets into the cockpit and attacks them, we will all crash and die."

These old political enemies spoke occasionally during Nixon's presidency. Nixon and his staff provided President Johnson with a weekly classified report sent to Austin each Friday on a presidential JetStar.

Whenever any logistical support was needed, it was always provided. Bill Gulley of the Nixon White House's Military Affairs Office was our primary link on requests for logistical support.

President Nixon even sent Air Force One to fly President and Mrs. Johnson to the Kennedy Space Center on July 16, 1969, to watch the launch of the mission that placed America's first man on the moon.

Later President Nixon told LBJ, "Lyndon, that plaque that was placed on the moon should have had your name on it, not mine. You supported America's space program when you were chairman of the Space Committee in the Senate. . . . You chaired the Space Council under Kennedy when you were vice president. You gave the space program your fullest support throughout your presidency."

I always have felt that was an example of true decency that President Nixon exhibited. I expressed to Bob Haldeman, John Ehrlichman, and Larry Higby of the Nixon White House staff how exceptionally grateful we all were for Nixon's thoughtfulness.

Nixon told me, "It was [Eisenhower] who told me I should treat Lyndon well in his retirement. Ike said that LBJ had been wonderful to him and to Truman during their time as former presidents. I expect you to do nothing less for him."

On this point, Nixon certainly was a man of his word.

Nixon himself would occasionally call me just to ask, "How's Lyndon?" It would only be a one- or two-minute call. Some people

Tom entering the Cabinet Room with highly classified documents in a black briefcase for LBJ to review with president-elect Nixon during the 1969 presidential transition. White House Archives.

LBJ, watching the *Apollo 11* moon launch from the Kennedy Space Center in Cape Canaveral, Florida, with VP Spiro Agnew on his left, Secret Service agent Clint Hill behind Agnew, and Tom behind LBJ. Wikimedia Commons.

said his calls were because LBJ knew about the Chennault affair and had never gone public with it. But I think it said a lot about Nixon, and it portrayed a level of thoughtfulness that isn't typically associated with him. He could be a genuine class act.

Before LBJ died in 1973, he and I took a car ride together—just the two of us—around the LBJ Ranch. The only others nearby were two Secret Service agents in a follow-up car. I asked him: "Mr. President, what would you have done differently if you could have during your time in the presidency?"

He told me, "I would have replaced more of the Kennedy people with my people early in my presidency. There were several very loyal staffers like Larry O'Brien, but there were several who never could accept me, like Bobby."

Robert F. Kennedy was extraordinarily loyal to his brother John. He never developed personal friendship or loyalty to LBJ as he had to JFK.

Quite the opposite. LBJ refused to name RFK as ambassador to South Vietnam, as he had requested.

I believe that RFK considered himself far better qualified than LBJ to serve as president. At times RFK seemed to look down on LBJ as a "southern wheeler-dealer," whom he treated with very little personal or professional respect.

LBJ continued, "I believe that I did what I had to do about Vietnam. We had signed a treaty," he said, referring to the SEATO pact of September of 1954, "that committed any signatory to come to the aid of any member nation that was attacked. I was convinced that, had we not tried to stop communism in North Vietnam, most of Southeast Asia would fall."

LBJ will long be remembered in different ways by many for his various policies and actions. One cannot expect anything different of an immensely complex man who led America at an immensely complex time.

What I will remember him most for was his overwhelming desire for peace in Vietnam and a better America for all of its people. That meant bringing more people together rather than dividing them, and nothing represented this more than his extraordinary commitment to civil rights—highlighted by his selection of Thurgood Marshall as justice of the U.S. Supreme Court.

On May 13, 1967, I was asked by President Johnson to attend an evening meeting in the Oval Office where he reviewed the three finalists for a vacancy on the Court. They were A. Leon Higginbotham Jr., Thurgood Marshall, and Shirley Hufstedler. Information was presented on each of the three prospective nominees, including FBI background checks and various supporting documents.

All three being considered for the seat had received the highest ratings of the American Bar Association and were extremely impressive.

No president had even proposed appointing a person of color, as both Marshall and Higginbotham were, and Hufstedler would be the first woman nominee.

Both LBJ and Lady Bird were passionate about introducing diversity to the Court, and it was a powerful display of leadership to the nation. However, Lady Bird Johnson very much wanted to see women on the Court, and she strongly encouraged President Johnson to name a woman.

Hufstedler was a female pioneer in the legal field. She had experienced an unstable childhood but went on to graduate with a degree in business administration from the University of New Mexico and was one of only two women in her class to earn a Juris Doctor from Stanford. Despite excelling in law school, she struggled as a woman to gain footing in the male-dominated legal field, and slowly but surely clawed her way to success.

Higginbotham pursued a career in law after starting off as an engineering major at Purdue University. As one of only twelve Black students at Purdue—all of whom were given student housing that did not have heat—he turned to law as a vehicle for change. He transferred to Antioch, where he met Coretta Scott, who would later marry Martin Luther King Jr. He also headed the school's NAACP chapter, worked to reduce the voting age in Ohio to eighteen, and worked as a butcher to support himself while earning his JD from Yale Law School.

Both Hufstedler and Higginbotham had exemplary records of public service in subsequent years.

Marshall was the son of a Pullman railcar steward. His mother was a kindergarten teacher. He had grown up in the racially segregated city of Baltimore and had been prohibited from attending the University of Maryland Law School because of his race. Choosing not to leave his fate to be decided by racist institutions, he went on to graduate first in his class from Howard University with an LLB in 1933.

While with the NAACP legal office, he helped found the Legal Defense Fund and successfully supported major efforts to overturn the historic *Plessy v. Ferguson* case which allowed for racial segregation in America.

Perhaps the crown jewel of Marshall's accomplishments was his successful 1954 school desegregation case, *Brown vs. Board of Education*, which legally ended the era of "separate but equal."

As solicitor general, a post to which LBJ had appointed him in 1965, he won 29 out of 32 cases before the U.S. Supreme Court.

After the three names were reviewed, President Johnson asked for comments from all the participants in the meeting. Then he dismissed the meeting and asked me to stay behind. I was completing my notes.

President Johnson said, "You know who I am going to pick, don't you, Tom?"

I responded, "No, Mr. President, I don't. They are all so exceptionally well qualified."

President Johnson continued, "Well, I'm surprised that you don't. You grew up poor in the South. You know what it takes to overcome hardship. I am selecting Thurgood Marshall. He is just as qualified as those other two. I also believe that when poor young Black boys learn that Thurgood Marshall could make it to the Supreme Court of the United States, they might see that they can make it too."

I almost cried.

As I look back on this episode, it was pure Johnson: both LBJ the man and Lady Bird the First Lady. Up until their last days in the White House, they wanted their decisions to inspire real change within the fabric of America.

Nominating Marshall was not easy, nor was it purely historic; it was concrete evidence that LBJ would move mountains to walk the walk. I was never prouder of him.

I do believe that LBJ was the leader that the nation needed during that time in history. For all the conflicts and crises that were thrown at him, he was steady. I would not use the word "calm" to describe him during a crisis, but totally steady. He simply didn't get rattled.

Unless you worked directly with him, it was almost impossible to truly understand the amount of experience he had from so many years in government. In a sense, he had seen it all.

His compassion was a major contributor to this steadiness.

The way that LBJ handled moments like the assassinations of Dr. King and Senator Robert Kennedy so effectively was a true testament to his character. Even in those bleak moments, he could pick up the phone, call their loved ones, and offer every ounce of support that the Oval Office could give.

One additional time in LBJ's later years that I will never forget is when a school bus in south Austin was in a major crash and many students died. At that time he wasn't responsible for protecting the nation, but he was calm and steady for the people who had trusted him as their representative for many years.

Someone asked him if he really needed to attend the funerals, and his response was so LBJ: "Their parents and grandparents have voted for me for years." He understood that politics was not just about power; it was about a shared sense of community with the people who had supported him.

I truly believe LBJ did his very best to lead America for civil rights, Medicare, for the poor, the homeless, the blue-collar, and all minority Americans. His dreams as a leader were my dreams too.

On his return to Austin after he departed the White House on January 20, 1961, for the final time as president, LBJ picked up a cigarette and lit it.

His daughter Luci looked up and said, "Daddy, what are you doing?"

With every bit of indignation LBJ could muster he said, "What does it look like I'm doing? For fourteen years I've wanted one of these, every moment of every day, but there was a job to do. There was a country to serve. But now the job is done, and hopefully you're grown."

And he smoked it.

There are many more stories I could tell, but I will conclude with a note Bill Moyers wrote to me many years later:

> You two shared an amazing kinship. He learned to trust you above all others except Lady Bird, and that trust was well served. You were the son he never [had], but even more important, you became the one he knew he could trust, which made it possible for you to help him through those hard and often melancholy final years. You're quite a guy, Tom Johnson, and I am so grateful our paths have crossed.

But for all that I write about Lyndon B. Johnson, one cannot ignore the enormous impact of Lady Bird. My tribute to her follows.

Tom and LBJ walking to Air Force One—in this case a Lockheed JetStar, not the Boeing 707. Courtesy of the LBJ Presidential Library.

CHAPTER 10

LADY BIRD JOHNSON

The true strength behind one of America's greatest presidents

Edwina and I first met Mrs. Johnson at a reception for the first class of White House Fellows in 1965. She was gracious, welcoming, and so thoughtful toward all of us. She made us feel completely at home. Pointing to the White House behind her, she said: "This is your house, too." She showed individual attention to every one of the Fellows and to their spouses.

However, at that reception, I will never forget how displeased she was that the President's Commission on White House Fellowships had chosen fifteen men and only one minority from a field of three thousand applicants.

That was the last time in the sixty-year history of the program that there was an all-male class of Fellows.

Since the White House Fellowship year of 1965 and until her death in 2007, Edwina and I have been very fortunate to be with her in Washington, in Texas, and on travels throughout the world. We had very special times together each August in a house on Martha's Vineyard.

Along with her daughters Lynda and Luci, I was at her bedside on July 11, 2007, at her home in Austin when she died. We were holding her hands.

For eight years I worked closely with Lady Bird and LBJ in the White House (1965–69) and in Texas (1969–73). However, during all of those years I reported directly to him, not to her. She had her own separate staff of assistants, particularly her press secretary, Liz Carpenter, and her social secretary, Bess Abell.

Once, after I had fulfilled a request that Mrs. Johnson had made of me, LBJ pulled me aside and said quite forcefully: "Tom, I want to make it clear to you that you work for *me*, not Lady Bird." I still don't know what it was that I did for Mrs. Johnson that upset him.

However, that was one occasion—a rare one—when I ignored his order, and I continued to assist Mrs. Johnson whenever I could. Besides, she often was much easier to work with than he was.

Along the way, Edwina and I also had become best of friends with the Johnson daughters Lynda Johnson Robb and Luci Baines Johnson. We remain close today.

Lady Bird loved watching the TV shows *Murder, She Wrote*; *Gunsmoke*; and *I, Claudius*. But her favorite—the one she called "my show"—was PBS's *MacNeil/Lehrer NewsHour*. Once, Lynda Robb approached anchor Jim Lehrer at a Washington dinner party to tell him that her own mother wouldn't even take her calls while his show was on the air.

Along similar lines, President Johnson once sent Jim Arness, the lead actor in *Gunsmoke*, a note that told him, "You're really messing up my Saturday nights."

Lady Bird was as unpretentious as she was complex. Trained as a journalist, she chose every word she spoke with extreme care.

You could give her caviar, and she would be thrilled, but she would be just as thrilled with a box of Cracker Jack.

One Christmas, she was even caught red-handed stealing the Reese's Peanut Butter Cups out of the children's stockings. She loved a little bit of candy.

Lady Bird also loved to read. William Faulkner, Eudora Welty, James Michener, and John Steinbeck were among her favorites. Following her death, Lynda and Luci distributed hundreds of her books to close friends and family members, many of them personally inscribed to her by the authors. Those of us who received them loved those special gifts.

But material possessions did not define the first lady. She often said: "The BEST gift you can give to another is the gift of a good memory."

She sure provided us with splendid memories of a lifetime. Trips to Egypt, Italy, Portugal, Spain, France, the Greek Islands, Acapulco, Martha's Vineyard, and more. Edwina became one of her favorite travel partners. She loved Edwina's optimism, her lust for adventure, her laughter, and her curiosity.

Mrs. Johnson also taught us the benefits of a "one-conversation table," no matter the size of the group. She said she wanted to hear what was being said all around the table. Often I was asked to announce her decree immediately upon being seated at a meal. It also was my responsibility to tap on a glass to remind violators when two or more guests or family members violated the one-conversation rule. We have continued that tradition throughout our lives, not always to the pleasure of every talkative guest.

There was no doubt by any member of the staff that LBJ's wife was the most influential of all his trusted advisors. When the going got tough about very divisive issues such as Vietnam, politics, budgets, legislative battles with Congress, and more, LBJ often would talk privately with her. Almost always.

He knew that he could trust her above anyone else. He also knew that she would provide wisdom and good judgment in straight, honest ways. She was no sycophant. There was no equal to her quiet power in the White House.

When LBJ would be at his worst, it was Lady Bird who could put her hand on his arm and say, "Now, Lyndon, now, Lyndon . . ." and it would calm him down almost instantly. White House speechwriter Bob Hardesty said, "She tempered his rashness."

One reason that they were so compatible was that, like Lyndon, Lady Bird understood the power of persuasion and competition.

Even when playing cards with her grandchildren, when the other adults would be going easy on them, Lady Bird never would. "These kids are going to have to learn how to compete on the real stage of life, and this is one thing I can do for them," she'd say.

As an environmentalist and fierce champion of women's rights, she worked on many projects, including the greening of the city of Washington and the nation's highways, but her crowning achievement was the Lady Bird Wildflower Center in Austin, Texas.

On her seventieth birthday, she gave the money and land to build the Wildflower Center.

On her eightieth birthday, she spent the day there.

Lynda and Luci say that their mother had three children: the two of them, and the Wildflower Center.

Just as she loved seeing groups of Americans of all ethnicities and colors and from all walks of life, she loved the diversity and contrast in nature. She felt the most beautiful site you could enjoy was one where you saw bluebonnets, winecups, gaillardia, yellow roses, bluebells, and countless others, all living amongst each other. The bluebell is what's on her gravestone.

In the last phase of her life, her family took a precedence that brought her the type of joy that she had never been able to give rein to, or receive from them, before. She had said so succinctly: Lyndon Johnson was more than a full-time job. But by the end, she made everyone know that she really loved them all best.

In her later years in Texas, Lynda and Chuck Robb occasionally brought her back to Washington, and they kept her informed on the latest news from the town she still loved. Luci and her husband, Ian Turpin, ran the Austin family business and were the family Lady Bird needed right there near home.

Every spring in Texas, people still rejoice over Lady Bird's wildflowers.

At the very end, when she could no longer speak after a stroke, she could still write shorthand in her beautiful handwriting.

One day when she couldn't get anywhere in a discussion with Luci, she grabbed her notepad, quickly scribbled some shorthand, and put a big exclamation point. She was exasperated.

As soon as she handed the note to Luci, Luci began to laugh.

Lady Bird motioned with her arms to express that she couldn't

believe Luci was laughing, and Luci said, "Mother, I'm not laughing *at* you, I'm laughing *with* you—I'm not smart enough to read shorthand!"

And with that, Lady Bird Johnson let out a belly laugh like you wouldn't believe.

I could write an entire book about Lady Bird, but there are four that others have written particularly well: *Lady Bird Johnson: Hiding in Plain Sight*, by Julia Sweig; *Lady Bird Johnson: An Oral History*, by Michael L. Gillette; *Lady Bird and Lyndon*, by Betty Boyd Caroli; and the best of them all, *A White House Diary*, which she authored herself.

She was truly one of a kind, a gentle warrior of a woman who deserves as much credit for the LBJ presidency as anyone, and who also blazed her own independent path.

CHAPTER 11

THE PASSING OF THE TORCH

Another mentor: Otis Chandler, California's golden son

George Cotliar, the splendid former managing editor of the *Los Angeles Times*, once said to me, "You have worked for three of the most important figures in America: President Johnson, Otis Chandler, and Ted Turner. You should write about them."

Just as I have written about LBJ, so much of my life has been influenced by Otis and Ted.

Until I went to work with Ted Turner at CNN in 1990, LBJ was the most complex man I ever had known. Close behind, however, was Otis Chandler, the publisher of the *Los Angeles Times*. He had personal characteristics that almost defied description, and a physique that could only be compared to that of a Greek god.

Otis wanted to win whatever competition he entered, with an equally awesome commitment to preparation. No matter if the topic was sports, business, journalism, surfing, auto racing, weightlifting, hunting, hiking, or anything in between, he always did whatever it took to come in first—always!

Otis and I first became acquainted through LBJ. A media deal between two of the most powerful families in America would lead to my leaving the mentorship of one giant, only to discover it with another.

By the end of 1968, with the LBJ administration soon coming to a close, LBJ was determined to persuade Edwina and me to go to Texas with him.

Almost every other White House assistant was moving on to impressive positions. Marvin Watson, who had already left the White House to serve as postmaster general, became executive vice president of Occidental Petroleum, Jack Valenti became president of the Motion Picture Association, Dean Rusk started to teach law at UGA, Jim Jones ran for a congressional seat from Oklahoma, Larry Temple took a position at a law firm in Austin, and Bill Moyers had already left to become publisher of *Newsday*.

I knew for a fact that LBJ had approached a number of them before asking Edwina and me to move to Texas in 1969. I was not his first choice.

When he asked me to go to Austin with them, I saw it as a serious personal loyalty conflict. I was still very committed to returning to Macon. My education at UGA and Harvard Business School had been funded by Peyton Anderson. He had approved my remaining in the White House after the White House Fellowship and been extremely patient and proud of me the entire way through.

At that point, I really owed it to Peyton to return to Macon. But LBJ argued that he needed us more than Peyton did.

Ultimately, we decided to move to Texas. It was a good decision.

I started as executive assistant to the former president, which was a big role but a small staff.

To my disappointment, LBJ reduced my compensation to $28,000 a year (down from $30,000) because, as he told me, “There are no personal state income taxes in Texas.” That hurt, but he always provided Edwina and me with at least a $3,000 financial gift each year, as well as many other gifts along the way.

Austin brought us closer to the LBJ family in many ways. Lady Bird invited Edwina and other friends to take memorable trips together with her. We continued to connect with the Texas LBJ circle of friends.

My first introduction to the Mayo Clinic—whose board I would later join—was in 1970 when LBJ took Edwina to Mayo Rochester. Texas physicians at Scott and White Clinic thought Edwina had leukemia. LBJ was a member of the Mayo Foundation board at the time—the only board he joined in retirement. The Mayo specialists immediately determined that she did not have leukemia but had cold urticaria—an allergy to cold temperatures.

On that trip, President Johnson also took Edwina as his guest to a Mayo Foundation board dinner. Known for his humor, LBJ introduced Edwina as "Mrs. Johnson" to other board members and their spouses. The wife of one of the board members said, "The audacity of that man! He is introducing that young blonde as Mrs. Johnson. I know Lady Bird. That is *not* Lady Bird!" Edwina did her best to clarify for every guest that she was "Mrs. Tom Johnson."

At the next Mayo board meeting, the chairman said, "Mr. President, you really created quite a stir at our last meeting. Introducing Tom's wife as Mrs. Johnson may have been technically accurate, but the board wives were certainly upset by it." That story has been retold many times among the Mayo board members and the LBJ family. Edwina was embarrassed beyond words. President Johnson loved it.

Unsurprisingly, as our time in Austin passed, I was introduced to more and more people through LBJ. One of the most significant was Otis Chandler.

It was in 1973 that I first met Otis. He had come to Austin to meet with LBJ and Lady Bird about the acquisition of KTBC-TV, the Johnson family television station in Austin. Otis's goal on that trip was to convince President and Mrs. Johnson to sell their CBS television affiliate, KTBC-TV, to the Chandler family business, the Times Mirror Company of Los Angeles.

Times Mirror had already purchased the *Dallas Times Herald* and KRLD-TV (later renamed KDFW-TV), a CBS-affiliated station in Dallas.

In making the *Dallas Times Herald* purchase, Times Mirror was required by the Justice Department and the Federal Communications Commission to divest itself of KRLD AM/FM radio stations in Dallas in order to keep the newspaper and the television station. However, because the divestiture of the radio stations was government mandated, Times Mirror received a so-called IRS tax certificate of $9 million, tax free, to invest in another media entity in a different market.

It was through LBJ's former aide Jack Valenti that Otis and Times Mirror president Al Casey learned of the LBJ family's intention to sell their Austin station. Under existing FCC rules, the Johnson family were required to sell either their cable system in Austin or their television station.

Jack had been one of LBJ's closest personal aides in the White House. He delivered that often ridiculed quote: "I sleep each night a little better, a little more confidently, because Lyndon Johnson is my president."

With LBJ's full blessings, Jack had been recruited to the presidency of the Motion Picture Association of America by the legendary Hollywood power broker Lew Wasserman, president of MCA, and Arthur B. Krim, chairman of United Artists—two of LBJ's closest friends, outside advisors, and influencers within the American Jewish community and the U.S. entertainment business.

At the time of their trip to Austin, Otis and Al Casey were leading Times Mirror into major expansions in cable, television, other newspapers, and more.

Otis and LBJ had already established respect for one another. Otis's *Los Angeles Times*' editorial pages cared deeply about social causes such as civil and human rights, clean air and water, public education, and public transportation. The *Times* largely supported a domestic agenda that was very much consistent with LBJ's presidential policies.

When Otis became interested in the Johnson TV station, I was executive vice president of Texas Broadcasting, the parent company of the Johnson family businesses. Texas Broadcasting encompassed television, radio, cable systems, banks, land development, cattle ranching in Texas and in Mexico (with former Mexican president Miguel Alemán), Muzak, Photo Processors, and other holdings. I'd even learned how to pregnancy-test a cow when I was president of the Comanche Cattle Company—another one of the LBJ family businesses.

Texas Broadcasting had been created with Mrs. Johnson's personal inheritance. She owned most of the shares of the parent company, and the two Johnson daughters, Lynda and Luci, each had significant ownership. The remaining shares were owned by longtime general manager Jesse Kellam, general sales manager Oscar P. "Bob" Bobbitt (who was married to LBJ's sister), attorney Donald Thomas, and a few others. I was never a shareholder myself.

Despite false reports that appeared in many newspapers, LBJ never personally owned a single share of stock himself.

While not a formal shareholder, LBJ treated the company just as he treated the White House. He always expected the absolute best from every employee, and he was regularly informed of the latest developments through conversations he had with Kellam regarding company matters.

By 1969 Mrs. Johnson was no longer confined to the role of First Lady and could take an important strategic role in the company. With a journalism degree from the University of Texas and with regular briefings by company management, she stayed well informed on company matters. She oversaw a number of decisions focused on new investments. I respected her enormously, especially her vision to look toward the future.

During the negotiations, I was in an administrative role, providing documents and briefings, as well as information regarding marketing, sales, and community relations. LBJ, attorney Don Thomas, and general manager Kellam were the actual negotiators.

After two days of intense negotiating with Otis Chandler and Al Casey, the television station was sold to Times Mirror for $9 million. The Johnson family retained ownership of the buildings and the television tower site, which they leased to Times Mirror at a very attractive rate.

After the sale was announced, President and Mrs. Johnson held a reception for Otis and his key Times Mirror executives to introduce the Californians to the major leaders in Austin, including advertisers of the television station.

Otis said I made a major impression on him during that reception.

President Johnson had me stand as the first person in the receiving line to greet the hundred-plus incoming guests. Following behind me was Chandler, then Lady Bird and President Johnson. My job was to make the introductions to Otis.

One of my most fortunate abilities during my younger years was an unusually retentive memory, and I introduced every attendee not only by name but also by their specific role in the Texas community and their personal association with the Johnson family.

I would tell Otis something such as "Mr. Chandler, this is Mr. Roy Butler and his wife Ann. Roy served as mayor of Austin. He owns the competing KVET radio station. His Lincoln-Mercury car dealership is one of our major advertisers."

Impressed by my introductions, Otis told me, "I've never seen anything like that."

Following the reception, Otis asked to meet with me privately. He wanted to know what I planned to do following the sale of the station.

I told him that I planned to return to my original profession—newspapering—and that I had an offer from Knight Ridder, thanks to Peyton Anderson. It was a chance to become a "general executive" in Miami, understudying the chairman of Knight Ridder, Alvah Chapman Jr.

I had never heard of the title "general executive" before, but it was planned that after serving as an understudy, I would be considered for the publisher role at one of their many papers.

Knight Ridder was wonderful to offer me such an important position. But Jack Knight, one of the two Knight brothers, made it very clear to me that he had concerns about my close ties to LBJ. He wanted to know if I could be as independent as Knight Ridder expected me to be.

Serving a president of the United States as an assistant is unusual in that way. It certainly put me on the map professionally—as it did once again in that moment with Otis—but it was also an albatross around my neck, always casting a doubt on my ability to remain independent of President Johnson's political positions.

While Jack Knight did not veto the Knight offer to me, I was put on notice that if I did join their company, I must be independent in the same fierce way that he was.

After I finished telling Otis of my future plans, he said: "I may have a better path for you to consider than Knight Ridder. Give me a few days to discuss my plan with our board."

Three weeks later, Otis presented me with a startling new proposal. He told me, "We want you to stay here in Austin as president of KTBC as long as needed for FCC approval of the transfer of ownership of the station to Times Mirror. I then want you to join me in Los Angeles at the *Times* or ask you to move to the *Dallas Times Herald* as executive editor." (The *Times Herald* was an afternoon newspaper, a competitor of the *Dallas Morning News*.)

"If you work out well as editor in Dallas, as I believe you will," he said, "I will then want you to become our Dallas publisher."

At that time the *Dallas Times Herald* had the tenth-largest circulation in the United States.

To put it mildly, I was stunned by the offer. I found myself thinking, "Could this actually be real?" Here was Otis Chandler, legendary publisher of the *Los Angeles Times* and leader of the Chandler family, asking me to serve as president of KTBC and describing a career path that could take me to the very top of my profession. I was only thirty-two at the time.

As I had told Peyton Anderson at the *Macon Telegraph* back in 1963, it was my ultimate dream to become publisher of a major American newspaper one day. Now Otis was offering exactly that: an opportunity to become executive editor of the *Dallas Times Herald* with a path toward becoming publisher.

Otis explained that following my presumed success in Dallas, I would be brought in as president and chief operating officer of the *Los Angeles Times*. After that, if I had worked out as president, Otis said he would step down as publisher to become chairman of the parent company, and I would succeed him as publisher in LA.

The offer felt more surreal by the moment.

Otis also proposed a second route, allowing me to skip Dallas and head straight to LA. However, I knew it would be better to go to Dallas and prove myself at a smaller, yet still significant, paper before trying to find my fit in LA. The Chandlers largely built that city, and the *Los Angeles Times* was their crown jewel.

Both paths that Otis laid out were focused not just on one amazing step in my career but on an entire future of incredible opportunity. During this moment I could see that the torch of mentorship first carried by Peyton Anderson, and then by LBJ, would now be held by Otis Chandler. He saw potential in me that was almost inconceivable.

Otis was a serious newsman, and progressive in many ways that set him apart from other leaders at that time.

Already in the mid-1980s, when environmental practices weren't often considered, he converted the entire *Los Angeles Times* truck fleet to run on propane rather than gasoline. Otis—not so different from Lady Bird Johnson in this way—made bold moves based on the future they wanted to help create.

Even though I knew the offer was too attractive to turn down, I couldn't say yes just yet. It was critical for me to discuss the situation with Edwina, as I have with every major decision in our six decades of marriage.

As much as we loved Austin and the friends we had there, Edwina thought the path described by Otis was just as compelling and exciting as I did. We also had many friends in Dallas, especially Deedie and Rusty Rose from Harvard, Barefoot and Jan Sanders from the White House, and Bea and Walter Humann from the White House Fellows program.

Several days later, after we had made up our minds, Edwina and I met with President and Mrs. Johnson at the LBJ Ranch. From other sources—perhaps Jack Valenti or Al Casey—LBJ and Lady Bird already knew of the Chandler offer. They also knew of my earlier offer from Knight Ridder.

It was a very emotional meeting.

Beginning the conversation, LBJ first confessed that he had blocked two executive job offers I had received while working for him in the White House. The one that I knew about had been from Coca-Cola to work in public and government affairs. The other was from Hearst Communications.

I always had wondered why Coca-Cola had withdrawn their offer. Originally I thought it might have been because of a comment by Edwina at a Washington dinner with Coca-Cola's top leaders.

This was an era when corporate wives were basically told to know their place, and often weren't even invited to speak up at dinners they attended. However, Edwina was *never* a corporate wife.

At some point during the meal, Coke's newest beverage, Tab, came up.

I can recall Edwina's words like I heard them yesterday. "That Tab tastes like tar, but Diet Rite Cola is good." Diet Rite wasn't even a Coca-Cola product—it was made by Royal Crown!

I wanted to slip beneath the table when she said that.

Later, Edwina said she didn't even know Tab was made by Coke—she thought it was a Pepsi product!

I'll admit that I didn't find any humor in her comment at all. In fact, looking back on it, I'm still somewhat embarrassed. The Coke executives didn't find any humor in it either.

The morning after the dinner, my offer from Coca-Cola was withdrawn. Edwina and I had very different feelings about the news.

She told me, "If you want to work for a company that can't take the truth, then it's your problem!"

It wasn't until that 1973 LBJ Ranch meeting to discuss Otis's offer with LBJ and Lady Bird that I learned the Coke executives met with President Johnson the following morning in the Oval Office. Apparently, with some pride, they told LBJ that they wanted to hire me to return to my home state of Georgia, where Coca-Cola has its global headquarters. Three of those attending that Oval Office meeting eventually told me what LBJ said:

"I have represented the Coca-Cola Company for many years in this town. Whenever Coca-Cola wanted something, I supported you. Now, in return, in gratitude, you are trying to steal my boy."

To avoid ending up on the bad side of LBJ—a man who demanded loyalty above all else—there was nothing for them to do but withdraw their offer to me.

Despite Edwina's faux pas not being the actual reason for the withdrawal of the Coke offer, I have continued to kid her about it for the last sixty years.

The second offer LBJ had blocked, he told us, was from William Randolph Hearst Jr., chairman of Hearst Communications, for me to become their "business manager."

Looking back now, these were two occasions when I felt personally wronged by LBJ.

After he confessed (my term for it), he presented Edwina and me with three checks totaling $25,000. He said the bonus was in return for my working four years for the LBJ family.

While generous, his gesture did not remove the dismay I felt for his blocking two very attractive job offers.

Having spent as long as I had with him, I did understand what he was trying to do by giving us those checks. Generosity was often LBJ's way of saying he was sorry—something that he never knew quite how to do.

He then said he wanted us to consider a counteroffer to the one made by Otis Chandler.

He said that if we would remain with them, I would become president and general manager of their family business, replacing Jesse Kellam when Kellam decided to retire. Until then I would serve as Kellam's understudy and would learn from him all the elements of the various holdings that the Johnsons still owned.

Kellam was a strong act to follow. He was a seven-day-a-week manager, who did a tremendous job running the Johnsons' business.

LBJ's proposal: The family would provide me with 1 percent of the equity in the company for each year that I stayed, up to twenty years, ultimately entitling me to 20 percent of Texas Broadcasting. If I left at any time, however, I would forfeit all of my equity.

As enticing as that offer *could* be, it also meant that if I worked for ten years and acquired a 10 percent stake, Edwina and I would lose all of our equity if we decided to resign for any reason.

Neither Edwina nor I liked that proposal.

It wasn't that the Johnson offer felt that unusual—many jobs in corporate America have packages tied to a length of service. Had I stayed for twenty years and acquired 20 percent of the business, I might have become a wealthy man.

However, with Edwina and me having two young children, aging parents, and a bigger world to explore, the LBJ position was no longer the right fit.

There were a few other key factors.

First, I was skeptical of working so long in a company that would inevitably be impacted by LBJ's daughters and sons-in-law. Every single one of them was absolutely wonderful, but I had always been told then, as I know now, that blood is thicker than sweat. With LBJ's heart issues growing more serious by the day, I knew family dynamics soon could change and I might find myself working for one of his two sons-in-law.

(Incidentally, Luci Baines Johnson has done a splendid job along with her husband Ian, managing the LBJ family businesses after Lynda and Chuck Robb decided that their focus would be more on Chuck's political career. A former United States Marine, Chuck Robb became governor of Virginia and a United States senator from Virginia. Lynda has been magnificent in many roles, including leading the organization Reading Is Fundamental.)

Second was my love for newspapers and print journalism. I found the prospect much more compelling than a corporate role overseeing many nonmedia businesses such as ranching, banking, Muzak, and photo processing.

Third was the matter of loyalty. I never wanted to be considered disloyal to LBJ by leaving him. I had seen up close and personal the way he had treated my close friend and early mentor Bill Moyers.

From the time Bill chose me to work for him during my White House Fellowship year in 1965, he and his wife, Judith, were always exceptionally thoughtful toward Edwina and me, and continued to be for decades beyond. During my time working for Bill, I was loyal to both him and President Johnson.

However, for reasons that I may never fully understand, President Johnson and Bill Moyers had a falling-out when Bill left the White House in 1967 to become publisher of *Newsday*.

In retirement, LBJ wouldn't return Bill's phone calls or answer his personal letters. He did not even permit Moyers to visit him when he was hospitalized in San Antonio shortly before his death.

On several occasions I tried to achieve reconciliation between these two strong-willed and powerful friends, but each time I failed.

My most significant attempt was in 1971. Bill had written an excellent book titled *Listening to America*. His publishers scheduled a nationwide book tour which included a stop in Austin, Texas. As any good friends would be, Edwina and I were thrilled to host a book party for Bill.

Although we knew there was a high risk that LBJ would not accept our invitation, the first guests we invited were President and Mrs. Johnson. I called LBJ at his ranch.

"Mr. President," I said, "Edwina and I want to invite you to a book signing party at the Headliners Club honoring Bill Moyers. I know Bill would be so pleased if you and Mrs. Johnson would attend, as would we."

There was total silence on the other end of the line. Not a single word was spoken. Rather than slamming the phone down as I had known him to do when he was mad, LBJ instead hung the phone up very quietly.

For the next several days, LBJ would not speak to me. I was frozen out.

To put it in perspective, I was executive vice president of the Johnson family businesses, his former executive assistant, and his closest male aide at the time. During this period, all messages that LBJ needed to send to me were delivered by Mary Rather, his longtime secretary.

Finally, after several days, I told Mrs. Johnson that I no longer could work under those conditions. She told Edwina and me that she would talk with him. As later reported to me by somebody present during their conversation, the message Lady Bird delivered is something that I never will forget:

"Lyndon, just because Tom is loyal to Bill does not mean that he is any less loyal to you. Bill gave Tom his first job in the White House. If anybody ought to understand loyalty, it is you! Tom will always be loyal to Bill, just as he will always be loyal to you."

The next day, without the freeze-out being acknowledged, our personal and professional relationship resumed as if nothing had ever happened.

Despite my enormous love for LBJ and Lady Bird, and all the opportunities for growth they had provided me, it was a lesson about just how quickly things could change in that world.

Edwina and I told them that it was time for our family's next chapter, and that I would be accepting the offer from Otis Chandler: a decision that President and Mrs. Johnson both ultimately understood.

The last dinner that Edwina and I attended with the Johnsons ended with tears and caring hugs. There were no hard feelings.

Our families had been together since my time as a twenty-four-year-old White House Fellow.

Only a few months later, on January 22, 1973, President Johnson died suddenly at the LBJ Ranch of a heart attack.

Mrs. Johnson called me and said, "Tom, we did not make it this time. Lyndon is dead. Please handle the announcement and the arrangements."

I called the two wire services, AP and UPI, and the three networks to notify the world of LBJ's passing.

Walter Cronkite was the first to take my call. I relayed the facts to Cronkite, and he announced the news of LBJ's death live to the world. At that point, it was the only time that CBS News had ever interrupted a broadcast for a live call-in report.

There is no question that I became a better newspaper editor and publisher because of my experience working with the Johnsons for those eight years. I became more proficient, and established relationships and support from others around the world that would not have existed without my roles working for a U.S. president. But when I left the LBJ family business, I was also proud knowing that I had given that role my very best.

New publisher Tom, in front of the *Dallas Times Herald* building in 1976. Courtesy of Times Mirror.

My decision to accept Otis's job offer also meant, once again, that I would not be returning to Macon. By then Peyton Anderson had sold his Macon newspaper anyway, in 1969 to Knight Ridder.

Peyton's grandson, Dr. Reid Hanson, a doctor of veterinary medicine at Auburn University, later told me, "You disappointed Peyton badly when you didn't come back." I will always have to live with that. But I also know that Peyton was very proud of my successes.

Likewise, as much as LBJ and Mrs. Johnson wanted me to remain with them in Texas, I believe they were very proud that they helped to develop a young guy into someone who became publisher of major newspapers in Dallas and Los Angeles.

Even after I left Austin, it wasn't the end of my and Edwina's relationship with the Johnson family. For thirty years I served as chairman of the LBJ Foundation, supporting the LBJ Library and the LBJ School of Public Affairs. I also continued to serve as an unofficial advisor to Lynda, Luci, and Mrs. Johnson. To this day, they remain family.

CHAPTER 12

THE RISE AND FALL OF TIMES MIRROR

Journalism's highs and lows—and my own

At the time I joined the Times Mirror Company, it owned many of the finest newspapers, television stations, magazines, cable television properties, forest products, and book publishing companies in America. Its holdings included the *Los Angeles Times*, the *Hartford Courant*, the *Baltimore Sun*, the *Dallas Times Herald*, the *Denver Post*, *Newsday*, and many others. It was a high-quality company with some of the best executives and employees in the industry.

My first positions as executive editor and publisher (1973–75) and then CEO (1975–77) of the *Dallas Times Herald* worked out just as Otis and I had hoped. It also was an exciting time to be in Texas. The state was booming, with new businesses and residents moving in. As a direct result, the *Times Herald*'s visibility, circulation, advertising, and profits were soaring.

We were in an intense circulation and advertising war with the other major paper, the *Dallas Morning News*. The *News* catered to upscale readers, while we were more blue-collar at the *Herald*, the evening newspaper.

Because of our readership differences, I never had much luck attracting high-end advertising accounts like Neiman Marcus. It drove me nuts, but we managed to build more new avenues to success than ever before.

The first thing I did when I got to Dallas was to bring in fresh perspectives—not replace the staff that we had, but add to it.

Tom as publisher of the *Los Angeles Times*. Courtesy of Times Mirror / *LAT*.

I hired high-level newsroom talent from papers like the *Washington Post* (editor Ken Johnson) and the *Philadelphia Inquirer* (managing editor Will Jarrett), and brought in young writing talent (Bob Dudney), who were excited about the dynamic new newspaper that we were building.

I also wanted to improve the status of women.

The paper had a women's section that was edited by Vivian Castlebury. I quickly promoted her to associate editor and a member of the *Times Herald* editorial board.

Vivian did a wonderful job infusing the paper with enlightening coverage of women's issues—something that was gaining some momentum, but still lacking at papers across the country. She was a fierce advocate of women's rights, the promotion of women into senior management, the inclusion of women on boards of companies, and equal pay for women.

I'm so proud to have worked with her.

To assist me at the *Times Herald* I quietly recruited the support of Nick Williams, the brilliant former editor at the *Los Angeles Times*. I would make sure that he had copies of the *Times Herald* on his desk in Los Angeles every day. I kept this relationship private, because I didn't want people to think that I was trying to turn the *Dallas Times Herald* into the *Los Angeles Times*.

Leaning into life in Dallas, I became quite active in the community—YPO, the Petroleum Club, Brook Hollow Country Club, the Dallas Assembly, Rotary. I also did my best to get to know every *Times Herald* staffer, especially leaders of the unions in the newspaper's production areas. It even became a family affair at times.

During my Dallas years, I received absolute support from *Times Herald* chairman and former publisher James Chambers and former executive editor Felix McKnight.

My wife Edwina and our two children, Wyatt and Christa, once went with me selling newspaper subscriptions door-to-door. Incidentally, Edwina and Christa outsold Wyatt and me by five to one. It was a clear lesson that women are far superior at sales and marketing. Pharmaceutical companies had learned that lesson by their deployment of female sales representatives to make their calls on physicians.

Not everyone in Dallas was happy about the changes I was making, such as bringing in new "outside editors" and reporters. Especially troubling for some community leaders was a new emphasis on stronger investigative reporting that could at times be critical of Dallas. We also changed older "puff sections" that were primarily advertorial, such as the automotive section, into straight news sections.

I believed that good journalism was good business. Since my college days at the University of Georgia's Grady School of Journalism, I had subscribed to the *New York Times*. I studied it—and its continued success—carefully. I still do, and I view it as the best newspaper, not only in America, but in the world!

I also had studied a variety of other newspapers while at Harvard Business School for my first and only other book, the one titled *Automating Newspaper Composition* (Nimrod Press, 1966) that I co-authored with L. Lee Moore III.

The publisher of the *Washington Post*, Don Graham, told me many years later just how revolutionary that thinking was. Don said it even took the *Washington Post* another sixteen years before they installed their first full computer system.

During our Harvard Business School research, I had been exceptionally impressed by the journalistic excellence of the *Washington Post*, the fierce civil rights positions of Ralph McGill, Gene Patterson, and Reg Murphy of the *Atlanta Journal Constitution*, the typography of the *New York Herald Tribune*, and the near absolute integrity of the Associated Press.

With that background, I believed I knew what good newspaper journalism was all about. Otis did too.

During my four years in Dallas, the *Times Herald* improved significantly, not only as a revenue producer but as a quality source for news. So much so that *Time* magazine recognized it as one of the "five best newspapers in the South." No other Texas newspaper was even mentioned.

That type of national recognition, paired with the *Times Herald*'s excellent performance in circulation, advertising, and editorial quality, propelled me higher and higher up the ranks of Times Mirror. Otis always made it clear to me, and to those running Times Mirror back in LA, that he was very impressed with what we were accomplishing in Texas.

"You cannot have financial strength without editorial excellence," Otis often told me. Occasionally he would reverse the order of the statement, which only further validated his point.

As hoped, my time in Dallas served as a successful testing ground of my abilities, and provided Otis and the Times Mirror board with the confidence they needed to bring me to Los Angeles with the support of the entire Chandler family.

While I was working in Dallas, Otis continued to invest in quality at the *Los Angeles Times*. It was his leadership that was taking the *Times* to new heights of financial and editorial excellence.

During his time as publisher, outstanding reporters and editors thrived. They were editors such as Nick Williams, Bill Thomas, George Cotliar, Dennis Britton, Noel Greenwoood, Narda Zacchino, and Jean Sharley Taylor; great columnists like Jim Murray; a world-class editorial cartoonist, Paul Conrad; a fiercely independent editorial page editor, Anthony Day; and strong Pulitzer Prize–winning investigative reporters like Washington bureau chief Jack Nelson.

After I became chief operating officer of the *Times* in 1977 and then publisher in 1980, we created new suburban and regional editions. With Otis's support, we expanded our delivery of the *Times* to Santa Barbara in the north and the Mexican border in the south, and built a full seven-day-a-week edition for San Diego County. In addition, we established a Washington, D.C., street edition, mostly for heightened visibility of the *Times*' splendid journalism in the nation's capital. *Washington Post* executives called it a PR stunt.

Otis approved construction of an expanded Orange County plant, a new San Fernando Valley plant, and a new Los Angeles downtown plant with state-of-the-art technology and highly efficient Goss color printing presses.

We opened many new domestic and international bureaus.

Most important, Otis put business executives in place who respected the wall between the news and business sides of our newspapers. Executives like executive vice president Vance Stickell and Don Maldonado sold record volumes of advertising and circulation without ever compromising the editorial integrity of the newsroom.

Otis was a heat shield, behind which the *Times*' news and editorial staff were well protected from Times Mirror corporate and Chandler family pressures.

At the end of the day, what mattered most to Otis was his desire to make Times Mirror into the best of all media companies, and the

Promoting the *Los Angeles Times*' new San Diego County edition.
Courtesy of Times Mirror / *LAT*.

Los Angeles Times into a paper that proved great journalism was not limited to New York and D.C. He wanted us to be at least as good as the *New York Times* and the *Washington Post.*

While it was professionally exciting to move from Dallas to LA, it was complicated for my family.

When we relocated from Washington to Austin, both Wyatt and Christa, then four and two, were too young to be troubled by the move. And when we moved from Austin to Dallas, we were still near many close friends. Los Angeles, especially because of how much our kids had grown, was a new type of transition for us.

It worked well for Edwina, who absolutely loved LA from the start, but the move was not easy for Wyatt, who was now in sixth grade, and Christa, who was in fifth. Wyatt loved his friends, sports, and school clubs in Dallas. As we were preparing for the move, he told me, "Dad, I know this is good for you, but it's not good for me."

I always felt terrible about dragging them away, and yet both of our children eventually grew to love California enough to make their permanent homes there.

Before activating his long-range plan for me, Otis wanted his parents to know me personally and to approve his choice and his plan for me to progress from Dallas to LA and from editor to publisher and CEO. He made it clear that each step was completely conditioned on my excelling in the earlier stages.

So, years before Otis brought me to LA, he arranged for me to meet with his father and mother, Norman and Dorothy "Buff" Chandler, at their splendid home in LA's Hancock Park. Not long afterward, in 1973, my first year in Dallas, Norman would die of throat cancer. I can still recall the scarf that Norman wore around his neck to hide a large surgical scar.

The newspaper had been in the Chandler family since the late 1800s. So when it came to the long-range possibility that I would one day succeed Otis as the first non-Chandler publisher of the *Times* since their reign began, his mother, Buff, was very blunt.

She said, "Tom, do not try to be like Harrison Gray Otis, Harry Chandler, Norman Chandler, or Otis Chandler. Just be Tom Johnson

Otis and Tom with a record polar bear Otis killed on one of his many wild game hunting trips around the world. Courtesy of Times Mirror / *LAT*.

and you will do just fine." She also said, "It's not just how powerful you will be, it's how interesting you will be."

Unforgettable words in an unforgettable meeting.

Buff was a major force within the company. From that point on, I had little direct contact with her or Norman, but Buff's presence was always felt, especially about stories she disliked in the *Times*.

For nearly a hundred years, the paper had been a megaphone for the Chandler family to shape Southern California as they saw fit. From water rights to labor unions to who got elected to go to Washington, the *Times* was a way for the Chandlers to make their own kings.

At the *Los Angeles Times*, a mecca for culture and conversation on the West Coast, Tom welcoming King Hussein of Jordan, with (*rear, left to right*) Times Mirror chairman Robert Erburu, vice chairman Phil Williams, and *Times* editorial page editor Anthony Day. Courtesy of Times Mirror / *LAT*.

During Otis's twenty-year term as publisher (1960–1980), high-quality independent journalism, rather than political favoritism, became the paper's true objective.

Buff's own personal mission was turning the Los Angeles Music Center into one of the best in the world. And she did it! Any criticism of the Music Center drove her mad. She occasionally wanted Martin Bernheimer, our music critic, fired for the way he would cover a performance at her beloved Los Angeles Symphony Orchestra.

Other times, Buff would complain about Pulitzer Prize–winning cartoonist Paul Conrad when he drew something scathing about her close friend Richard Nixon.

Luckily for me, Buff and Otis had an understanding that she would always take her blistering complaints directly to her son, which protected me and others on the staff. She would call Otis, furious. Otis would listen to her, but then he would not proceed to do anything that troubled me or editor Bill Thomas based on his mother's slashing tirade.

For my first three years at the *Los Angeles Times* (1977–1980), I was in the role of president and chief operating officer. That included advertising, circulation, production, new technology, promotion, finance, legal, human resources, and security. While I had no direct news and editorial responsibilities, that did not stop Otis from involving me in those areas. He insisted that I sit in on the daily editorial board meetings, which was an unusual move.

I wasn't welcomed by everyone on the news staff in the early days.

Bill Thomas, then executive editor at the *Times*, told Otis that in picking me, he had "chosen a guy from the bush leagues." Over time, I did what I could to earn the staff's trust. Eventually even Bill Thomas came around, writing me a wonderful note before he retired saying that he would have picked me as publisher, too.

Otis and I spent a great deal of time together.

We spoke as often as we could. Frequently we would travel together, at times with Otis driving his turbocharged Porsche at high speeds along the Pasadena Freeway. Other times, we would fly together to handle Times Mirror business across the country.

At the race track, Tom with Otis Chandler's son Harry and Otis, suited up in his driving gear. Courtesy of Times Mirror / *LAT*.

He was a great mentor. Otis was one of the most impressive strategic thinkers and planners that I ever have known. He could have been an outstanding professor at Harvard Business School.

During my time in LA as publisher and CEO, one hell of a lot was assigned to me, including eventually overseeing the brilliant Dick Schlosberg, publisher of the *Denver Post*, and the former Knight Ridder superstar Lee Guittar, publisher of the *Dallas Times Herald*.

Adding responsibility for two hotly competitive Dallas and Denver newspaper wars to my already heavy load as CEO of the *Los Angeles Times* was far too much for me, and it took a heavy toll. Many times, I would be in my LA office in the morning and then take an American Airlines evening flight to Dallas to assess the situation at the *Dallas Times Herald*, get a few hours' rest at a nearby hotel, and then spend two or three long days addressing crisis issues—primarily circulation—before returning to continue running the *Los Angeles Times*. Dick Schlosberg certainly did not need me overseeing his leadership in Denver. *Dallas Times Herald* publisher Lee Guittar went on to become the president of *USA Today*.

Serving as CEO of the *Los Angeles Times* and also overseeing Denver and Dallas almost broke me psychologically. I never should have agreed to do it.

In addition, Otis and the Times Mirror board members were pressuring me to identify and select a new editor of the *Los Angeles Times* to succeed Bill Thomas.

Bill was perhaps the least well known of any editor of any major newspaper. He never sought the spotlight for himself. His passion was for great writing. He served as editor from 1971 until his retirement in 1989. Under his leadership, the *Times* opened eleven domestic and international bureaus and won eleven Pulitzer Prizes. Daily circulation rose significantly during his tenure—up to 1.1 million in Bill's final year.

I wanted to replace Bill with an editor who would articulate a vision for the future. There were three highly qualified internal candidates: managing editor George Cotliar and deputy managing editors Dennis Britton and Noel Greenwood.

Another was Shelby Coffey III, a protégé of the legendary Ben Bradlee at the *Washington Post* for seventeen years before serving as editor of *U.S. News & World Report*. Otis Chandler had met Shelby when both of them were lifting weights in a Washington gym years earlier.

In my opinion, there was no better young editor in the nation.

At Otis's urging, I had recruited Shelby to become editor of the *Dallas Times Herald* when that position opened. Later I convinced Shelby and his family to move to Southern California, where he worked with associate editor Jean Sharley Taylor at the *Times*.

I asked each of the four to write a "Future of the *Times*" report, outlining their specific recommendations if chosen as editor. All four were superb. Coffey's report was 126 pages filled with innovative ideas on coverage, new design, and significantly improved reporting on minority issues—especially within the growing Latino, Black, and Asian communities.

After consulting with Otis, I chose Shelby as executive editor. All three finalists continued as leaders at the *Los Angeles Times*, and Coffey chose Cotliar to continue as managing editor.

Throughout my time in LA, I tried to be as connected with the community and our customers as I had been in Dallas. For instance, if someone called to say their paper had not arrived, I would occasionally drive a copy over myself. Nothing would surprise them more than to see the publisher personally delivering a paper to their door.

I knew how those types of actions could appear as self-promotional, so I would always do them in absolute privacy, telling no one other

Tom in front of a *Los Angeles Times* fleet delivery truck—one of the first vehicles powered by propane, not gasoline. Courtesy of Times Mirror / *LAT*.

Tom and Mary Ann Dolan, editor of the *Los Angeles Herald Examiner*. The *Los Angeles Times* printed the *Herald Examiner* when the competing LA newspaper lost power. Courtesy of Times Mirror / *LAT*.

than our circulation director. I did not want to be accused of being a showboat.

It was also important to me that the *Los Angeles Times* be an unwavering pillar of the California community—and that meant supporting great journalism in all its forms. Just as we had an incredible rivalry in Texas between the *Dallas Times Herald* and the *Dallas Morning News*, there were very strong competitors in California.

Once, one of those local competitors—the *Los Angeles Herald Examiner*—had a massive power outage at their unionized printing facility. Almost immediately I invited them over to print their paper at our nonunion plant. Otis's trust in me to do the right thing was so absolute that I didn't even bother asking him if we could accommodate the needs of the *Herald Examiner*. He believed in great journalism and great competition just as much as I did.

While I loved my work, there is no doubt that I was spending too much time with work and too little with my family—just as I had done in Washington, Austin, and Dallas.

Beginning at Harvard Business School, I became convinced that I wasn't in the same intellectual league as many people, but by being the hardest worker around, I could excel. As a result of my earned success, I enjoyed the recognition that I had sought since childhood, as well as exceeding my early financial goals, but I definitely should have spent more time at home with my family.

Fortunately, I had a magnificent wife who was supportive of me, but my children didn't have the father they deserved. I wasn't around enough to help them or enjoy them.

One time during those years, I remember my daughter Christa saying to me, "Don't forget that you're a daddy too."

Not listening more to Christa's advice is one of the biggest regrets of my life.

Even though I was a workaholic, our family certainly did enjoy many benefits that came with my position. Having helped to build the city of Los Angeles, the Chandlers had access to everything, and Otis and his wife Missy would often invite our family out to events. Anything else that Edwina and I wanted to do together or with our children only required that I ask.

We had the best seats at Dodger Stadium, the Music Center, and the Hollywood Bowl. Those were wonderful perks of working for Otis and Times Mirror, but the comfort of my relationship with him—and the media empire we were running—sadly did not last forever.

Along the way, Otis encountered serious crises in his own personal and professional life.

Once, he helped a friend in a financial venture called Geotek, which almost resulted in Otis being indicted for fraud. He had encouraged friends to invest in Geotek, and those friends lost money. That deal ultimately cost Otis several longtime friendships and distracted him seriously while Geotek was investigated.

Living the LA life: (*front*) L. R. MacKenzie Colt and Linda Thompson; (*second row*) great friends Kenny and Marianne Rogers with Tom and Edwina.

Wyatt and Christa at the 1984 Summer Olympic Games in LA.

With the *Times* track team during an *LA Times* track meet. We won! Courtesy of Times Mirror / *LAT*.

He also ended up divorcing Missy, his wife of twenty-six years, for another woman, Bettina Whittaker.

My wife Edwina certainly wasn't happy about their separation. She's always been a strong member of the "first wives club." Edwina made her thoughts very clear to Otis when she learned about his relationship with Bettina.

Otis told me he just wanted a quieter life with Bettina than the very dynamic and public one he had lived for many years with Missy.

Other serious troubles struck Otis as well.

His oldest son, Norman, developed inoperable brain cancer in 1989 and died in 2002. There were times when Otis thought that Norman might succeed me as publisher.

An additional crisis: Otis's youngest son, Michael, hit the wall while driving in high-speed racing trials for the Indianapolis 500. He almost died, but recovered.

A wild musk ox almost killed Otis while he was hunting in Alaska.

He and Bettina were thrown from Otis's motorcycle when a tractor pulled in front of them while they were on a vacation trip, nearly ripping off Otis's toe. He and Bettina miraculously survived.

Otis's mother, Buff Chandler, spent several years confined to her Hancock Park home in seriously declining health before her death in 1997.

In the 1980s, Otis pulled back. "I've had enough of it," he told me one day.

He had been "at it" for thirty-two years, fighting for quality, for diversification, for expansion. A seven-year apprenticeship at the *Times*, twenty years as publisher of the *Times*, and five years as chairman of the board of Times Mirror. He had fought against bias, mediocrity, and some selfish relatives—including two who were members of the highly conservative John Birch Society.

Otis had the highest expectations of world-class performance in himself and in others, but there were too many family members constantly trying to wrestle for power.

The decline of Times Mirror began when Otis Chandler left the company in 1985, while I was still in the role of publisher. Sadly, for those of us who cared about the company, Otis by then had removed himself from major positions of influence.

Several Chandler family members had become unhappy with what they saw as the financial underperformance of the company (not the *Los Angeles Times*, which had its best year in 1989), especially the value of their stock and dividends. They were equally displeased with what they described as "Otis's liberal *Los Angeles Times*."

Initially I thought that he had been forced out by the much more conservative Chandler family board members. I no longer feel certain about that.

Family members Harrison Chandler, Bruce Chandler, Warren "Spud" Williamson, and Chandler brother-in-law and family lawyer Dan Frost, among others, placed intense pressure on Otis, Times

Mirror president (later CEO) Robert Erburu, and chairman Dr. Franklin Murphy to improve the financial performance and "rein in" the liberal *Times*. How do I know? Because I attended many of those board meetings and heard their complaints firsthand myself. I was a Times Mirror board member.

When Otis did pull back, members of the Chandis Trusts and the Times Mirror board were better positioned to influence the company and the *Times*.

I think Otis simply "had enough" of the stresses and controversies within the company, and he wanted a new life, with a new wife. That is exactly what he told me privately.

In fairness to the Chandler family, Times Mirror had made a number of genuinely questionable decisions. Among them:

1. Buying afternoon daily newspapers in Dallas in 1970 and in Denver in 1980 at a time when evening newspapers had begun to falter all across America and television news was soaring. People were beginning to get their evening news from TV, certainly not evening newspapers like the *Times Herald*.
2. Selling excellent cable television systems rather than expanding them and buying more cable systems, when the cable business was dynamic and growing rapidly.
3. Selling highly profitable television stations rather than expanding that high-margin television group. (This decision was made not by Otis but by Times Mirror president Robert Erburu and the board.)
4. Failing to seize many major growth opportunities, including a chance to buy a large share of Ted Turner's rapidly growing Turner Broadcasting System when others like John Malone of TCI, Jerry Levin of Time Warner, and Ralph Roberts of Comcast seized that moment. (Times Mirror did purchase a relatively small stake in TBS but passed up an opportunity to purchase 50 percent of CNN for $300 million. That was a huge mistake. Some analysts later put a $7 billion value on CNN.)

5. Selling their newsprint and forest products division, Publishers Paper Company, to Jefferson Smurfit, at the bottom of the market and, even worse, with a binding provision that the *Times* buy its tonnage from Jefferson Smurfit *at market newsprint rates.* Our volume of 600,000 annual tons would have otherwise enabled the *Times* to purchase newsprint at a 10–15 percent discount below market prices in many years.

Clearly, the Chandler family looked on with envy as well-led media companies like Gannett continued to report higher earnings and stronger profit margins. But what some people failed to realize was that Gannett operated primarily in cities where there were no competing newspapers. The *Los Angeles Times* was in direct competition with Hearst, Tribune, Copley, Freedom, and Knight Ridder in Southern California.

On March 21, 1989, Dr. Franklin Murphy, then chairman of Times Mirror, came to my office after I had been ordered to replace Anthony Day as editor of the *Times*' editorial pages, because "certain family members and leaders in the business and religious community consider Day ultra-liberal."

I refused to do it.

In fairness to Murphy, he was the only Times Mirror board member that provided me with a specific reason for my being removed as publisher of the *Times*. During the afternoon of Thursday, July 27, 1989, in the publisher's office, Murphy and I had the following exchange:

"I will deny that I ever said it, but it was simply that you were Otis's fair-haired boy. There are those who could not accept that fact. That is the reason for the action."

"Dan Frost, Bob Erburu, a few TM board members?" I asked.

"You said that. I did not. I will not deny that; however . . . I would say there were personality differences, policy differences . . . that your interrelationships with Bob [Erburu] and Dave [Laventhol] were not the same as those with Otis. I think you did a splendid job as publisher."

Murphy finished with one final conciliatory remark: "I would not replace Tony Day, either."

I never understood why I was considered a safer, less liberal voice than Day. After all, I had been hired in part due to my experience working directly with Lyndon Johnson for eight years. LBJ certainly was known as a champion of liberal ideals, especially civil rights.

However, as the *Times* increased its strong support for the growing Latino community, opposition to harsh LAPD policing tactics, the benefits of public transportation, and environmental quality, the Chandlers began to see that I was more liberal than they initially had thought. Yet Otis and I had nearly identical views on all of these issues.

As a former university chancellor at UCLA, Franklin Murphy understood the value of academic and journalistic independence, despite also being regularly upset by the *Times*' editorial content, and by Paul Conrad's cartoons.

The Los Angeles religious leader who was most critical of me and the *Times*' liberal editorial pages was Archbishop (later Cardinal) Roger Mahony. Times Mirror CEO Erburu was a leading Catholic and a close friend of Mahony.

There were some very critical business leaders as well. Among them were Howard Allen, then chairman of Southern California Edison; Phil Hawley, chairman of the Carter, Hawley, Hale department store chain; and David Packard, chairman of Hewlett-Packard. Allen disliked the *Times*' outward support of various environmentally minded editorials that focused on clean air and antipollution efforts, as well as our concerns about the safety of SoCal Edison's nuclear power plant being constructed near an earthquake fault line near the Pacific Ocean at San Onofre.

(Proving the impact of our news coverage, that San Onofre nuclear power plant was eventually closed.)

In what would be my final year, even though certain divisions of Times Mirror were not flourishing, the *Times* was having an incredible year by all measures. We were reporting record earnings, record profit margins, and its highest circulation levels ever. Still in the role of publisher, I kept on leading the *Times* the way Otis and I felt it should be run.

TIMES PERFORMANCE DURING TJ YEARS ('77-'89)

- Times 1989 operating income 1st half up 22% from '88.
- Times 1989 pretax up 27% in 1st half.
- Times 1989 pretax margin is 20.5% in 1st half.

	1977 (Yr. TJ named Pres.)	1989 (est.)
LAT Revenues	$332.7 million	$1,054
LAT Pretax	$ 49 million	$188.5 (was $203 in '87 before off '88)
LAT Pretax Margin	14%	*20.5% (*actual 1st half 1989)
Daily net circulation	1,002,000	1,127,000 (despite 10 price increases)
Sun. net circulation	1,293,000	1,441,000 (despite 11 price increases)
Per cent of TM earnings per share contributed by LAT	24.6%	39.3%
TM EPS growth '77-89		9.5%
LAT EPS growth		13.5%
LAT Net Income growth '77-89(e)		12.8%

Times performance report for 1977–1989, during Tom's years as president and then publisher. Courtesy of Times Mirror / *LAT*.

During a lunch with Howard Allen at the California Club in 1989, he said to me: "Tom, either you start running the *Times* the way Dan Frost and the Chandler family want it run, or you will be out as publisher." I told him I would continue to run the *Times* as Otis and I felt best.

Thanks to Howard, I did get fair warning. Incidentally, Howard Allen was a good personal friend. He and I shared a tent for many years at the Lost Angels Camp of the Bohemian Grove. I really enjoyed my times with him, except for this one.

On Friday, June 30, 1989, I hit rock bottom.

Erburu summoned me to his corporate office, where he told me he was "making a change." I would be promoted to chairman of the *Times*, chairman of the newspaper group's marketing, and vice chairman of the board.

I was crushed by his decision to remove me as publisher. A severe period of depression began.

After my departure from the publisher's position, Anthony Day was removed as editor of the editorial pages.

In my new role as vice chairman of the parent company, I was responsible for coordination of the marketing at all of the newspapers Times Mirror owned across the country. It was still an important job, but not one that I loved nearly as much as my role as publisher. I knew it was time for me to explore other opportunities outside Times Mirror.

During this time my depression was in full swing, and I was having a hard time both at work and at home.

Thank God for the support from Edwina and a few of our closest friends, as well as my wonderful executive assistants Joan Klunder and Ingrid Farmer, who would move my schedule around when I wasn't well. There were times when I would literally rest under my desk to recharge my batteries.

This was the late 1980s, and corporate executives weren't supposed to suffer from mental illness. That was perceived as a weakness in corporate America. Suffering largely in silence made it an immensely difficult period.

Not long after I began my new role, Erburu offered me a good (not great) financial separation package.

Since it was clear to me and others that he wanted me out, I accepted.

I considered Otis a giant among men, a hero. I still do. But it didn't mean that our relationship was perfect, either.

I was tremendously disappointed when Otis did not oppose the decision to replace me as publisher in 1989.

I asked Otis why he approved Erburu's decision. He simply said, "Because Bob [Erburu] asked me to." That was the last I ever heard about his decision.

With Otis gone, Anthony Day gone, and me gone, the Times Mirror corporate takeover of the once highly independent *Los Angeles Times* was in full swing.

However, I was pleased with the choice of David Laventhol to replace me. I admired David immensely. He had a strong journalism background and was extremely creative and respected. He had formerly been publisher of *Newsday*, the dominant newspaper on Long Island. He had served as editor under my White House mentor Bill Moyers and then was promoted to publisher when Bill left in 1978. When the announcement was made that he would replace me as publisher, Laventhol said to me, "Tom, I always thought I'd be reporting to you."

Unfortunately for Laventhol, the hounding by right-wing community members did not stop. Mere months into his new position, Archbishop Mahony wrote to him saying, "What I find particularly distressing is the arrogance of your extreme liberal editorial policy. You do not even credit intelligence to those with a more moderate approach to many issues and concerns."

More changes at the *Times* were to follow, even though splendid leaders such as Dave Laventhol, Dick Schlosberg, Don Wright, Bill Niese, Jim Boswell, Don Maxwell, George Cotliar, and Shelby Coffey continued to lead the paper magnificently. The *Times* remained financially and journalistically strong until the Tribune Company bought Times Mirror in 2000 and then in 2007 sold it to Sam Zell, who loaded huge debts on the balance sheet. In 2008 the *Chicago Tribune* filed for Chapter 11 bankruptcy.

After sixteen years of hard work at Times Mirror, and then being replaced as publisher of the *Times* in 1989, the darkness of my depression grew even deeper. Being ousted was the true breaking point, but my constant workaholic ways and lack of time with my family were contributing factors, many of which I brought on myself.

The first person I told of my ousting was my son, Wyatt. My exact words were "They got me today." I was in tears. Wyatt was a great comfort to me then, as he often has been over the years.

Never before had I experienced failure in either my academic or professional life. To say I was emotionally crushed would be a massive understatement. There were times when I seriously contemplated suicide.

On July 8, 1989, I received a handwritten, highly confidential letter from Otis. He wrote it while at his Keystone, Colorado, ranch home.

I have decided that I am now free to disclose its contents since the Times Mirror Company no longer exists, and since all of the Times Mirror executives mentioned by Otis in the letter have died. I did consult several of my most trusted friends, who also believe that I am not betraying any personal trust by including it in this book.

The actual text follows.

> Dear Tom,
>
> This is a personal letter from me to you—and it is not intended to be shared with anyone but your immediate family.
>
> However, if at some point in your future business career you find yourself wanting to share these thoughts with a new employer, please feel free to do so.
>
> The only point I wish to make as strongly as I can is that I request you never share this letter with anyone associated with the Times Mirror Co., or any of its units, including the Los Angeles Times. I know you understand this plea.
>
> During these past few weeks of relaxation and reflection in and around our home in the majestic Colorado mountains, I have had the opportunity to think long and hard about our personal relationship and our business association which both go back some seventeen years.
>
> It is hard for me to realize how fast these years have gone by, and how much has happened to both of us during this important period in our lives.
>
> I find myself at age 61, 62 in Nov—sounds pretty old, yet I am content and healthy and enjoying my always-new business, family, and athletic challenges.

You aren't 39 anymore, it seems, yet I always think of you as that age—young, dynamic, enthusiastic, articulate, successful, devoted to family, friends, and career . . . someone who could easily be President of the U.S. someday, or anything he wanted to achieve . . . "potential unlimited" should read your biography!

You have always seemed like an older son to me, or that younger brother I never had.

I feel so blessed and fortunate to have crossed your path in Austin when you were still serving President Johnson at KTBC. I was tremendously impressed from the beginning with your obvious leadership qualities. When you agreed to move to Dallas to become our new editor, I had no reservations whatsoever that you would succeed in your new post.

You became an outstanding editor in a relatively short time. You were my only candidate for the Times Herald Publishership. You and your new team moved the paper forward on all fronts.

The outside media took national note of your papers' new reputation.

Then, I wanted you in Los Angeles, to begin your preparation to become my successor as publisher within a few years. I had decided to complete my twenty-years as publisher, and then move to corporate as Chairman for the remainder of my Times Mirror career.

You were my only choice for the publisher of The Times . . . and there was no dissent by any of the senior officers or directors of Times Mirror.

There was some considerable surprise, however, that I wanted to step down after twenty-years (no one, not even Missy or my best friends at the time had any concept of the personal stress and pressure that I had willingly accepted and endured since I first went to work at The Times in the summer of 1947).

Your career as Times President was exactly as I had quietly predicted, and had hoped and prayed for. You were fully prepared to be named Publisher in the spring of 1980.

I wanted to continue to work with you, and be available to you as you tackled a wide range of unfinished projects, and assembled your own new list of priorities.

I also made certain while I was chairman that you were relatively free from corporate interference with The Times, and its exciting new future.

I have been most proud and pleased with all that you have accomplished during these past nine years as The Times publisher.

I wanted my successor to successfully complete all those important projects you and I had begun (or planned for) when we worked together as Publisher/President—like the SF plant/expand, OC plant/expand, the San Diego edition, and so on. As I recall you and Charlie [Chase] and I also came to the conclusion that someday we needed a single, expanded new downtown plant—and what a plant you conceived and have now built!

You also worked long and hard (at great personal sacrifice) to save Dallas and Denver, but they probably had sunk beneath the survival level even before you undertook your heroic efforts. You certainly didn't deserve the media criticism that came your way (others in Times Mirror did, but that's a long story).

You also represented The Times and Times Mirror on a national level in superb fashion—the national awards for the paper (and its publisher), the speeches, important contacts, service on the AP and NAB boards, ANPA convention chairman as well, and so on.

Although, as you well know since we talked about it frequently, I wish you had moved faster on key executive appointments, you now have in place a great new team to help you lead the paper into the next century.

There are enormous problems (and opportunities) that lay ahead, but so were there in my day—there always will be in this business and in Southern California.

You have led The Times to record performances in all measurable criteria. Your circulation, ad revenues, total revenues, and profits are absolutely astounding!

So where have you failed? If, indeed you have in any significant areas of management, I guess I could suggest a few significant points where I would have acted more swiftly, or taken a different road, or been more bold (careless perhaps?).

But who is to judge? The best person to make those calls has been you, our publisher!

If the future is unclear, if the rewards seem less exciting with our newly constituted Times Mirror senior management group (team, no!) then perhaps you need to contemplate a move on into the unknown where another even better opportunity lies in wait for the great Tom Johnson—and you are a great man, my son, my brother, my great and good friend.

> What you know in your heart you have accomplished no man, no company, no outside media, no one on this earth can take that away from you, and your wonderful family.
>
> Most importantly of all, God knows what and who you are and what you have done. Never forget that! I love you, my friend!
>
> —Otis

Mark Willes was recruited from General Mills in 1995 and was announced as president at the Times Mirror annual meeting on May 2, 1995. He was elevated to chairman on January 1, 1996. In 1997 he took on the additional duty of publisher of the *Los Angeles Times*.

Even after more than thirty years since my departure, I remain very saddened by the subsequent dismantling of the Times Mirror Company.

The sale to Tribune Company was negotiated privately behind Willes's back by a representative of the Chandis Trust. Rather than creating an equal to the *New York Times* or the *Washington Post*, the disastrous transaction with real estate titan Sam Zell eight years later put the company into bankruptcy.

There are those within the newspaper and business worlds who have blamed the disintegration of Times Mirror on Willes. That is not my view.

In fact, there were many reasons why the company declined and eventually was sold to the Tribune Company. Some were operating mistakes. Some were strategic errors. Some were driven by rapidly changing market conditions and by radically new digital technology.

My opinion is that certain members of the Chandler family had a greed for money. They were the ones who set the sale to Tribune Company in motion, as well as the eventual collapse of Times Mirror.

It is my belief that Times Mirror and the *Los Angeles Times* would be among the top two or three media companies in the world today had Otis Chandler remained as chief executive officer and the *Times* stayed committed to the highest degree of unbiased, hard-hitting journalism.

Otis demanded the very best in himself and in those who worked with him. I am so grateful I had the honor to have been chosen by Otis as the first non-Chandler publisher of his *Times*. It was an incredible ride.

When I reflect back on my turbulent ending with the *Times*, I take comfort in one of the greatest gifts that I ever received from anyone. It was a letter written by my son, Wyatt, in the *Jewish Times*, in defense of my integrity as a newsman.

Our coverage of the Middle East had been terrific for the years I was publisher. However, just as it does today, covering major events in that turbulent region, such as the 1982 Sabra and Shatila massacre, could cause major reactions in both the Jewish and Arab communities.

I had grown accustomed to being criticized by someone or some group at any point in time—including Buff Chandler and her Music Center friends—but in 1988 I was being disparaged as antisemitic because of our very independent coverage of Israeli-Palestinian issues.

The *Times* confronted a boycott by many Jewish-led advertisers and temporarily lost thousands of subscribers.

Wyatt learned of the personal attacks on me and wrote the following letter in my defense.

> Editor: I have boycotted grapes and Gallo wine, been arrested at the Nevada Test Site against nuclear proliferation, supported the rights of our gay brothers and sisters. I am against any sort of racial or religious persecution. I try and do all I can to make our world a better place.
>
> I'm not Jewish and can never know what you have been through despite the Shoahs that I'd see, all the survivors I may meet.
>
> I have read time and again of Arabs killing Indians bombing Russians, Lebanese, Ugandans, shooting and destroying. I also know of American finance murder in Central America.
>
> I'll do anything (non-violent), and you can call me on that to stop anti-Semitism. It is wrong and makes me sick—the one prejudice I still hold is towards bigots. This is hard to stomach.
>
> From my perspective, the Times coverage seems fair. Is Israel Nirvana—does it not suffer from some of the same ills as other societies? Are not some of its actions as ill as those that oppress Blacks in South Africa? Armenians in Russia? Jews here in the U.S. today? Asians in my little conservative San Marino?

I just ask you to look at the Big Picture.

Also, I am biased. My father, Tom Johnson, is the Times publisher. We do not stand head-to-head on many things—and I know the Dallas paper had a writer recently very guilty of prejudice towards Blacks (he was fired).

But I tell you this: my father is a wonderful, enlightened man—though perhaps not radical. I know of no prejudices he holds towards any man due to one's creed, color or faith. He's not going to slant anything to make any group happy.

He will do anything he can to stop anti-Semitism, but there is also a lot of concern about racism towards other groups, Palestinian included.

Thank God for that. It hasn't always been so.

Please let me know if I am wrong and what I can do as an individual.

Peace.

Wyatt Johnson

San Marino

It is Wyatt's letter that reminds me to this day that we did our best to provide accurate, fair, and comprehensive coverage, no matter who it angered or pleased.

A quality newspaper doesn't cater to any one group; a quality newspaper reports the news.

CHAPTER 13

THE OSWALD NOTE

Kennedy's assassination, and the note that might have saved a president

Of all the revelations during my years in government and media, the single most shocking one came in the summer of 1975. It concerned the assassination of President John F. Kennedy twelve years earlier, on November 22, 1963, in Dallas, Texas—an event that was always surrounded by speculation and conspiracy theories.

While serving as publisher of the *Dallas Times Herald,* I was at a dinner with many of the city's power brokers. Sitting next to me was a high-ranking federal law enforcement officer.

Prior to that dinner, my source and I already had become friends.

He was well aware of my position as publisher of the *Times Herald.* He also knew that I had been an aide to President Johnson in the White House and afterward. While I had built my career in media and public service, my source had risen up the ranks in U.S. federal law enforcement.

Over dessert, our conversation turned to the assassination of President Kennedy.

He and I were both convinced that Lee Harvey Oswald was the lone gunman, which had long been a major debate both in public and government circles. But I asked him if there was any undisclosed information that might eventually be revealed. My notes show that the exact question I asked was "Is there anything we do not know about the Kennedy assassination?"

Oswald threat revealed

Note to FBI destroyed; Kennedy not named

Lee Harvey Oswald . . . . . . warned FBI agent

By TOM JOHNSON
Staff Writer

Lee Harvey Oswald personally carried a "threatening" letter to the Federal Bureau of Investigation office here several days prior to the assassination of President John F. Kennedy, The Dallas Times Herald has learned.

The letter, which apparently did not mention President Kennedy, was destroyed by FBI personnel shortly after the assassination and its existence never was revealed during intensive investigation by the Warren Commission, according to sources within the FBI.

The FBI has launched a full internal inquiry into the Oswald visit and possible criminal violations in connection with destruction of the note and failure to report its existence.

In response to inquiries by The Times Herald, FBI Director Clarence M. Kelley said Saturday that an investigation "tends to substantiate that Lee Harvey Oswald visited the Dallas FBI office several days prior to the assassination of President Kennedy."

Kelley said Oswald visited the office "apparently as the result of an interview by an FBI agent of his (Oswald's) wife Marina, in connection with the FBI investigation of Lee Harvey Oswald prior to the assassination."

FBI agents had made contact with Oswald's wife, Nov. 1, 1963, only 21 days before the assassination. Another attempt to interview her was made on Nov. 5, but it was not successful.

The FBI probe into Oswald's visit was launched as a result of questions asked by The Times Herald during a July 6, 1975, meeting with Kelley in Washington FBI headquarters. The Times Herald has been checking the previously unreported incident for more than two months.

In a statement prepared for The Times Herald Saturday, Kelley said: "Oswald left a note addressed to this agent, and, although recollections vary as to the wording of the note, it was for the purpose of warning the agent to desist from further interviews with his wife."

"Prior to the current FBI inquiries, there had been no information concerning this visit and note recorded in FBI records, and inquiries tend to corroborate that shortly after the assassination, the note in question was destroyed," he said.

Kelley said Saturday that "inquiries are continuing to determine the full facts concerning the handling of this matter." Kelley said Attorney General Edward Levi is being kept informed on the progress of the investigation.

Apparently those personnel in Dallas FBI offices at the time who knew of Oswald's visit and his letter have kept the incident secret for almost 12 years, sources told The Times Herald.

A person assigned to the FBI office at the time of the assassination said of the visit: "Oswald left a threatening note . . . he wanted the agent in charge of his wife's case to quit harassing Marina."

"I didn't actually see the note

See OSWALD on Page 18

Times Herald query prompted FBI probe

The FBI internal investigation was initiated as a result of a July 6 meeting between The Times Herald and FBI Director Clarence M. Kelley and Associate Director James Adams.

The Times Herald had uncovered information concerning the reported Oswald visit to the Dallas FBI offices prior to the assassination, as well as information on a "threatening letter" and the reported destruction of that letter.

Because the newspaper has received hundreds of unsubstantiated reports challenging the findings of The Warren Commission Report, a decision was made to delay publication until the story could be verified both independently and at the highest level of the FBI.

THE DALLAS TIMES HERALD

96th Year—No. 243 ★★★ ★ DALLAS, TEXAS, SUNDAY MORNING, AUGUST 31, 1975 Classified: 748-1414 Circulation: 748-9711 Other Depts.: 748-9711 15 Parts Price Thirty-Five Cents

—Staff Photo by Phil Huber

COSMIC COWBOYS—About 20,000 "redneck rock" fans had gathered by mid-afternoon Saturday for the beginning of "48 hours in Atoka," an Oklahoma country-western rock festival that is expected to draw 100,000 "cosmic cowboys." See story, more photos on Page 8-B.

School tax rate hiked by 14 cents

By ERIC MILLER
Staff Writer

The Dallas school board Saturday approved an unexpected 14-cent tax rate hike, eight cents of which will be applied toward the implementation of a school desegregation plan later this school year.

Trustees voted unanimously to adopt a $164.5 million 1975-76 school operating budget that will set aside $5.6 million specifically into a desegregation contingency fund. The total budget, including federal projects, is more than $211 million.

The board had been expected to adopt a $158.9 million operating budget, calling for a 6-cent tax rate hike, but that was prior to a two-day retreat of closed discussions concerning the drawing of a new desegregation plan to present to U.S. Dist. Judge William M. Taylor by Sept. 10.

The new tax rate has been set at $1.51 per $100 value, based on 75 per cent of fair market value. Of that total, $1.31 will be directly used for the operating expenditures, while 20-cents will be devoted to interest and sinking fund payments.

Last year's tax rate, converted to the 75 per cent assessment rate, was $1.37. Last year's operating budget totaled $125 million.

The tax hike means the owner of a home with a fair market value of $30,000 will pay $31.50 more in taxes, $328.75 as compared to $308.25 under this year's rate schedule.

According to a budget report the school district sent to the Texas Education Agency Saturday, a $2,270,233 fund balance exists from the preceding year's budget.

Trustee Charles Fletcher, who voted for the 8-cent additional tax rate hike under "protest", said he is unsure that amount will be necessary.

Fletcher told The Times Herald the topic of desegregation costs did not receive much discussion at the closed desegregation retreat Thursday and Friday.

"I heard figures of between six and eight cents discussed," he said. "If we're not sure we won't need all the money, why take it from the taxpayer?"

Fletcher said the $5.6 million likely would be used to purchase additional school buses to implement the plan, as well as for upgrading a number of substandard schools in various parts of the city.

In adopting the budget, trustees also took a number of other actions.

All high school coaches were given 11 per cent salary increases and were placed on 200-day contracts, opposed to their present 180-day term of employment.

Trustees also declined to contribute $100,000 in local funds to KERA-TV (Channel 13) for instructional television.

Gasoline price expected to climb after decontrol

By WILLIAM L. CHAZE
Times Herald Washington Bureau

WASHINGTON — Government controls on domestic oil prices are set to expire at midnight tonight, making higher gasoline prices this fall almost a certainty.

A slim chance remains for controls to be resurrected within the next several weeks. Ford has delayed vetoing an extension of the controls to give Congress more time to work on the problem.

The extension would impose controls for another six months. Ford met last week with the Democratic leadership of Congress and said he had decided against immediately vetoing the legislation.

Senate Majority Leader Mike Mansfield said the veto "probably will take place, but in the meantime we stand a good chance of developing an alternative."

The controls, which have held 60 per cent of U.S. oil under a relatively low price ceiling since winter 1973, have been the object of a year-long tug-of-war between Congress and Ford over energy policy. The two have been unable to agree on a gradual phaseout of controls on 5.5 million of the nation's 8.5 million barrels of daily domestic crude oil production.

The Federal Energy Administration says that without controls, there eventually will be a 3-cent price increase for gasoline, home heating oil and other fuel. The oil industry generally agrees, but Saturday company spokesmen — reacting to the possibility of a sudden compromise — were denying that immediate price rises are in the offing.

One company official put it this way: "No one is going to be stupid enough right now, when it looks like we might get some kind of decontrol, to raise prices and enrage consumers and create a political condition where there might not be any decontrol."

However, Rep. John Dingell, D-Mich., who heads the House Energy subcommittee, has predicted a 7-cent

See OIL on Page 1?

—AP Wirephoto

OIL WORRIES — Rep. Carl Albert, foreground, and Sen. Mike Mansfield still plug for oil compromise.

WEATHER REPORT

(National Weather Service Forecast)

Dallas and vicinity: Clear to partly cloudy and warm today through Monday. High both days 95. Low tonight 75. Wind light southerly. (See details on Page 10B.)

8 am...76 2 pm...94 8 pm...90
10 am...85 4 pm...96
12 N....90 6 pm...96

WHERE TO FIND

Brownsville watchful as storm nears

BROWNSVILLE, Tex. (AP) — Disaster teams arrived Saturday in South Texas to prepare for a possible strike by Hurricane Caroline, but except for watching the situation closely residents took little action.

The storm, packing winds of 80 miles per hour, churned towards the sparsely populated northeast Mexico coast Saturday, but weather forecasters warned that even a slight northward deviation could bring Caroline into Texas.

Most commercial fishing vessels had returned to harbors by Saturday when the Red Cross began bringing in teams, including nurses and first-aid specialists, from Oklahoma, Kansas and Missouri.

One had to look carefully to see any hurricane preparations. A few businesses placed masking tape on windows and some car dealers stored new cars inside.

But except for rain and winds gusting to 28 mph, it appeared to be an ordinary Saturday afternoon. Shopping center parking lots were full and traffic was heavy.

The storm virtually wiped out Labor Day weekend business in South Padre Island while it was still swirling two hundred miles off the coast. The

See [illegible] on Page 12

Bureau of Census says Dallas losing population

By BILL WALDROP
Staff Writer

The federal people counters, better known as the U.S. Bureau of the Census, Department of Commerce, say Dallas' population has been shrinking at an annual rate of 3.4 per cent since 1970.

Local people counters — the City of Dallas and the North Central Texas Council of Governments (NCTCOG) — say the growth loss estimate just is not so.

Growth is slower, certainly, than the boom years of the 1960s — that decade racked up a 24.2 per cent increase at a 2.2 per cent annual growth rate — but the city is still growing, local officials say.

Obviously, maybe there has been some mistake, one official says. But also, maybe everybody is right but just about different things at different times, says another spokesman.

Federal census figures estimate the Dallas population at $15,866 as of July 1973 while COG's figures total 912,960 as of January of this year.

City estimates put the population figure at 890,100 as of April 1974 and at 893,000 as of last April. The 1974 figure represents a 5.4 per cent change in the 1970 census total of 844,401.

The first-time study estimate of city populations on such a massive scale by the bureau of census was done at the request of the federal office of revenue sharing.

The estimates were to be used in computing 1975-76 revenue-sharing allocations.

Cities around the country began receiving the updated figures early in the year and objections were raised almost immediately.

In the case of Dallas, the new totals did little to change the city's share of the federal money pot.

Dean Vanderbilt, the city's management services director, said last week that Dallas' current revenue-sharing appropriation is in line with previous years.

Population estimates were reviewed for accuracy after the protests but, at least in the case of Dallas, they remained unchanged when released last week.

"The census bureau has a long-standing reputation for estimating procedures," said Bob Greer, chief of urban analysis for the City of Dallas Department of Urban Planning.

"They're a very competent group of people but we are all using different methods.

"What it really comes down to is both of us have some very sound methods for estimating population figures and some very sound data, but we

See DALLAS on Page 11

Courtesy of Times Mirror / *LAT*.

He startled me with his answer.

"The biggest one that will be disclosed one day, Tom," he said, "will be that Oswald came by our FBI Dallas offices and left a threatening note days before the assassination."

When Oswald arrived at the FBI's Dallas field office on November 12, 1963, my friend told me, he asked to speak with Special Agent James Hosty.

The receptionist, Nannie Lee Fenner, told Oswald that Hosty was not in the office at that time.

Oswald left a note with Fenner for Hosty and left.

That visit to the FBI office was not reported to the U.S. Secret Service or to other Dallas law enforcement agencies prior to the president's visit on November 22.

Following the assassination, no details of Oswald's visit or his note were reported by the FBI to the Warren Commission—the government body that conducted the official investigation into JFK's murder.

To understand the breadth of this intelligence failure that may have ultimately resulted in the death of President Kennedy, it is important to understand the reason that Oswald delivered that note ten days before he assassinated JFK.

Oswald had a history of trouble throughout his life. In his youth, he bounced between a dozen schools. He was jailed during his time as a U.S. Marine. And in 1959 he defected to the Soviet Union.

While living in the USSR, Oswald married a Russian citizen, Marina, with whom he had a daughter. In 1962 the young family of three moved to the United States and settled in Dallas.

Together, Oswald and Marina made for a classic counterespionage case, and they were in fact on the government's radar.

In Dallas, Oswald and Marina sometimes lived apart due to marital issues. When separated, Marina and their two daughters (the second was born in October 1963) would often stay with a friend, Ruth Paine, about ten miles away in Irving, Texas.

The tension between Oswald and the FBI that led to Oswald leaving his note for Agent Hosty stemmed from visits that Hosty paid to

Marina at Paine's home on two separate occasions: November 1 and November 5.

The FBI had only recently located Marina, after she and Lee separated (the status of their marriage was unclear), and Hosty was attempting to make contact with Marina and to establish her identity, address, and place of employment.

In November 1963 the FBI had no confirmed evidence that either of the Oswalds was a Russian agent, but the Cold War was at its height, when the possibility of nuclear war between the United States and the Soviet Union was all too real.

In the FBI's eyes, Marina was of higher security interest than Oswald, given her education and communist upbringing during the Cold War era. It wasn't until later that Agent Hosty learned Oswald had been a subscriber to a communist newspaper, the *Daily Worker*, which elevated the FBI's interest in him as well.

While Marina and their two daughters were living with her friend Ruth Paine in Irving, Oswald was living during the workweek in an eight-by-eleven-foot room in Dallas. He would visit Marina and the children on weekends.

When Marina saw Oswald on the Friday after Agent Hosty's second visit, she told him she was terrified that he was a KGB agent there to force her back to Russia. She was so scared that she even tried to hide behind the refrigerator during the FBI agent's visit.

Marina's recounting of the FBI visit infuriated Oswald to the point where he went to the Dallas FBI offices and asked to see Hosty. When the receptionist Nannie Lee Fenner told him Agent Hosty was not there, Oswald left the threatening note with Fenner, for Hosty's return.

Why the Dallas field office did not act quickly following the threatening note is a matter of speculation. Several former FBI agents have told me it was simply "a bureaucratic failure." Other agents have said that threatening notes and messages come into large field offices like the one in Dallas "by the hundreds."

Following JFK's assassination and the arrest of Lee Harvey Oswald for the crime, receptionist Fenner recalled, she immediately recognized Oswald's face when it was shown on television. She had given Hosty the note on November 12, but she was uncertain if he had informed anyone else in the FBI offices.

In near panic, she notified Dallas FBI superiors of Oswald's visit and the note he left. These men included the assistant special agent-in-charge, Kyle Clark; Hosty's direct supervisor, Ken C. Howe; and eventually the special agent-in-charge, Gordon Shanklin.

Hosty was *not* present when Mrs. Fenner informed the other agents about Oswald's visit and the note. Hosty was at the Dallas Police Department when she told the story to his higher-ups.

Agent Ken Howe immediately searched Hosty's desk and found the note, which he showed to Shanklin.

As another source of mine related, Shanklin exploded in anger and immediately called FBI headquarters in Washington to determine what action he should take.

When Hosty returned to the Dallas field office in the early evening, Shanklin confronted him with the note and demanded a full explanation.

That is where matters stood until things became even stranger.

Late on Sunday morning, November 24—only two days after JFK's assassination—Oswald was murdered by Jack Ruby in the basement of Dallas police headquarters while he was being escorted by Dallas police officers to a vehicle waiting to transfer him to jail.

Shanklin promptly summoned Agent Hosty into his office and said: "Jim, I don't ever want to see that note again. Oswald's dead, and there can't be a trial now."

According to my source, as well as three additional agents, the command to destroy the note—"flush it"—was a direct order that came from Washington, likely from FBI director J. Edgar Hoover.

While I consider those sources reliable, I have never been able to officially confirm their account.

Because the source of the original information obtained at that dinner in Dallas is now deceased, and because more than sixty years have passed since JFK's assassination, I feel comfortable disclosing that the source *was* a ranking FBI agent in the Dallas bureau. I will also confirm that it was *not* Gordon Shanklin.

Although I have never revealed the source to anyone, even in confidence, reporter Hugh Aynesworth wrote to me on December 3, 2014, with this message: "Your source was Vince Drain. He told me many years ago that he was your source on that important story. And, he was critical of at least two other agents, blaming Shanklin and his top assistant for telling Hosty to destroy the note. . . . It seems totally logical that had Hosty, Howe or those who knew of the note—recall we were told that half a dozen staffers or agents were aware Oswald had left it—had they followed through, it might at least have scared Oswald into not shooting President Kennedy that day."

Aynesworth continued: "Either the Secret Service or the Dallas Police would have closely watched Oswald. There is not much doubt about that."

While many reporters and editors feel that the confidential agreement between journalist and source ends when a source dies, I do not share that view. Out of my original pledge of confidentiality, I still hold firm even now in refusing to confirm whether FBI agent Vince Drain was my original source.

Following the Dallas dinner, I returned to the nearby offices of the *Times Herald* and advised editor Ken Johnson and managing editor Will Jarrett of what I had learned. I typed a summary of the information. The three of us agreed that a single source was not sufficient for immediate publication of such historic and controversial news.

The next morning, a Cadillac arrived unannounced at our home in north Dallas. It was my source from dinner the previous night.

The visit was in no way threatening, but Edwina and I were surprised by his stopping by uninvited. He expressed his regret for not speaking to me the night before at the dinner "off the record," and asked that I refrain from publishing the information he had provided.

I told him I would not.

To be clear, he knew I was publisher of the *Dallas Times Herald*, and he certainly knew that he had not clarified that our conversation was to be kept off the record.

Aware of the seriousness of the situation, I took an unprecedented step, one that I had never taken before nor ever took again. I contacted my friend James Adams, FBI deputy director, and asked for an urgent meeting with him and FBI director Clarence Kelley in Washington. Both men agreed. (I happened to know Adams, a Texan, during the time that I worked for former president Johnson in Austin.)

On July 6, 1975, I flew to Washington, where the three of us sat down in Director Kelley's office. I found the office eerie, given it had been occupied by J. Edgar Hoover when I was last there with the LBJ administration.

As I told Kelley and Adams what I had learned, both men appeared to be genuinely shocked.

I asked them to either confirm or deny the information, and requested that any findings be made available first to the *Dallas Times Herald* before being released to any other news organization. They agreed to those terms, and assured me they would begin an immediate internal investigation.

The investigation authorized by Director Kelley involved ranking FBI supervisors from around the nation to serve as inspectors. All Dallas agents, including Shanklin, Hosty, and Howe, as well as my source, were interviewed.

On Saturday, August 30, 1975, Director Kelley contacted me with a statement. Over the phone, he said, "Tom, I regret to confirm that the information you provided to us *is* accurate."

Statement from the FBI

Saturday, August 30, 1975
Statement by Federal Bureau of Investigation Director Clarence M. Kelley, issued to The Dallas Times Herald Saturday by Associate Director James B. Adams:

FBI Director Clarence M. Kelley confirmed today that inquiries conducted in response to questions asked by The Dallas Times Herald tend to substantiate that Lee Harvey Oswald visited the Dallas FBI office several days prior to the assassination of President Kennedy, apparently as the result of an interview by an FBI agent of his wife Marina in connec-

> tion with the FBI investigation of Lee Harvey Oswald prior to the assassination which was documented in the Warren Commission report. Oswald left a note addressed to this agent and although recollections vary as to the wording of the note, it was for the purpose of warning the agent to desist from further interviews of his wife.
>
> FBI inquiries to date establish that the note contained no reference to President Kennedy or in any way would have forewarned of the subsequent assassination. Prior to the current FBI inquiries, there had been no information concerning this visit and note recorded in FBI records, and inquiries tend to corroborate that shortly after the assassination, the note in question was destroyed.
>
> Inquiries are continuing to determine the full facts concerning the handling of this matter.
>
> The Attorney General has from the inception been kept informed of the progress of FBI inquiries to date. Director Kelley has indicated that there will be no further comment for publication until all inquiries have been concluded and the matter considered by the department.

I personally wrote the story for the following day's edition, with significant editing help from the *Times Herald* editors Ken Johnson and Will Jarrett. Reporters Hugh Aynesworth and Bob Dudney secured interviews with FBI Dallas Agent-in-Charge Gordon Shanklin and with Agent Hosty that were included in the story.

Before the story went to print, every element had been fact-checked with then FBI director Clarence Kelley and assistant director James Adams. It ran across the top of the front page of the *Times Herald* and was picked up by news organizations around the world.

Over the many years since the end of the FBI's internal investigation, I have not dealt with any JFK assassination reports other than the Oswald note.

However, I do believe that Oswald should have been interrogated by the FBI in the days immediately prior to the assassination. Certainly, the Secret Service should have been notified of the threatening note Oswald had left at the Dallas FBI offices.

Clint Hill—the heroic Secret Service agent who climbed on the back of the presidential limo seconds after the shots were fired at JFK—decades later told me that Secret Service agents in Dallas, prior to and on November 22, 1963, were continuously checking with sources and examining information pertinent to the president's security.

Hill told me that when the presidential party arrived in Dallas, the Secret Service was unaware of any specific threats to the president, Mrs. Kennedy, Vice President Johnson, or Mrs. Johnson in the Dallas area.

Despite their efforts, he said, nobody had ever mentioned Oswald's visit to the Dallas FBI offices or the note he left.

It is not unreasonable to believe that had the FBI advised either the Secret Service or the Dallas Police of the potential danger that Oswald represented, he would have been under close law enforcement surveillance instead of being allowed to hide on the sixth floor of the Dallas School Book Depository with a rifle, awaiting a clear shot at the president's car.

In fact, the Dallas police chief once told reporter Hugh Aynesworth, "If the Dallas Police had been informed that a man working the motorcade route had the ties to Russia that Oswald had, we would have sat on his lap."

Had that taken place, the history of America could have been written in a vastly different way.

Many conspiracies continue to tie Oswald to outside groups, but my overall confidence in the Warren Commission has never been shaken regarding its conclusion that Lee Harvey Oswald was the sole assassin.

In particular, Cuba's relationship with the USSR had given skeptics good reason to believe that Cuba or Cuban president Fidel Castro might have been tied to the assassination. Even LBJ had his suspicions about Cuba, but no connection has ever been proven.

In the aftermath of JFK's assassination, a major question I continue to ask myself is: Do U.S. intelligence agencies communicate better with each other now than they did in 1963?

Several investigations concluded that the attacks on the World Trade Center and the Pentagon on September 11, 2001, could have been prevented if those federal agencies had communicated more openly and more effectively. We will never know with certainty.

However, the massive Department of Homeland Security was created after 9/11. The U.S. government has expanded its intelligence-gathering capabilities immensely, including programs that I fear infringe on personal privacy rights of American citizens, especially journalists.

Today the National Security Agency and other agencies gather massive amounts of data. The 2013 classified information leak by Edward Snowden also shows the vulnerability of our private information. Making the threats of this Big Brother reality worse, the Chinese, Russians, Israelis, Saudis, and other foreign governments are building high-technology systems that can penetrate even the most highly encrypted programs.

This is a new world—far more technologically advanced than it was prior to the breakdown in communications between the FBI and the Secret Service in 1963, or even before September 11, 2001.

Is America safer?

Do our billion-dollar intelligence agencies communicate well enough to prevent a nuclear device from exploding in downtown New York, or Washington, or your hometown?

Have we learned the lessons of the Oswald note?

Have we learned the lessons of September 11? Or the January 6, 2021 attack on Washington, when right-wing militants overran our nation's Capitol Building?

I hope and pray that we have. Our lives depend on it.

CHAPTER 14

INTO THE DARKNESS AND OUT INTO THE LIGHT

"Depression is a treatable illness."

My battle with chronic depression is by far the most personal topic that I discuss in this book. I write very openly about my depression in hopes that it may be of value to those who are suffering with it themselves, as well as their friends and families.

In my opinion, nobody understands that mysterious illness better than those of us who have experienced it.

It has been one of the most challenging issues of my life, as well as one of the most rewarding to speak about openly.

Almost everybody knows of a family member or friend who battles depression. The World Health Organization reports it is a leading cause of disability worldwide, with some 280 million people suffering from it globally. This understates the impact that depression has on families.

From my own research and my own experiences, I've learned that depression can be a result of a family history (genetic predisposition); a traumatic event in life such as the loss of a loved one, lack of financial security, or a serious illness (situational); the damage we inflict on our bodies through alcohol, harmful drugs, excessive smoking, or even simply natural aging (chemical changes); or an unbalanced lifestyle with too little time for relaxation and fun (stress). Often it's a combination.

Common symptoms frequently include a prolonged period of being down, continuing feeling of sadness, irritability, and feelings of guilt or worthlessness. Many people report a loss of interest in activities they once enjoyed, excessive sleeping or insomnia, pulling back from family and friends, a loss of sex drive, and a loss of energy and enthusiasm for life.

Many also report thoughts of suicide, as I once did myself.

Suicide has been in the top ten causes of death in the United States for many years. Until the COVID pandemic, suicide was the only one of the top ten causes of death that was increasing compared to heart disease, stroke, and cancer.

As my friend the columnist Art Buchwald said, "Suicide is a permanent solution to a temporary problem. It is the only decision that, if acted upon, cannot ever be reconsidered."

You can change what college you go to, who your friends are, or who you're married to, but you can never reverse the act of death by suicide. Please do not do it!

Sadly, two of my very best friends, Rusty Rose of Dallas and Jerry Lindauer of Austin, took their own lives because of depression. Experiences like those inspire me to keep fighting.

There are treatments today that can enable you to become healthier. If you or anybody you know is suffering from depression, please go to a professional and get help. You can also call the National Hotline for Mental Health Crises and Suicide Prevention at 800-273-TALK (8255) or dial 9-8-8.

The most important message that I want to convey is this: *Depression is a treatable illness.*

At the time I was diagnosed by a psychiatrist at UCLA, I was publisher and chief executive officer of the *Los Angeles Times*. As expected for the publisher of a major newspaper, my job was very stressful, but life in California was wonderful. The city was booming, and the Chandler family for whom I worked were at the heart of that growth.

In spite of the beautiful weather, the excitement of the city, and my enjoyment of being publisher, there were a variety of personal problems, especially with my temper.

My anger was never directed at members of my staff. Instead it was often vented at home, where my wife Edwina, son Wyatt, and daughter Christa at times would see the worst of me.

As a result of my depression, I retreated from friends, from activities I loved, and from my family. It's true what they say—when you're not your best self, it's those you love the most that you hurt the most. That certainly was my experience when I was in the early days of my depression.

I thought my depression began while I was in LA, but my wife Edwina believes that many of my symptoms had been a part of our marriage and early family life for many years. Neither of us was educated on the symptoms of depression at that time, but Edwina knew something was wrong.

As is the case with many people who experience mental illness, I had a genetic predisposition toward depression.

My uncle Foreman Brown—my mother's brother—was hospitalized for most of his life with depression in the Milledgeville (Georgia) State Hospital for the Insane. That name alone is a reminder of how far we've come on issues of mental illness.

He was placed there by his parents, John Brown and John's second wife, Olivia, who was not the biological mother of either my mother or my uncle. John and Olivia found that Foreman's behavior was seriously erratic, so they had him committed and confined there for most of his life.

On occasion, he was administered electric shock treatments, now known as electroconvulsive therapy (ECT).

About once a year, especially when I was young, I would accompany my mother on a drive to Milledgeville to visit him. When we arrived, he would be permitted to come outside and sit with us.

I showed considerable interest in him as a relative, and he was a wonderfully sweet man.

Perhaps because of my young age, I was somewhat bewildered by the fact that he was hospitalized. He always seemed so normal to me. He was thoughtful, kind, and responsive in a very gentle way. There's a chance it was a result of his medication, but I never knew for sure.

Based on what I saw firsthand at that Milledgeville hospital, and what I later learned from reading a Pulitzer Prize–winning exposé written by Jack Nelson of the *Atlanta Journal-Constitution*, that state mental hospital looked much like the one in the movie *One Flew over the Cuckoo's Nest*.

Nelson exposed the inhumane conditions and treatments, which were often forced on patients, including primitive forms of ECT.

Fortunately, ECT is very different today. When used properly under medical supervision, it's become a proven remedy for some serious cases of depression, with a high rate of success, according to various experts I know and trust.

My mother never showed symptoms similar to those of her brother. She had "down days" like everyone but was never stricken by depression. However, the genetic path of depression was passed down to me, as well as to another close relative, our daughter Christa.

When my ousting from the *Los Angeles Times* triggered the worst of my symptoms, Edwina really became assertive. She "forced" me to go to a psychiatrist at UCLA by giving me an ultimatum: "Go see the psychiatrist, or else."

After only three sessions, the UCLA psychiatrist said, "Mr. Johnson, you have chronic depression."

I always had a Superman mentality that I could leap over any building or fly at any speed to conquer whatever situations life threw at me. My whole life had been lived with the idea that even if I was not more capable than others around me, I could outwork anyone.

For reasons that I didn't fully understand, depression was a very different type of challenge. I could not simply outwork it.

Various medications were recommended, beginning with lithium. But lithium left me in a zombielike state.

Two other antidepressants made my mouth so dry that I could barely speak. Another had the side effect of excessive perspiration, especially if I become uptight and anxious, as I often am before delivering a speech.

The time between medications, and the difficulties associated with switching from one to another, were absolutely terrible.

Much of this was during the early days of psychopharmacology.

Treating people accurately for their very nuanced forms of depression has improved significantly as the field has advanced. We now know that lithium, for instance, can be effective for bipolar disorder.

When medicine wasn't working, I turned to exercise and diet.

I was running as much as five miles, five days a week, with friends Jack Liebau, Ron Olson, or Dr. Richard Nalick. At one point my weight dropped to 172 pounds.

During this same time, Edwina also demanded that Wyatt and I go with her to see a child psychologist. Neither Wyatt nor I wanted anything to do with it, but I finally agreed because of her persistence. Wyatt never went. He and I clashed.

The psychiatrist opened the conversation with me by saying, "Mr. Johnson, I understand that I only have a short period of time with you. I also understand that you wish you were not here." I told her both of those statements were true.

She offered very explicit advice: "I will summarize some points for you that I usually do not get to until I've reached perhaps six months of sessions with patients. . . . First, back off, Mr. Johnson. You cannot manage your son the way that you manage the *Los Angeles Times*. Second, let him become what he would like to become in life, not what you want him to become. Praise him more often. What he hears from you is mostly criticism. Third, show him how much you love him. Provide him with unconditional love."

To her third point, I thought, "Unconditional love, my ass. Sometimes I'd like to knock him through the wall."

But the doctor was right.

She explained to me that if Wyatt didn't know how much I loved him, he would go find love in a bottle or with a gang. This hit me especially hard, since Wyatt was already running away from home.

Before meeting with professionals, I felt like I had tried everything, but it was clear that everything I was doing was not working.

Following the meeting, I wrote all of the doctor's instructions down on a notepad in my car and decided that I would follow her advice. I adopted everything she had told me.

It wasn't a perfect solution, but my new approach was better than before.

Her advice also made me realize how I didn't have all the answers as a parent.

Yes, I had degrees from UGA and Harvard Business School. Yes, I had learned a great deal about management and people through my profession. And yes, I had learned valuable lessons from my own childhood. But I had never been trained to be a father.

I finally began to comprehend that there was still so much more for me to learn.

The most important lesson I learned from the rocky process was that my self-worth had become too intertwined with my own positions of power. I had to learn that I was much more than a publisher. I was also a husband, a father, a friend, a good citizen, and hopefully a mostly good man.

It was only after a new beginning as CEO of CNN—back in my home state of Georgia—and a new antidepressant that I began to recover from my depression. I found a wonderful new psychopharmacologist at Emory University, Dr. Charles Nemeroff. He is now at the Dell Medical Center in Austin, Texas.

Edwina was the hero in my personal life who threw me a lifeline.

Her persistence to get me the professional help I needed to save both myself and my relationship with my family was the support that I needed to get back on track.

Ted Turner—the absolutely brilliant leader of CNN—was my professional hero. Ted was the one who helped me once again find my purpose when he recruited me in 1990 to the best job of my life, president and CEO of CNN Worldwide.

Thank you, Ted!

CHAPTER 15

TED TURNER

"I want to make CNN the absolute best news network on the planet! That's it, pal!"

Until I met Ted Turner, I thought President Lyndon Johnson was the most complex person I ever had known.

As I've described, LBJ could often be kind, thoughtful, generous, loving, dynamic, forceful, funny, persuasive, and the best storyteller I ever have known.

But he also could be mean, cruel, harsh, petty, depressed, anguished, and angry. He was a workaholic who drove his staff to accomplish every project as quickly and as professionally as possible. He also drove himself relentlessly. I've never known anyone who drove himself as hard as he did, with the possible exception of Bill Moyers.

By comparison, Ted Turner could be totally outrageous and was a tremendous visionary. Ted could see the future in ways that few people can, and he had the drive and talent to turn his ideas into reality.

Like LBJ's, his commitment to success extended far beyond expectations of himself.

After I was ousted as publisher of the *Los Angeles Times* in late 1989, I began to search for a position that would bring me a sense of public service and new opportunities in journalism.

My close friend Joe Allbritton had offered me a major executive position with his Allbritton Communications Company, which included the *Washington Star*, multiple television stations, and other businesses.

Ted and Tom in the CNN newsroom at Atlanta headquarters, with journalist Chris Turner, son of CNN's EVP of Newsgathering, Ed Turner. Courtesy of CNN.

Other friends of mine, Jim Batten, Alvah Chapman, and Lee Hills of the Knight Ridder media company, had offered me the position of publisher of their *Philadelphia Inquirer*, even though Batten told me, "You are not interviewing well." I knew I wasn't.

I'd been offered the position of publisher at the *International Herald Tribune*, which was based in Paris and jointly owned by Katharine Graham of the *Washington Post* and Punch Sulzberger of the *New York Times*. That offer was so tempting that Edwina had even begun taking French classes at a junior college near our home in San Marino, California.

Another possibility came from the newly appointed chairman of Cox Enterprises, James Cox Kennedy, who discussed my becoming president of Cox. However, after consulting with two of his Cox board members, Jim was told, "If you hire Tom Johnson, he will be running the company instead of you," as that board member later told me.

I would have accepted Jim Kennedy's offer had he extended it. Cox was then—as it remains now—a splendid organization that values excellence in its products, in its operations, and especially in its people. It also was located in my home state of Georgia. Edwina and I often had dreamed of returning home, and the Cox position would have been a wonderful opportunity to do just that. I was disappointed that a formal Cox offer never came.

I eventually narrowed my search to two offers: publisher of the *International Herald Tribune*, or a senior management position with Time Warner in New York, which then CEO Jerry Levin discussed with me.

As Edwina and I weighed Paris and New York, a spectacular offer came in. It was from Ted Turner at CNN.

I did not know Ted well. We had only met during one major dinner in LA when I was publisher of the *Los Angeles Times*.

I certainly knew who he was; in fact, much to my dismay, Ted was famous for publicly predicting the demise of newspapers in many of his speeches.

Now, in 2025, it looks as though Ted's prediction was mostly accurate. Newspapers have been closing across the nation, especially their print editions, as readers and advertisers turn to phones and other devices for online news.

When Ted founded CNN in 1980, many conventional leaders, including Otis Chandler, did not think CNN would succeed. The other three networks—NBC, CBS, and ABC—did not initially see CNN as a threat, either.

It was called by some "CNN: The Chicken Noodle Network," yet in only a few short years, Microsoft would approach CNN with a $1 billion offer for 50 percent ownership.

At the time of CNN's establishment, network news was broadcast on television only in the mornings and evenings. Ted saw a demand for twenty-four-hour news and convinced the cable TV industry to distribute CNN. CNN brought new shows like *Moneyline* with Lou Dobbs; it had segments on fashion and sports; and breaking news would always be covered by the twenty-four-hour model.

Next came satellite distribution, which HBO was the first to use in 1975. CNN was in the wave that followed, distributing via satellite by June 1, 1980.

I loved CNN from its earliest years in the 1980s. I'd often watched CNN in my *Los Angeles Times* office or at our home in San Marino, and especially during my travels. I would only stay in hotels that had CNN and HBO on their hotel TV systems. I was then, and am now, a CNN news junkie. It brought me news, especially breaking news, when nobody else did.

The most vivid impression of what CNN could do came during its coverage of the Tiananmen Square massacre on June 4, 1989. Sitting in my *Los Angeles Times* office, I was stunned by the coverage.

Protests had been taking place for months in Beijing, and the military eventually began to advance on the protesters. Leading up to June 4, Chinese media had told people to stay away from protest gatherings, and news networks, including CNN, were ordered by the military to leave the square. Two days earlier, the Chinese Communist Party had even shut down a remote CNN workspace in Beijing.

Instead of following the orders of the Chinese Communist Party, CNN kept its crews in place and continued broadcasting some of the most iconic scenes of that movement, including Tank Man, who stood alone in front of the Chinese tank, and has never been heard from since.

On June 4, CNN was only able to get audio and still images out, but it went on to smuggle video from Beijing to Hong Kong that was then transmitted. Eason Jordan was the one who oversaw this incredible coordination of coverage.

It was through Jerry Lindauer—my closest Austin, Texas, friend—that the CNN job offer from Ted originated.

Jerry was then chairman of the National Cable Television Association and an executive of Prime Cable, based in Austin. Jerry and his then wife, Posy, had become close friends of Ted's through cable industry meetings and travels together to Moscow and Havana.

The president of CNN, Burt Reinhardt, was approaching age seventy, and Ted thought he should identify a successor to Burt. He had narrowed his search to four insiders: Ed Turner (no relation), CNN's head of news; Lou Dobbs, head of CNN business news; Jon Petrovich, head of Headline News; and Paul Amos, a brilliant vice president and executive producer.

Ted told all four finalists he *never* would pick a newspaperman for the job, especially since he thought NBC had made a major mistake by naming Pulitzer Prize–winning newspaper editor Michael Gartner as NBC News president. Gartner's reputation had been damaged by an NBC News crew placing igniters beneath a test automobile to "prove that it would explode on impact." It did. So did Michael's career.

Aware of Ted's search, Jerry Lindauer told Ted that I "was interested in the CNN job if Ted had an interest in me." This was something that Jerry and I had discussed.

Not long after, Ted called me and asked, "Would you really take the position as president of CNN?" Ted knew that his maverick status made hiring a traditional leader like myself somewhat unlikely.

I was skeptical, but also intrigued by Ted's vision for the future of media. I told him, "Ted, you need to know me much better than you do, and I need to know you better than I do."

Ted arranged for the two of us to meet in his Century City offices in Los Angeles. Expecting an hour-long meeting, I was surprised it lasted less than twenty minutes and was interrupted at least once by a phone call from his then girlfriend, Jane Fonda.

In the meeting I asked Ted, “What is it that you expect of your next president of CNN?”

His answer: “I want to make CNN the absolute best news network on the planet!”

“What else?” I asked.

“That’s it, pal.”

I would come to learn that Ted really meant what he said, but I told him I still needed more time. Some of my friends, including Otis Chandler, thought Ted was a nut.

Our meeting in Los Angeles was on a Thursday. The next day Ted’s vice president of human resources, Bill Shaw, called me.

“Did Ted offer you the job?” he asked.

I responded: “Yes, I think so, but I told him I need more time to think about it.”

Shaw proceeded to tell me about a baseball player whom Ted had offered a million-dollar contract to play for the Atlanta Braves, provided the player would give him an immediate answer. When the player failed to respond within a day or two, Ted withdrew the offer.

Shaw’s message was clear and blunt, as I’d come to learn was his typical style.

Even after the warning, I told Shaw to convey to Ted that I simply needed more time. I fully expected that Ted might withdraw the offer, but he did not.

I appreciated Shaw reaching out, and he would end up becoming a friend.

My due-diligence inquiries included talks with Atlanta’s Roberto Goizueta, chairman of Coca-Cola; J. B. Fuqua, chairman of Fuqua Industries; my college roommate, Don Rountree of Towers Perrin; and former president Jimmy Carter.

It was along River Road at the Bohemian Grove that President Carter and I spoke about Ted. President Carter strongly recommended that I accept Ted’s offer.

I also sought advice from my longtime friends Bill Moyers, then at PBS, and Walter Cronkite of CBS.

Finally, I called Jane Fonda. "Tell me about Ted," I said.

She responded: "He is the most remarkable man that I've ever known."

Over the course of my considering whether to join Ted at CNN that summer, I flew from New York to have dinner with Ted, Jane, and my wife Edwina in Los Angeles. I knew that more face time was the only way I might understand Ted better. I also wanted Edwina to know him and for Ted to know Edwina.

Unfortunately for our meeting, during the flight from New York to Los Angeles, I began to feel ill.

Later, with Edwina driving her white Jaguar, we picked Jane and Ted up at Jane's house in Santa Monica. The first significant error I made was suggesting that Ted get in the front seat with Edwina, and I sit in the back seat with Jane. They were too much in the throes of teenage-style love for that arrangement to have worked. I never did that again.

As Edwina drove up Highway 1 and then into the hills going north, I became progressively nauseated.

Despite not feeling well, I asked Ted more about the CNN position. He made it clear that I would have full control over news content, news personnel, and the hiring and firing of news staff.

Ted said he had only one rule when it came to news: "Be fair."

The way he saw it, reporters were supposed to report, not editorialize. Anchors were supposed to anchor, not provide personal opinions. I agreed completely.

By the time we got to the restaurant, I was going repeatedly to the restroom to throw up. Fortunately, Ted and Jane were so preoccupied with one another that only Edwina knew how sick I really was.

Describing Ted and Jane this way might sound like they were being rude, but it was actually wonderful. Later, Edwina even said to me, "Why isn't our romance more like that?"

Leaving the restaurant, I knew to let Jane and Ted share the backseat, putting me up front with Edwina while she drove.

Incidentally, at that fateful dinner Edwina and I had with Ted and Jane Fonda at a restaurant in the Santa Monica hills, I said to Ted: "Ted, before you hire me you need to know that I battle depression." His answer, which he has since told me he does not remember with the same crystal-clear memory that I do, was: "Hell, pal, let me tell you about me."

Within the first few miles of our drive home, I quickly asked Edwina to pull over to the side of the Pacific Coast Highway and let me out.

Sick on the side of the road, I yelled back at Edwina to keep going, and to come back and get me once she had dropped Ted and Jane off at Jane's Santa Monica home. To that, Ted shouted, "We're not going to leave you out here, pal!"

I yelled back at him, "Ted, haven't you ever been so sick you really didn't want to see anybody?"

He said, "I sure have, pal."

As Edwina was driving them away, Ted shouted out the window, "If you still want the job, you've got it!"

Edwina took them home and returned as soon as she could to find me. She assumed I'd be across the street at a service station by then, but I was still lying on the slab of concrete where she left me. When I saw her white Jaguar pull up, I could barely raise my hand to flag her.

We drove off to stay in a terrible hotel with green shag carpet covered in cigarette burns. Edwina still laughs about how she was afraid the woman at the hotel check-in counter would think she was a hooker trying to get a room for her pickup.

Despite my illness, that evening with Ted and Jane was the beginning of a personal and professional relationship that has now spanned more than three decades.

To this day, I so admire what a difference Ted has made in the world, especially with CNN. While I had worked earlier for one major U.S. domestic media company, Times Mirror, the impact that CNN was having on the entire world was unlike anything I had ever known. It was truly global.

Most of my friends, especially Bill Moyers and Walter Cronkite, urged me to accept Ted's offer. "The future of information is television, and the future of television news is CNN," Moyers said.

Edwina and I were vacationing with Lady Bird Johnson on Martha's Vineyard, as we often did in August. The decision about accepting Ted's offer dominated every waking hour and several sleepless nights.

Lady Bird wanted us to return to Austin to manage their LBJ family businesses. Yet she understood that I had left that career path definitively in 1973 after deciding to join Times Mirror in Dallas and later in Los Angeles.

Finally, I took a quiet walk with my close friend Art Buchwald, who also suffered from severe depression. Art was under a long-term contract with the Los Angeles Times Syndicate and lived a few houses away from the house that Lady Bird Johnson rented on Martha's Vineyard.

After hearing my thoughts about CNN, Art said: "DO IT!"

Even though I had been lucky to have so many great job opportunities offered to me, ranging from the *New York Times* through the *Washington Post*, Gannett, Time Warner, and others, Art was right.

I was forty-nine years old and had done the best I could at one of the greatest print-media companies in the world. This was simply one of those moments that I knew could turn into a tremendous adventure. I was deeply inspired by Ted's vision for the future of news, and going to CNN would also mean that Edwina and I would finally return to our home state of Georgia for the first time since we graduated from UGA in 1963.

At the Martha's Vineyard rental house where Lady Bird and her guests were concluding breakfast, my first call was to Jerry Levin at Time Warner to tell him I had decided to accept Ted's offer. I did so because Jerry had been incredibly kind in offering me a position in New York, and also because Time Warner owned a very big chunk of Turner Broadcasting.

Jerry said he had learned just how much Ted wanted me at CNN, and that my decision was the right one.

With Edwina sitting beside me on an upstairs bed in the Martha's Vineyard house, we called Ted with our decision. I heard him shout: "Jane, Tom accepted!"

Tom and Art Buchwald on Martha's Vineyard.

My start at CNN would begin an eleven-year relationship with the network and its leader, during which time I reported directly to Ted.

However, my hiring was not without opposition.

Nearly everyone at CNN was surprised by the announcement of my new role. Two executives were particularly upset: Lou Dobbs and Paul Amos, both of whom had been on Ted's shortlist for CEO.

One of the other finalists, Ed Turner, the longtime senior news executive, came to my office shortly after my arrival. "Tom, I should have been chosen as president of CNN, not you, but Ted made the decision that you're the guy. I just want to tell you today that I will support you completely." Ed stood by that promise.

Unfortunately, Dobbs and Amos never really accepted me. Amos left. Dobbs stayed but always felt that he would have been a better choice.

Even though I was still dealing with my depression, I was in a far better place than I had been during my last days at the *Los Angeles Times*. I believed in treating others the way I wanted to be treated, and I always have tried to do so.

Tom and CNN's EVP of Newsgathering, Ed Turner, in a helicopter over Haiti. Courtesy of CNN.

Ted showing his wonderfully humorous side. Courtesy of CNN.

Tom, Ted, and Jane Fonda at an Atlanta Braves home game. Courtesy of CNN.

As soon as my tenure at CNN was under way, I made it my mission to respect and learn from everyone. Not only did I know it would be the best way to earn the staff's trust, I genuinely needed to educate myself on the new technology.

It had been many years since I served as a television executive in 1971–73 at KTBC in Austin, Texas. Unlike the experienced staff at CNN, I didn't know the modern satellite technology and how it worked. Luckily, everybody reached out to be helpful.

Anne Williams, a technically skilled CNN executive, presented me with a basic 101-type book on television production. Satellite director Dick Tauber schooled me on satellites and the latest communications systems. It was a terrific example of CNN people working with me as a team.

Even though I needed help with the technical aspects of cable news, others understood that I had solid news judgment and was successful at booking high-profile guests. I had what they called "the golden Rolodex."

All my prior years of relationship building also taught me who really ran the show. One of those was Gail Evans, who had also worked as a policy assistant during the LBJ administration, and who been at CNN since its inception in 1980. Gail was one of the highest-ranked female executives at CNN and would turn out to be a most trusted advisor. What a force she was!

Most important, the staff also saw that I would work my butt off alongside them. I was then, and always had been, a workaholic, driven to excel. This was one of many major reasons that Ted and I got along so well.

Ted expected every meeting to start on time. Being late was a sure way to piss him off.

He expected you always to be prepared about your own area of responsibility. Mine was news.

You knew that you were in trouble with Ted if he said, "You don't know what the hell you're talking about, do you, pal?" He wanted concise answers delivered crisply. Any effort to con Ted with BS did not work. Those who tried did not last long.

Ted also could be funny. I'll never forget his crawling up on a large circular conference table in the Turner boardroom so he could retrieve a quarter. He held it up and said, "That's the way you become a billionaire."

There was one occasion when Ted needed me for a deciding vote at an important Turner board meeting. Edwina and I were on a river raft vacation down the majestic Colorado River. Ted urgently ordered that a helicopter be sent to airlift me out so that I could cast the deciding vote. Unfortunately, helicopters were only permitted for rescue emergencies, not for any urgent business matters. That didn't satisfy Ted. He asked that a small skywriter aircraft fly over the Grand Canyon with a message saying, "Tom call Ted." In the end, my vote was not needed at the Turner board meeting, and no skywriter aircraft was deployed.

On another occasion, before my joining CNN, Ted was astounded by the soaring ratings of CNN when it covered the story of "Baby Jessica in the Well" in 1987. A young girl had fallen into an uncovered well in Midland, Texas, and CNN showed the rescue live for all of the hours that it took to retrieve her.

At the next CNN Executive Committee meeting, Ted congratulated the group on the spectacular CNN ratings from the Baby Jessica story. He laughingly suggested that CNN should place candy bars around open wells across the country so that more children would fall in, and CNN could have more highly rated televised rescues. Many in the room thought that was about as terrible a joke as anybody could deliver. But it was just pure Ted.

As outrageous as he was, Ted was, and remains, an absolute genius. I do not expect there ever will be another quite like him. I love the guy.

Each morning, no matter where in the world he might be, Ted would call his executive assistant, initially Dee Woods, later Debbie Masterson. He would then speak separately with three of us—president Terry McGuirk, Entertainment Division head Scott Sassa, and me—and at times with other of his direct reports, such as Chief Financial Officers Paul Beckham and Wayne Pace. We were expected to be available for that phone call, or else!

This was just one of a number of policies that made CNN unique, all of which were "Ted's rules."

At CNN you weren't allowed to smoke at work, and if you needed help quitting smoking, the company would provide you with support.

There was no Styrofoam anywhere in the office because of Ted's strong environmental views.

The word "foreign" was banned because Ted said it translated as "alien" in some languages. As a global company, everything was titled "international." Even when the Council on Foreign Relations wanted to come to Atlanta, Ted was willing to join and donate only if they changed "foreign" to "international."

There was no BS-ing. Ted liked straight shooters who knew what they were doing.

Once, an extremely high-powered marketing firm came down to Atlanta to pitch an advertising campaign to Ted. We all felt that it was a big deal to have them there. Unfortunately, they also felt like we were lucky to have them. Regardless of how good Ted thought their ideas may have been, he disliked their attitudes. That was the end of it.

Lastly, if you ever told Ted anything, and I mean *anything*, you had better remember you said it. An opinion you gave him in 1980 could come back to bite you in 1990 if it had changed without reason. He had a steel-trap memory.

His rules were a part of his visionary thinking. He was one of the rare breed of leaders who took calculated risks when traditionally smart people were not as bold.

Once, Ted ordered me to either purchase or lease several blimps. I said, "Ted, why in the world do we need to buy or lease blimps?"

He said that blimps had a lot of benefits over helicopters. They could stay in the air longer, they were much more stable platforms for aerial photography, and we could advertise CNN logos on both sides, much as Goodyear does with its blimps.

Ted said, "Think of it, pal—our blimps can fly over areas hit by hurricanes, earthquakes, floods, and even sporting events like the Augusta National Golf Tournament and the Super Bowl."

One of the CNN executives in the room reminded Ted that we could not fly over golf tournaments or football stadiums, since those events would require us securing expensive television rights, and we would be in competition with the major networks that had exclusivity to sports coverage.

This was a classic example of Ted's "out of the box" creative thinking, always searching for the next way to take CNN to the moon. There were many more. He was a visionary.

The main reason we did not pursue leasing blimps was the outbreak of Desert Storm, the United States' 1991 war in Iraq, and the resources it required of CNN to cover it.

Incidentally, this was before the introduction of drones, which are now being used effectively by CNN for the same purpose. CNN now has ninety FAA-registered drones and many drone pilots used across the globe for worldwide operations.

As I settled into my role, just as I had done at other media companies, I found young people to promote and to mentor, including Eason Jordan, whom I later recommended as my successor as CEO of CNN. *Time* magazine editor Walter Isaacson was chosen instead. Walter has written several blockbuster books, including biographies of Elon Musk, Steve Jobs, Leonardo da Vinci, Henry Kissinger, and Benjamin Franklin. Eason is now senior vice president of the Connected Leaders program at the Rockefeller Foundation. In this position "he focuses on growing, engaging, and energizing the Foundation's network of convenings and fellows to advance partnerships and alliances that amplify action in support of its mission to promote the well-being of humanity."

During my years at CNN, the network did amazing things, but it was also there that I made my biggest mistakes as a news executive.

One of them was naming Cardinal Bernardin of Chicago in a 1993 story that portrayed him as a pedophile. After we televised the allegation, the young man who made the initial charges of sexual abuse against the cardinal completely renounced his allegations.

Another huge mistake was incorrectly naming Richard Jewell as "the suspect" in the 1996 Atlanta Olympic Park bombing. A senior

Tom meeting with the Chinese leader Jiang Zemin in Beijing. Courtesy of CNN.

FBI executive had assured me, "Tom, he is the guy." CNN should have described him only as a "person of interest."

Third was falsely reporting that U.S. Special Forces had used sarin gas in Operation Tailwind in 1970 in an attempt to rescue captured American POWs, when in fact an internal investigation concluded that there was insufficient evidence that sarin or any other poison gas was ever used.

As a result, CNN set up an excellent Standards and Practices department headed by Rick Davis, a veteran CNN executive, whose staff had responsibility for vetting controversial stories and ensuring that our reporting was absolutely accurate before it went to air.

An example of the controversy that at times shadowed our decisions concerned Panamanian president Manuel Noriega. Arrested for major illegal drug activity, Noriega had once been a primary source of U.S. intelligence in Panama. There was no disputing Noriega's record of corruption, but after his arrest and transfer to a federal prison in Miami, Noriega's jailhouse conversations with his attorneys were taped, transcribed, and made available to the federal prosecutors.

I believed then, as I do now, that no matter who prisoners are or what they've been arrested for, they should have the privilege of private conversations with their attorneys.

Noriega was not given such treatment.

Tapes of his conversations with attorneys from the Miami prison were acquired confidentially by CNN. It was those tapes that the prosecutors were using, supplied to them by the FBI.

U.S. federal judge William Hoeveler instructed us not to broadcast any parts of the tapes—an order that we defied on the advice of several attorneys who stated that we did have the right to broadcast the tapes. Seven lawyers said it would be "prior restraint" by the government to order us not to broadcast. I learned then that lawyers are not always right.

In a statement at the time, I said, "CNN considers the district court orders against telecast of the actual content of General Noriega's recorded conversations are unconstitutional prior restraints. Legal counsel has advised CNN that it has the right to air the content while we pursue an appeal." We did.

Judge Hoeveler said in no uncertain terms that we were wrong to air them, holding us in contempt and even threatening to take away the law licenses from the CNN attorneys who advised me we could broadcast the tapes.

In federal court in Miami, Judge Hoeveler told me that CNN had two options: pay a significant fine, or apologize to the court every thirty minutes for an entire twenty-four-hour period on air.

Asking for a brief recess, I stepped outside to an adjoining private office and called Ted. I explained that the fine would likely be $10 million—a number that never has been officially confirmed.

I recommended to Ted that we apologize to the court. Ted agreed, and we did.

Along my journey at CNN, I began to understand several major differences between newspaper journalism and television news, and sometimes that meant learning new ways to correct mistakes.

One of the most important differences is what you could chalk off as the newspaper's advantage of having many "column inches."

Newspapers generally have extensive space in which to publish complex, major stories. Television news does not often have that benefit. Fortunately, I supervised three twenty-four-hour channels, CNN USA, Headline News, and CNN International. We could run longer pieces and more extensive live coverage on CNN USA while broadcasting shorter reports of news, weather, sports, and even a local news insert, twenty-four hours a day on Headline News.

However, there were still times when the audience expected more. Much more.

An example of that occurred in 1999 during the O. J. Simpson trial.

Across the country, people were absolutely fixated on the murder trial. It was about the rule of law, but it was also about issues of race and how the justice system applied differently to people of color. It was made even more dramatic by O. J. Simpson's own celebrity, the trial lawyers and witnesses, and the graphic nature of the murders themselves.

During the height of the Simpson trial, anytime that CNN would cut away to announce other breaking news, our phones would begin ringing off the hook and our email systems would be overloaded. It made for near meltdowns with the Public Affairs department.

I had seen these types of public reactions before, but never on this scale.

Even though the nation was totally enthralled with the O.J. trial, it wasn't as if the rest of the world was suddenly placed on hold. During that time, other news was breaking around the world every minute, including historically significant events, such as Bill Clinton's impeachment and the tragic death of Princess Diana.

I learned this to be a hardship of TV that just doesn't exist the same way in print: you can only give viewers one story on their television screens at a time (or two with a split screen).

Even though the O. J. Simpson trial *was* news, it had become equal parts entertainment—a reality that did not fit my vision, or Ted's, for CNN.

That was when sound journalistic judgment was paramount.

I learned to never let ratings or popular appeal alone force what you cover. Doing that can lead to becoming like a tabloid newspaper. Our job was to be as responsible as we could be without exploiting tragedies. Unfortunately, in the heat of the moment, too many bad decisions still are made, and news has become much more focused on entertainment than in my days at CNN.

When I first began working there, CNN had no major competitors. The only other news outlet that was broadcasting at a similar pace was the BBC, but they were primarily radio then. Even still, I recruited some of the BBC's top news executives to come to CNN.

I also tried to hire Bill Moyers and Walter Cronkite.

Cronkite did a few shows with CNN after his retirement at CBS. He anchored at least two space shots for us, including John Glenn's return to the heavens. But little else.

Moyers loved the independence he had at PBS. Commercial television did not offer him the autonomy and freedom his spectacular long-form shows received at PBS. I couldn't blame him.

It wasn't until years later, in 1996, that Fox News began broadcasting. It appealed to the conservative market, finding ways to become the channel of Republicans and of many in the military. Roger Ailes was brilliant in the way he captured anti-mainstream media viewers.

Even though Fox's slogan was "Fair and Balanced," it certainly was not. Their talk shows and political commentaries definitely were conservative.

At one point Roger named CNN the Clinton News Network, and far too many viewers and analysts tagged us as liberal.

This was Fox's way of trying to fabricate balance—by making us seem as liberal as they were conservative. I didn't agree, and neither did Ted.

As Ted had demanded, we always worked to be truly fair and accurate.

Despite not wanting to be viewed as left or right, we couldn't control the way the media landscape had changed, or the way many in the public viewed us. As Fox continued to build its rapport with the right, its mere presence ultimately made us look more and more left-leaning.

This change in how the public was consuming news was not lost on Ted. To increase our reach, Ted considered creating another channel for conservative viewers that could still be far more balanced than Fox, but ultimately he decided against it. However, I did call Rush Limbaugh to discuss with him the possible creation of a conservative channel or show for Ted. Only a very few CNN staffers knew of that initiative. One of them, Gail Evans, almost threw up over the thought of bringing Rush to CNN.

While we had to compete for viewership, CNN was able to flourish in a way that our competition often didn't. That success tended to be directly tied to Ted's brilliance and leadership.

Five years after the fall of the Berlin wall, I was in Saint Petersburg, Russia, for the 1994 Goodwill Games—an event that Ted created in 1980 after the United States and other nations chose not to attend the 1980 Olympics in Moscow. I was sitting in a meeting with Pat Mitchell, the brilliant head of Turner Productions, when Ted burst into the room, slammed his coffee cup on the table, and simply said, "Cold War."

That was the inception of what would be Pat's definitive documentary on that historic period, no matter the cost. Ted was a major history buff who did not feel that the Cold War had been properly documented from all sides—the Americans, the Europeans, the Russians, the Cubans, and so many more. He wanted a forty-hour series, one hour for each of the forty years. There ended up being more than six hundred interviews with leaders, which together with archival footage made for twenty-four vivid episodes. These projects were Ted's way of making sure that critical moments in history didn't wane into a few lines in the textbooks of our children. The *Cold War* series he funded is undoubtedly the best documentary on the subject ever made.

During major events happening around the world, Ted was always there with another new idea.

He was also brilliant when it came to expansion.

A perfect example was his idea for the CNN Airport channel. CNN had already reached the homes of millions of people worldwide, but Ted saw a niche to expand even further. In an era before tablets and smart phones, Ted thought CNN should be there to supply news both in the airports and on aircraft. It was a terrific innovation.

We worked with airports, mayors, and authorities of all types to get CNN Airport into as many airports as possible. We even installed the wiring and TV installations in the airports.

Once, I took Henry "Hammerin' Hank" Aaron, who was a VP at Turner Broadcasting at the time, to visit the New York City Port Authority with me. We felt Henry's presence would help us as we pursued a contract to place the Airport Channel in all three New York Port Authority airports. NBC had seen how successful the CNN Airport channel had become and wanted a piece of the action. They simply figured their city's three major airports—LaGuardia, JFK, and Newark—would be theirs to own. To NBC's dismay, Henry Aaron and Airport Channel president Debbie Cooper charmed everyone in that room. We walked out with another deal for CNN Airport, and everyone else got to take home a signed "Hank Aaron" baseball. (We did not break any ethical rules.)

Henry wasn't from New York, but he had an amazing track record as a baseball legend and civil rights advocate, who had lived under intense racial scrutiny and threats for many years while with the Atlanta Braves. Ted Turner had the highest level of respect for him, and Henry helped us do such wonderful things at CNN that Ted placed him on the Turner Broadcasting board.

The only real policy difference between CNN Airport and other CNN channels was our decision not to broadcast live aircraft crashes, fearing that it could lead to panic aboard aircraft or in airports. It was a terribly difficult exception to approve, but considering it was for people's safety, we agreed.

Across the world, we could use all of CNN's extensive resources for global news to break stories, entertain travelers, and even insert news clips from their local cities and countries. It was marvelously dynamic for its time.

Even though CNN Airport slowly lost its dominance during the era of smart devices, it had a tremendous run, airing from 1991 to 2021.

As the years went on, the structure of the company changed. In 1996 Turner Broadcasting was bought by Time Warner, and Jerry Levin was placed at the helm of all operations. Two years after that, America Online (AOL) bought Time Warner.

At the time of my arrival at CNN, Ted owned 200 million shares of AOL Time Warner stock, was vice chairman of the parent company, and had been exceptionally loyal to Jerry Levin. But over the course of three years, Ted's relationship with his new "bosses," paired with other reasons, simply created too much tension. In 2001 Jerry Levin removed Ted from all responsibilities at Turner Broadcasting.

For the *Guardian*, reporter Edward Helmore wrote of the ousting: "Ted Turner, the most voluble and compelling media titan of his time, now cuts a ghostly figure. In the last month, the billionaire founder of CNN, erstwhile husband of Jane Fonda, the largest private landowner in the U.S., environmental campaigner, United Nations benefactor, yachtsman, and irrepressible loud mouth, has been cut adrift from the U.S. media empire he created by rivals with no tolerance for an outspoken individualist."

Much later, I asked Jerry to tell me why he removed Ted. Jerry would only say: "Tom, I never will disclose who advised me to do that." He never did.

To this day, Ted maintains that he still does not know who fired him.

Speculation has long been that Ted could embarrass Jerry and other Time Warner board members. In their defense, Ted did have a knack for that.

Others said Ted went on a rampage about the expenses of helicopters, executive jets, and retreats at Acapulco and Aspen that AOL Time Warner owned. Ted considered those things wasteful—something that he never tolerated at Turner Broadcasting.

Ted also considered the executive pay packages of the Warner Brothers cochairs equally wasteful.

On an AOL Time Warner board trip to China, one of the most prominent board members pulled me aside and said: "Tom, you and Terry [McGuirk] must get Ted under control." He didn't provide any specifics, but I inferred that it concerned Ted's exceptional dismay about all the excessive spending under the new Time Warner leadership.

Years later at the Bohemian Grove, I asked former AOL chairman Steve Case again why Ted was ousted. He told me: "Tom, Ted simply wasn't there. He wasn't running the company. That's the reason why."

In fairness to those concerned, Ted—as brilliant as he was—was a maverick, and being controlled by others simply did not suit him. He was accustomed to being captain of his own ship.

At one time Ted had been diagnosed as manic-depressive. This diagnosis was later retracted.

Regardless of how his mental health condition should be described, it helped make him the brilliant businessman that he was. Ted's high periods were so creative and so full of excitement.

He even had a tape produced that he ordered to be played in the event of the apocalypse. Every Turner network president was supposed to be aware of the tape. It includes a recording of the navy hymn "Nearer My God to Thee."

That's only one of the many stories about Ted Turner's eccentric behavior that are absolutely true.

As important as Ted was to the media world, he was also an inspiration to many outside the field of journalism. He cared deeply about our planet—the air we breathe, the water we drink, and the safety of the world in which we live. Think of this: at times Ted, one of the few billionaires of his day, could be seen walking down the street with his arms full of trash, picking litter up off the street.

This commitment to ideals larger than himself and CNN eventually manifested in Ted giving the United Nations one billion dollars in 1997. It's still a huge sum of money, then amounting to one-third of Ted's wealth.

Not once in eleven years did Ted and I ever have a major dispute. Ted supported journalistic excellence as strongly as Otis Chandler did at the *Los Angeles Times*.

Ted simply cared about things in a way that was utterly genuine. He didn't need a camera focused on him to try to impress anyone.

Had Ted not sold Turner Broadcasting to Time Warner, I am convinced that TBS would have become one of the three or four most successful, most creative, and most respected media companies in the world. I also believe CNN would have eclipsed most, if not all, of the other network news channels we have today.

With certainty, we would have far higher standards of quality and of ethics than those exhibited by Fox News.

In one of the greatest and saddest ironies of my life, both Ted Turner and Otis Chandler were diagnosed with the same illness—Lewy body dementia. After a hard-fought battle, Otis died of it in 2006. At the time of this writing, Ted continues to struggle with the condition.

Like Otis before him, Ted is a giant of journalism, a hero of my life, and one of the most remarkable men I've ever known. I love them both.

CHAPTER 16

CNN GOES TO WAR

The boys of Baghdad, and indomitable Ted: "You will not overturn me, pal!"

Not long after I began working at CNN in 1990, I learned Ted had really meant what he said when he told me, "I want to make CNN the absolute best news network on the planet!"

It wasn't just that his vision was extraordinary. He was willing to spend the money necessary to enable CNN to become the world's first genuinely global news channel. At first, CNN was distributed by satellites and cable only in English. By the time I retired, it was distributed in Spanish and several other languages around the world.

Once I began my work with CNN, I was blown away by the staff. It was a dynamic, competitive group of both young people and experienced journalists.

I was further impressed by the tremendous number of women in important roles at the company. Women were editors, reporters, vice presidents, and even executive vice president (Gail Evans). In the field, women were working as combat photojournalists and reporting from dangerous war zones.

The whole staff shared Ted's vision of being the best news network anywhere. I call it the Ted Turner spirit. He simply believes in winning.

Ted had built Turner Broadcasting; he had won the America's Cup, one of the biggest sailing races in the world; he had won the heart of Jane Fonda; and he would go on to take the Atlanta Braves from being one of the worst teams in baseball to the number-one team. Ted was a winner, and he made other people want to win with him.

Left to right: International Desk editor Simon Vicary, Tom, and line producer Charles Caudill in the CNN master control room during the 1991 Gulf War. Courtesy of CNN.

August 1, 1990—my first day at CNN—was one of the quietest days I had ever experienced in journalism. It was so dull, in fact, that Headline News ran a segment about horses jumping off high-dive platforms into the water.

On the second day, however, everything changed.

It was August 2, 1990, and Iraqi leader Saddam Hussein invaded Kuwait. Days later, U.S. president George H. W. Bush proclaimed: "This will not stand, this aggression against Kuwait."

President Bush's words clearly meant that Saddam must decide to withdraw voluntarily from Kuwait, or the United States and its allies would drive him out militarily. Too much oil and too many U.S. allies in the region, such as Saudi Arabia, were at stake.

It was clear to me that CNN must be prepared for military conflict in the region.

U.S. secretary of state James Baker III would begin diplomatic negotiations with Iraqi deputy prime minister Tariq Aziz on January 9, 1991, in Geneva. Within a few days, Secretary Baker made an announcement with two components: First, that Iraq had no intention of withdrawing from Kuwait voluntarily, and second, that the United States stood by its conviction that Iraq would not be permitted to remain in that oil-rich nation.

The White House and its allies were further alarmed that Saddam Hussein might push beyond Kuwait with an invasion of Saudi Arabia and other nations in the region. A third great concern was that Israel might unleash its powerful military in the event that it was attacked by Iraq.

During the war, the Iraqi military did fire multiple Scud missiles into Israel. It took strong diplomacy by the Bush administration to prevent Israel from counterattacking.

CNN executive vice president of news Ed Turner and I met with Ted in his fourteenth-floor office at CNN Center. It was a short meeting, but historic.

I explained to Ted that we needed to lease strategic communications equipment in the region, which meant placing portable ground stations (uplinks) and staff in as many locations as possible, and as quickly as possible. We also needed to book communication circuits ahead of all the other networks.

I told him: "Ted, if we are to own the story of a possible war between the U.S. and Iraq, we will need to spend a great deal of money over our budget."

"How much more?" Ted asked.

Ed and I told him that war expenses could range between five million and thirty million dollars more than we had budgeted for 1991.

Ted's answer—and I quote him exactly—"You spend whatever you think it takes, pal."

That was when I knew without question that Ted really meant it when he said he wanted CNN to become the best news network in the world.

Later that afternoon, the CNN senior network leaders gathered in my windowless sixth-floor office. I relayed the same message to them that Ted had told Ed Turner and me: We will spend whatever it takes, and do whatever it takes, to give CNN the competitive edge over all the other networks.

Every one of us had an unrelenting sense of urgency. We were working to secure all the infrastructure necessary, not just to receive information about the war, but to broadcast live coverage on all three CNN networks—CNN USA, Headline News, and CNN International—and to serve all our affiliates (such as TV Asahi in Japan) around the world.

It's important to remember that in 1991 the infrastructure was far more primitive than it is today. Information often needed to uplink from Amman to London, then to New York, and finally down to Atlanta.

Giving us the technological edge, CNN vice president and international editor Eason Jordan and satellite desk leader Dick Tauber arranged for uplinks to be positioned in as many locations in the Middle East as possible. Tauber also was authorized to lease multiple transponders and to book whatever satellite circuits and other transmission links CNN would need.

Joint Chiefs of Staff chairman General Colin Powell (later secretary of state)—a former White House Fellow and friend—helped us to convince Saudi leaders through the Saudi ambassador to the United States, Prince Bandar bin Sultan, to permit CNN to position an uplink at King Fahd Air Base—a joint Saudi-U.S. location in the Saudi desert.

As the contractual and political connections were secured, we began to assemble the necessary equipment and deploy many of our reporters and technically talented people to the region.

Positioning the uplinks was no small feat. Each one required expensive equipment, boxed and trucked into place: a task far easier said than done in a war zone.

We eventually began painting "CNN" in giant letters on the rooftops of our trucks that transported equipment between Amman and

At CNN Center, examining a satellite coverage map, Tom with Joint Chiefs of Staff chairman General Colin Powell. Courtesy of CNN.

Baghdad. We advised the U.S. Air Force of what we'd done, but I was constantly worried that some hotshot U.S. pilot would fire missiles before they could see "CNN" written on the truck's roof. Thankfully, that never happened. We were so lucky in so many ways.

Being new to television after thirteen years at the *Los Angeles Times*, I relied on the highly experienced, superb team of CNN executives who were already in place: Burt Reinhardt, my predecessor as president; Ed Turner, head of news gathering; Jon Petrovich, head of Headline News and eventually all new online CNN.com ventures; VP Paul Amos; VP and senior executive producer Bob Furnad; business editor and anchor Lou Dobbs; domestic editor Earl Casey; vice president and head of research and bookings Gail Evans; International Desk editor Parisa Khosravi; and, in particular, international editor Eason Jordan.

Despite the fact that two of my most senior direct reports, Lou Dobbs and Paul Amos, were exceptionally disappointed that they had not been chosen by Ted as president of CNN, the entire executive team was united in a fierce resolve to win the Gulf news war.

From the top down, CNN had a terrific, proactive staff that took initiative. Decision making was swift and decisive.

For instance, when executive producer Bob Furnad needed to take live breaking news to air, he simply did it, knowing he didn't have to check with me to interrupt coverage or to drop commercials. That type of confidence throughout the organization kept our coverage moving.

Perhaps the most important personnel decision regarding CNN's coverage in Iraq was the choice of Robert Wiener to be the senior executive producer and fixer extraordinaire in charge of our Baghdad operations.

Earlier, Ed Turner told me, Ted had ordered him to fire Wiener over what Ted felt was conduct unbecoming a bureau chief when Wiener was based in Israel. However, believing that Wiener was indispensable to the network, Ed had repeatedly "delayed" firing him. That decision certainly turned out to be the right one. Without Robert Wiener, CNN never would have accomplished what it did in Iraq.

Wiener was like a three-ring circus master. He thought big, and he was highly experienced. With CNN's fullest support coming from Atlanta headquarters, Robert was able to manage the CNN Baghdad staff and the Iraqis in a way that no one else could.

Supporting our efforts were the countless connections with Iraqi officials who actually were government-controlled "journalists." That friendly relationship had been established through the annual CNN World Report conference that CNN held in Atlanta. The conference was an opportunity for newspeople from around the world to come together and take workshops, listen to prominent speakers, and network with each other over dinners and drinks. Those were relationships that helped tremendously when we would need international cooperation. In short, they were our friends.

The most important operational decision was CNN's establishment of an independent communication channel—a "four-wire"—that would enable CNN to transmit audio from Baghdad back to Atlanta if coalition bombs and cruise missiles destroyed the Iraqi telecommunications and power systems.

CNN engineer Nic Robertson, who later became a producer and a splendid combat correspondent, had been working on arranging technical capacity for CNN in Baghdad during the buildup to the war. It was Robertson who suggested the four-wire. He had used four-wires and two-wires for several years at IBA, TV-am, Sky Channel, and NBC. He booked them to coordinate feeds from faraway places in the days before cell phones, and when landlines were unreliable.

With a four-wire, both parties could talk and listen at the same time, whereas with a two-wire only one party could talk at a time. Working together, Nic Robertson, Robert Wiener, and Dick Tauber established a dedicated phone circuit. It went from our ninth-floor room in Baghdad's Al-Rashid Hotel to our tenth-floor room at the Philadelphia Hotel in Amman, Jordan, to Rathbone Place at CNN London, to CNN Center in Atlanta.

What a historic technological and journalistic triumph it turned out to be!

This four-wire bypassed the Iraqi public switch telephone network, so there were no operators or automated telephone switch gears in the path of our connection. As complicated as that may have seemed, it sure worked.

Eason Jordan said, "Arguably the biggest hurdle in getting the four-wire was convincing the often difficult, hostile Iraqi authorities to authorize and facilitate use of the four-wire—prompting a challenging and relentless series of appeals over weeks that involved several CNN-ers pleading with Iraqi officials in person, by phone, and telex. Many of us actually were surprised when Iraqi officials finally relented, providing CNN with permission and the technical means to proceed with the four-wire."

Eason deserves unquestioned credit for organizing the historic coverage that came out of Iraq, but Steve Cassidy and Larry Register were also absolutely crucial for our success. They moved field teams and equipment all over the region, adjusting to constant changes and dangers. Their efforts provided CNN with coverage from multiple locations.

For instance, Larry Register conducted live interviews in Jerusalem with Benjamin Netanyahu, who was deputy foreign minister at the time, as they both wore gas masks. Steve Cassidy led coverage both in the field and in Atlanta. When there was an emergency, I often asked Cassidy to take charge of resolving whatever hot issue we were confronting. His work in Amman, Jordan, was terrific, and a precursor to his crucial assistance in Sarajevo. He also coordinated assistance when photojournalist Margaret Moth was gravely injured in Sarajevo during another global crisis.

In Iraq, there were many lesser-known moments when producer Robert Wiener was instrumental in helping to keep our operations working 24/7. At the time, I had little idea just how wide the parameters of our "supply" list were, with the occasional "beverages" coming in from the airport duty-free, but I had no problem with that—the crew needed downtime and I was glad to reward them.

Without the four-wire, CNN would not have been able to transmit an exclusive audio signal from the first moment that allied bombs fell on Iraq. These capacities were doubled when we later switched to a big Inmarsat phone that Nic Robertson smuggled into Iraq.

Receiving Ted's approval to "Spend whatever you think it takes, pal!" and the successful installation of the four-wire were two of the most momentous decisions assuring our historic coverage.

As great as Ted's approval was to spend whatever it took, another decision by Ted was even more consequential.

Many days I called Ted, often finding him at his Montana ranch. The calls were informal but succinct. I would give him a summary of what was going on at CNN Center, and he would give me an overview of the way he saw our coverage on TV. There was never any BS with Ted.

During one historic conversation, I informed him that I had received warning calls from the highest levels of the U.S. government to get all of our personnel out of Baghdad. The calls had come from the White House presidential press secretary, Marlin Fitzwater, from Joint Chiefs chairman Colin Powell, and even from President George H. W. Bush himself.

In the first call, Fitzwater told me, "Tom, President Bush asked me to call you. Your CNN staff in Baghdad is in serious danger. You risk loss of control of your coverage and the lives of all of your staff." He continued, "I don't know exactly when we're going to do it, or how, but it will be soon."

Shortly after Fitzwater's call, General Powell called. He said, "Tom, you should get your staff out of Baghdad now. They are in very serious danger. Having them remain runs the risk of their being killed, and their presence compromises my mission."

Within an hour of General Powell's call, my assistant Ashley Van Buren—who remains my most important aide even as I write this book thirty years later—rushed into my office where I was meeting with senior CNN executives.

"The president is on the line," Ashley said.

One of the executives in my office made a smart-ass comment: "The president of what?"

Tom with assistants Joan Klunder (*left*), who came along from Los Angeles to Atlanta, and Ashley Van Buren, a mainstay for more than thirty years—including on this book! Courtesy of Gittings Photography.

"President Bush," Ashley replied.

President Bush said, "Tom, CNN has been very thorough in its coverage—fair, but tough, even though many of our coalition partners feel that Saddam is 'using' CNN for propaganda purposes. . . . I know you already have spoken to Marlin and to Colin. I simply want to emphasize their message. Tell Bernie [Shaw] and your team not to stay around [Baghdad] too long. CNN's staff is in serious danger."

He ended the conversation by saying, "If at any time you need to speak directly with me during this crisis, call me at this number . . . and ask for my personal assistant, Patty Presock."

I briefly described the warnings from Fitzwater, General Powell, and President Bush over the phone to Ted. I told him that I thought we had three choices:

One: Pull everyone out of Baghdad and reposition them in Amman, Jordan, until it was safe enough for us to return to Baghdad.

Two: Move the team from Al-Rashid Hotel in downtown Baghdad to an area outside of the immediate war zone where they would be safer.

Three: Leave them in place.

Before I could even finish giving Ted my recommendation, he shouted at me over the phone line: "Tom, our decision is those who want to stay can stay. Those who want to leave can leave."

Then, in an even louder voice, he said: "And you will not overturn me, pal!"

I was jolted by his intensity, considering I had no thought of overturning Ted's decision.

Next, Ted went on to say something I never will forget:

"I know that you lost two correspondents when you were publisher of the *Los Angeles Times*, and those deaths had a very profound effect on you. I am taking total responsibility for the lives of our staff in Baghdad. I am taking that off of your conscience and placing it on mine."

It was true that I had lost two members of my *Los Angeles Times* staff. Joe Alex Morris was killed while covering the overthrow of the Shah of Iran. Dial Torgerson was killed on the Honduran-Nicaraguan border, even though his car had large letters identifying him as press. Their losses troubled me deeply. I never liked sending staff who worked for me into exceptionally dangerous situations, but I often did.

Ted addressing that concern and taking responsibility for their possible deaths is an example of the leader he was.

Within minutes, Eason Jordan advised Robert Wiener, who was in Baghdad, of Ted's decision. A few members of our team in Baghdad were clear that they did not want to depart. In fact, most did not, especially Peter Arnett, who told me: "Tom, if you order me out, I will quit CNN and go to work for somebody who will permit me to stay here to cover this."

As it turned out, the staffers who did want to leave were unable to do so at that time, since Baghdad International Airport was already closed. By that point it was far too dangerous for them to set out by car on the highway between Baghdad and Amman.

It was a stressful situation, and there was deep concern about the safety of our team.

From Atlanta, I was not only speaking with the White House but also with the spouses of our Baghdad reporters, trying to keep everyone as calm and informed as possible.

Privately, however, I was doing my damnedest trying not to indicate to those around me how very worried I was that they might not live through the night.

At Al-Rashid Hotel where our staff was staying, there was a basement that appeared to be an underground bunker. There were times

Left to right: Eason Jordan, producer Simon Vicary, and Tom in the CNN newsroom during the 1991 Iraq War. Courtesy of CNN.

when we thought Saddam himself might take refuge there for his own protection.

At 6:35 p.m. Eastern, January 16, 1991, these were the words that CNN announced live at the beginning of the war: "This is Bernie Shaw. Something is happening outside. . . . Peter Arnett, join me here. Let's describe to our viewers what we're seeing. . . . The skies over Baghdad have been illuminated. . . . We're seeing bright flashes going off all over the sky."

Via the four-wire, NBC, ABC, and CBS were able to interview our anchors during the first night of the war. The voices of Bernie Shaw, John Holliman, and Peter Arnett were rippling across everyone's airwaves. Incidentally, Ted approved our competing networks using brief segments of our live reporting from Baghdad.

Unluckily, on day two of the war, I received a report from NBC that Al-Rashid was on the target list for coalition bombing that day. I immediately called Colin Powell to speak to him urgently about that report.

Powell angrily responded: "You should not know anything about our targeting," but added, "Do you think I would bomb the hotel where my good friend Bernie Shaw is staying?"

It was one of the toughest ass-chewings that I've ever experienced.

I later learned that Al-Rashid had been a targeting point for the U.S. cruise and Tomahawk missiles that were being fired. In other words, they were programmed to go over the hotel and then take a left or right to their next destination. One did malfunction, however, striking near the hotel and injuring a number of people.

As Nic Robertson had predicted, the entire Iraqi power and communications systems were immediately destroyed by U.S. stealth fighter jets and cruise missiles.

Every media company based in Baghdad except CNN lost all its transmission capabilities. Only CNN was able to broadcast live audio to millions of people worldwide. All channels turned to CNN, most with no permission from us to do so, for our live, exclusive coverage. They had no place else to turn.

Tom and Eason standing among construction crews repairing rocket damage in front of Baghdad's Al-Rashid Hotel. Courtesy of CNN.

The coverage that CNN provided during the conflict was exceptional.

Tom Brokaw praised our coverage as "daring," and added: "CNN used to be called the little network that could. It's no longer the little network."

President Bush reportedly criticized CNN for "giving a megaphone to the Iraqis to voice their propaganda," which included an interview with Saddam Hussein.

I disagreed with the president.

Having been in the White House Press Office as a young man, I generally trusted that information coming from the White House, the Pentagon, or the State Department was being delivered in good faith, but I knew it could also be skewed. After all, I had been a part of the administration that had the infamous "credibility gap."

I knew that CNN was being "used" by both governments to some degree. My perspective was that it remained better for Iraq and the United States to be exchanging statements on CNN than firing missiles at each other.

CHAPTER 17

A TRULY GLOBAL NETWORK

Two stories that showcase the international reach of CNN

My professional life has been full of interesting work with some of the world's most interesting people.

I was so fortunate to love all the jobs that I've had, ranging from the White House to newsrooms and to boardrooms of many splendid philanthropic organizations. My service on the Trilateral Commission, the Rockefeller Foundation board, the Mayo Foundation, the MD Anderson board, and the White House Fellows board all provided me with a genuine sense of public service.

Sometimes my work was public and exciting. Other times it was private and very stressful.

Perhaps the most satisfying role I ever had was as CEO of CNN. So much of that was because of the exceptional vision, wit, talent, and passion that Ted Turner possessed. Ted was committed to bringing independent and honest coverage, not just to Americans, but to people all around the world—especially those living under oppression. I thought that type of dedication to the news was magnificent.

Over the course of my media career—especially at CNN—there were moments that were just as historically significant as anything I ever did with the LBJ administration. Sometimes there were even events that brought experiences full circle.

The press is often referred to as the fourth estate: a critically important bridge between the general public and governments at all levels. The press is essential to a democracy, and I believe careers in journalism are some of the most noble pursuits that any of us can undertake. CNN was perhaps the most important bridge during the late 1980s and 1990s, as it developed cable news during a period of immense global change.

Because of his passion for worldwide impact, Ted had established relationships with some of the most important national and global leaders at the time. Cuba and the Soviet Union were two of the most fascinating, given their tensions with the United States. Those stories are below, and would not have been possible without CNN, or the unmatched leadership of Ted Turner.

A Coup, a Pen, and the Dissolution of the Soviet Union

As an independent media organization, CNN has always brought accurate and trusted information to areas of the world where freedom of expression was prohibited. China, Russia, Cuba, and Vietnam are among those countries where a free press does not exist.

In founding CNN in 1980, Ted Turner was determined to distribute open, honest reporting to as many countries as possible. He also was willing to spend the millions of dollars to provide the global newsgathering infrastructure needed to do it.

The job as CNN CEO was central to this mission. The role of a network news executive often includes serving as a "booker" who assists in arranging important interviews—especially those of great significance—when the network is in fierce competition with other news services for exclusivity.

A year of historical global significance, 1991 really put our network capacities to the test. It proved to the world that the letters "CNN" were synonymous with breaking news worldwide.

Since the end of World War II, East and West had been locked in the Cold War. It was a topic that dominated everyday life for decades. Ordinary citizens built bunkers, and children practiced "duck and cover" drills in their classrooms.

My own time serving in the LBJ White House occurred in the shadow of the Cuban Missile Crisis—the tensest nuclear moment in history—and the war in Vietnam was very much a "hot" part of that "cold" war.

Since the Bolshevik Revolution in 1917, Russia had been ruled with an iron fist. The USSR's infamous second leader, Joseph Stalin, is thought to have caused the deaths of anywhere from twenty to sixty million people, squashing every threat to his empire.

Over the decades that followed Stalin's death in 1953, Soviet citizens began demanding more freedom and better lives for themselves. In 1985 Mikhail Gorbachev was elected to be a great reformer and bridge to the Western world.

Gorbachev introduced policies of glasnost (greater openness) and perestroika (reconstruction) that gave the Soviet people not only a gradual taste of what life could look like with more freedom but a clearer understanding of just how repressed they had been for so long.

He also served as a peacemaker between the Soviet people and the Communist Party's deeply held secrets of the past. Reform, he knew, began with amends—but this path forward threatened the survival and material comforts of other party leaders around him.

In many ways, by giving the people more of what they sought, Gorbachev fueled their hunger for more. By 1990 the Soviet Union had entered a phase of full-scale collapse. The Baltic republics had declared independence from the empire, and that same feeling of liberation was boiling over from Russia to Poland, Ukraine, East Germany, and beyond.

In May of 1990 there was even greater change beyond Gorbachev. Boris Yeltsin, a democratic populist who both disliked and worked closely with Gorbachev, was elected chair of the Russian Supreme Soviet, which for the first time since 1938 gave significant power to an outside body. In many ways this position made Yeltsin the true face of change.

On August 19, 1991, the rift between the people and the most devoted wing of the Communist Party leadership boiled over in what CNN called the "seven days that shook the world."

While Gorbachev was recovering from a "health issue," a team of eight hardline Communist Party leaders declared a state of emergency and staged a coup to overthrow him. In contrast to Gorbachev and Yeltsin's "party of hope," they became known as "the party of fear," and they were determined to remove Gorbachev and Yeltsin and return the Russian people to a state of political submission.

Security forces put Gorbachev under house arrest at his dacha, and Yeltsin was barricaded by tanks inside the Russian White House. The coup was formidable, but with no single leader, the "party of fear" floundered in their attempt to take control. Most notably, they had grown isolated from the feelings of liberation that had swept across Russia during those years.

When the coup began, CNN had three reporters based in Moscow: bureau chief Steve Hurst and correspondents Eileen O'Connor and Claire Shipman, all supported by additional TV crews and producers.

Following news of the coup, I raced home from CNN Center in Atlanta to quickly pack a bag and fly with Eason Jordan to Moscow. Roughly sixty additional staffers got on planes from other locations to join us.

The coup was not the only reason to rush. ABC had announced plans for a joint interview with Gorbachev and Yeltsin. We at CNN decided to compete vigorously for those interviews.

The day that we arrived, Eason and I met with Yegor Yakovlev, who was Gorbachev's head of Soviet TV. He agreed to arrange an interview between CNN and Gorbachev on one condition: that it be a joint interview, with the two interviewers being Steve Hurst and Yakovlev himself.

CNN won that competition with ABC for a number of reasons.

Through his creation of the Goodwill Games in 1980, Ted Turner had become friends with Gorbachev and other high-ranking Soviet officials, especially those in the sports sector.

Then in 1989 CNN became the first non-Soviet broadcaster to transmit independent news programming into the Soviet Union, through a cooperative relationship with Gosteleradio, the Soviet state commission for TV and radio.

Originally CNN programming was only available in select Soviet ministries and in a few hotels such as the Savoy, a gilded hotel frequented by elites in the heart of Moscow. But over time the network signal reached many Russians in their homes.

During this same period, CNN had established friendly relationships with Russian officials because of its Moscow bureau. One of the most significant CNN bureau chiefs to have served there was Stuart Loory, a Russian-speaking former print journalist who had a tremendous reputation for independence, integrity, and competitiveness.

Our final and most important edge was CNN's satellite coverage. Eason and I had satellite maps with us that showed our network's reach across the globe. It was unmatched by any other news organization.

On the night of August 19—the first night of the coup—Yeltsin declared himself the new leader of Russia and made a call for massive social resistance. As he stood with protestors outside the Russian White House, Yeltsin's call to action reverberated across the land, with leaders from republics across the USSR recognizing him as the new head of state and calling for protests in their own capital cities to show support for Yeltsin.

Yeltsin was a political leader from a poor Siberian upbringing who had always aligned with the working class. He was known for making spontaneous visits to factories as a means of understanding his country, and he had vast popular support, including with members of the military and KGB. The armed forces were not against him.

By the next day Yeltsin commanded all Russian military forces, and millions of citizens were in the streets across the empire, crying out in support.

In a matter of mere hours, Russia had changed. The Soviet Union had changed. The world had changed.

CNN's coverage was a major triumph. We secured a number of first "post-coup" interviews, including with the head of the KGB, the defense minister, the foreign minister, and Boris Yeltsin himself.

These were the moments that CNN was built for. Our teams were very strong and our coverage was complete. By being able to report

Tom holding camera lights as CNN photographer films former U.S. senator Sam Nunn on the roof of CNN's Moscow bureau in August 1991. Courtesy of CNN.

directly to TV sets around the world, CNN brought the people not just news but the feeling of revolution that had swept the USSR.

As the coup subsided over the following days, a new feeling of liberation came to Russia, but the power struggles were far from over.

Gorbachev was still leader of the USSR, but Yeltsin was now the clear leader of the Soviet people and had called for Gorbachev to step down. It would take four long months for the Soviet leaders to agree on a transition of power.

In December, reporting from Moscow began to captivate the world once again.

Having always been a fierce competitor, I decided to pull out every resource I could mobilize to run circles around Ted Koppel and Rick Kaplan of ABC, just as we had done in August.

Departing again for Moscow, I took several copies of a CNN satellite map that displayed the distribution of our coverage. It showed that CNN reached virtually every part of the populated land surface of the planet in English—capacities that over time would include Spanish and many other languages.

Our main goal was securing the final interview with Gorbachev after he dissolved the Soviet Union, and the first interview with Boris Yeltsin as the new president of Russia.

The first visit we made after landing in Moscow was with the Russian information minister, Mikhail Poltoranin. We showed Poltoranin the same CNN satellite maps that we had taken to Moscow in August. I told him emphatically, “No other news organization on earth reaches as many nations.”

“I know that!” he snapped back at me.

I was careful to mention that while ABC had a larger U.S. audience than CNN, CNN’s international audience levels consistently spiked dramatically higher in times of crisis. In addition, CNN reached millions of international viewers that other U.S. domestic news organizations did not.

Stuart Loory and I proposed to Poltoranin that we provide the exclusive interview with Boris Yeltsin in Russian via Russian TV so that the entire world would see it in ways that no other news organization could. Even after decades have passed, I cannot overstate the value of having the seasoned, Russian-speaking Stuart Loory with me.

Moscow bureau Chief Steve Hurst and the CNN Moscow staff were also meeting regularly with government officials. As a former Associated Press reporter, Hurst possessed a streak of diplomacy that worked well with his hardline independent journalism skills.

We also had the help of terrific local resources—namely Yuri Somov and Zoya Conover. Technically they were both interpreters, but we depended on them both for far more than that. Zoya in particular had a strong background with Gosteleradio and had deep connections with Russian leadership. She was an attractive, intelligent, and fierce young woman. With Zoya by our side, we could walk past any KGB guards with ease.

It probably didn't hurt that we also gifted boxes of chocolates and bottles of whiskey to some of the Soviet staffers. Unit manager Frida Ghitis recalled, "We were under great pressure to beat the competition." We still worried that the name recognition of Ted Koppel and the ingenuity of Rick Kaplan somehow would enable them to win.

With a great deal of determination, and surely a bit of luck, we were able to arrange with the Kremlin for CNN to have exclusive rights to both interviews. The only issue was that we were still dealing with Soviet bureaucrats during a very tumultuous time. Even though Yeltsin needed Gorbachev's support for a smooth transition into total power, and Gorbachev needed Yeltsin to ensure his comfort and well-being after stepping down, the two men were often at odds, and Gorbachev had not confirmed which day he would officially resign.

Knowing how ready we had to be at any moment, CNN had dispatched a total of seventy-five executives, producers, directors, camera operators, sound operators, managers, and interpreters.

Our main concern was that Gorbachev would resign ahead of schedule. Fortunately, there was only one major false start.

On the afternoon of December 24 we rolled personnel and our equipment into action with five or six trucks, cameras, and other equipment after hearing word that Gorbachev was going to suddenly make an announcement. I handed my business card to a guard at the entry gate who had absolutely no idea what was going on.

The Kremlin offices were dark, but we were ready.

After a while of waiting, we realized that nothing was set to happen. We returned to CNN's Moscow bureau, where I hosted a Christmas Eve party for all the staff.

Prior to the party, I had asked Frida Ghitis to find me a Santa Claus hat. She couldn't find one in a store, but she saw a newspaper photograph of a Norwegian Santa Claus delivering presents to children in a Moscow orphanage and somehow managed to buy his. Sometimes it's better not to ask too many questions.

Despite doing our best to have a terrific Christmas Eve, word came right in the midst of the party that the big announcements of Gorbachev stepping down and of Yeltsin assuming leadership of Russia would take place the following day, December 25, 1991. That news certainly reduced any celebratory vodka consumption ahead of the most internationally historic Christmas Day of our lives.

The first interview we were set to hold that day was with Boris Yeltsin. We were advised that President Gorbachev's interview would then follow in one of his offices in the Kremlin, where he would sign the necessary papers to dissolve the USSR and give his farewell address.

The next day, as the CNN crew was getting everything set up in the Russian White House, Yeltsin was nowhere to be found.

Zoya phoned Yeltsin's handler to find out where he was. Unaware that the live, globally broadcast interview was supposed to take place in under an hour, they were heading back to his dacha for a few hours of rest.

Somehow Zoya was able to persuade Yeltsin to turn the car around and keep our appointment. "CNN has spent millions of dollars and is going to be broadcasting live," she reminded him in Russian.

While Yeltsin agreed, he had one condition: Zoya would personally apply his television makeup before the cameras started rolling. She relented.

As Yeltsin was getting ready, CNN producer Charlie Caudill checked with Russian officials to make sure that all the arrangements had been made for simultaneous translations.

He asked an aide which ear Yeltsin preferred for his earpiece.

"He's deaf in one ear," the aide said.

"Which ear?" Caudill asked a Russian technician.

The technician didn't know, so Caudill told him to find out.

"Hell no, I will not ask the president of Russia which ear he's deaf in!" the technician replied.

It was Zoya who ended up helping with yet another smooth transition. "Whisper in his ear it is nice to meet you. If he smiles that is the correct ear." Through this trial and error, we discovered it was his left.

There were so many little moments like this that combined preparedness, talent, and outright luck to keep our operations moving steadily. All of this was the result of the excellent CNN Moscow bureau working closely with CNN Atlanta leadership.

The interview with Yeltsin was conducted by Moscow bureau chief Steve Hurst and CNN correspondent Claire Shipman.

Shipman later recalled that despite the day's earlier confusion, she found Yeltsin in a happy mood, and aware of the power he held.

In retrospect, the fact that Yeltsin arrived totally unprepared made it one of the best interviews that we could have ever hoped for. He was honest, ambitious, and showed his humanity. Unlike close-lipped Kremlin leaders of Soviet days, Yeltsin's demeanor was emblematic of a new Russian era.

On policy, Yeltsin assured the global audience that the breakup of the Soviet Union did not mean that nuclear weapons would fall into the wrong hands. He assured the world that there would not be a single second after Gorbachev's anticipated resignation announcement that the nuclear codes would be unsafe.

Then, in a thoughtful way, he said: "Today is a difficult day for Mikhail Sergeyevich [Gorbachev]," hinting that the transfer of power might be imminent.

Despite their differences, Yeltsin acted as a gentleman, declining to answer questions about mistakes Gorbachev had or hadn't made. He also conveyed to Western leaders that the new Russia was eager to cooperate on the global stage.

After completing Yeltsin's live television interview, the entire CNN crew immediately started our race across town to televise Gorbachev's final appearance as president at the Kremlin. All the equipment had to be broken down and loaded into multiple vans in thirty minutes.

Ensuring the quickest route through the city, we gave "donations" to Moscow police to facilitate a full lights-and-sirens escort through Moscow's rush hour.

Charlie Caudill and I were seated in the lead car, leaving some spectators to think we were Yeltsin and Gorbachev themselves! They yelled and waved to us as we drove.

When we arrived at the gates of the Kremlin, even though the guards were smitten with Zoya and another miniskirt-clad interpreter, we were delayed until several mobile phone conversations were completed among the Russian chain of command.

At 5:35 p.m. our crew was directed to Room 4, where Gorbachev was set to make his final address. It was a separate office that had been furnished to look like the real presidential office sixty feet down the corridor.

Oddly enough, Gorbachev was unaware we were to use Room 4, and when he learned of it, he swiftly objected.

"Why not in my office?" he asked Aleksandr Yakovlev, who was the secretary for propaganda.

Yakovlev told him that CNN had already set up in Room 4. "CNN broadcasts to 153 countries," he reminded Gorbachev.

"Well, let's not take the risk of changing the location," Gorbachev conceded.

Just as we had done for Yeltsin, CNN had an agreement with Gosteleradio that we would transmit the resignation address live both in Russian and in English worldwide.

As Gorbachev entered Room 4, staffers from both CNN and Russian Television filled the space, spilling over into the corridor.

Among the staffers were two Associated Press personnel. One was AP Moscow bureau chief Alan Cooperman, and the other was AP photographer Liu Heung Shing. As a member of the board of the Associated Press, I added their names to our list of CNN staffers and smuggled them in. I felt that there was so much history in the making of this event that both an AP reporter and an AP photographer should be there to record it.

There were no Russian journalists or TASS photographers present.

After making his way through the crowded room, Gorbachev shook hands with me. He asked me about CNN's global distribution before amusing both of us with a point about the matters at hand.

"Is your empire doing well now? It is not being dismantled, is it?" referring to the dissolution of the former Soviet Union that he was about to orchestrate.

I answered: "Mr. President, at the present time it is not."

He replied, "Well, it means you have structured your empire quite well, but be sure to give enough power to your republics."

Shortly before live airtime, Gorbachev opened the green folder in front of him that contained his speech and two documents. One was his resignation as president of the Soviet Union, the other the transfer of command and control of the armed forces to Boris Yeltsin.

Gorbachev looked up and said in a quiet voice, "If you have to go, you have to go. It's that time."

Then, as Gorbachev attempted to write on the side of his green folder, his pen failed to write.

Patting his coat and pants pockets, Gorbachev told his press secretary, Andrei Grachev, "Give me a good pen." Grachev was also without one.

With only a minute to go until we were broadcasting live, I reached into my jacket pocket and pulled out a Mont Blanc ballpoint that Edwina had given to me for our twenty-fifth wedding anniversary.

With my hand inside my coat, all three nearby security officials became alarmed. "They did everything but draw their AK-47s," Charlie Caudill later joked.

Gorbachev immediately yelled out to the guards: "Nyet! Nyet!"

Here we were about to broadcast live around the world with the resignation of the president of the Soviet Union, the dissolution of the Soviet Union, and the conveyance of the nuclear codes and power to Boris Yeltsin, and I somehow nearly managed to get myself shot.

As the moment cooled, I smiled and handed Gorbachev my pen. "Mr. President, you may use mine."

"Is it American?" Gorbachev asked.

"No sir, it is either French or German," I told him.

"In that case, I will use it," he replied with a smirk.

As soon as he signed the papers and closed the folder, Liu Heung Shing made another piece of history.

A Russian security guard had already spotted the AP photographer raising his camera and ordered him to leave. Standing near the CNN tripods, Shing had enough distance to disobey orders until the final second.

Just before taking a punch to his kidney from behind, Shing snapped a photograph that would appear on the front page of nearly any media organization covering the historic event, and his photo coverage of the collapse of the Soviet Union would go on to win a Pulitzer Prize.

On that historic day, the world watched Gorbachev deliver his remarks. They were insightful, heartfelt, and—to Boris Yeltsin, who was watching from a different room—infuriating. It was not a sheepish speech that offered full submission to Yeltsin; Gorbachev outlined the progress that the USSR had made over the last six years and openly expressed that he felt the disbanding of the Soviet Union was imprudent. Yet he left peacefully.

It was the second time in my professional life that I had stood to witness a historic leader stepping down from power, running parallel to LBJ's announcement in 1968 that he wouldn't be running for a second term. Both men had lost popular support, but I truly felt that both men had done their very best to leave the world a better place. I respected both leaders for knowing when their time was up.

Gorbachev was gracious in his CNN interview that followed. He was a changed man, to be sure, but he was composed.

Pulitzer Prize–winning photo of Gorbachev by Liu Heung Shing, Associated Press, 1991 (APNews.com).

Reflecting on his time as leader and all the changes that were under way across what was the Soviet Union only moments before, he was pleased that, under his leadership, reforms had begun, and he was ready for a long rest.

After the interview was over, Gorbachev placed the pen in his pocket preparatory to leaving the room.

Moving quickly, I acted to intercept him. I knew the significance of that pen. Once a cherished gift from my wife, Edwina, it had now become a piece of history that literally was used to sign the end of the Cold War.

A smiling President Gorbachev (*right*) examining Tom's Mont Blanc pen, with which he would sign documents dissolving the Soviet Union and conveying power in Russia to Boris Yeltsin, as Tom and Gorbachev's press secretary Andrei Grachev look on. AP photo.

As Gorbachev returned the pen to me, one of his aides also understood what the pen meant and tried to convince me to leave it.

"No way!" I told him.

Years later I would donate that pen to the Newseum in Washington, D.C.

Colin Powell later wrote, "That Christmas Day, the unimaginable happened. . . . The Soviet Union disappeared. Without a fight, without a war, without a revolution. It vanished . . . with the stroke of a pen."

Fidel Castro Denies Role in JFK Assassination

Another major historic event for me was my meeting with Cuban president Fidel Castro in Havana. This meeting was made possible in large part because of Ted Turner's friendship with Fidel.

I had the historic opportunity to speak personally with Castro about JFK's murder by assassin Lee Harvey Oswald and other issues.

Accompanying me were several CNN executives, including Eason Jordan, Larry Register, and Lucia Newman.

We were there on a mission to request Cuban approval for CNN to open the first independent Western news bureau in the years following the Cuban revolution. To the dismay of all the other American news organizations, President Castro eventually did approve our request.

During our conversation, Castro told me that there were absolutely no connections between the Cuban government and Lee Harvey Oswald or the Kennedy assassination. His exact quote to me, in the presence of several CNN executives, was "Had Cuba been involved in any way, you would have incinerated my little island."

Fidel Castro meeting with Tom in 1996. Courtesy of CNN.

Earlier, in December 1991, after the collapse of the Soviet Union, I was granted access, along with reporter and Russia expert Stuart Loory, to the KGB's official file on Oswald.

Loory was a veteran correspondent who had covered the Soviet Union for thirty years. He'd been the last Moscow bureau chief for the *New York Herald Tribune*, White House correspondent for the *Los Angeles Times*, and CNN's first Moscow bureau chief in the 1990s.

Together Loory and I viewed the secret Oswald files at KGB headquarters in downtown Moscow's Lubyanka Square. While we were allowed to read through the files, we were not permitted to take notes.

Although it was noted that Lee Harvey Oswald had defected to the USSR and married a Russian wife, there was no evidence in the KGB files that he had ever been a Soviet agent. In fact, Oswald had been monitored closely by the KGB as a possible CIA agent, and the KGB files indicated that the Russians considered Oswald mentally unstable.

One specific point of contact between Oswald and the USSR was when Oswald had visited the Soviet embassy in Mexico City on October 1, 1963. During the visit he asked for a transit visa through Cuba to Moscow, for both him and his wife.

Many of Oswald's phone calls and visits to the Soviet and Cuban embassies were recorded and photographed by the CIA and other intelligence agencies. The CIA routinely photographed visitors to the Soviet embassy in Mexico but did not ever manage to photograph Oswald himself.

No official evidence linking Cuba or the Soviet Union to the assassination has ever been discovered or released, and based on all my accumulated knowledge, I remain unconvinced that Cuba or the USSR was involved in any way.

However—and it is a big "however"—President Johnson did remain suspicious of a possible Cuban connection with JFK's assassination until his death in 1973.

A book by historian Max Holland, published in 2004, reported that LBJ was suspicious of a Cuban connection primarily because he learned directly from CIA director Richard Helms in May 1967 about the attempts to kill Castro during the Kennedy administration.

This is a brief segment of the CBS transcript from a 1969 Walter Cronkite interview of LBJ that was not aired on CBS at the formal request of President Johnson—a request that I personally made to CBS management on LBJ's behalf. Reluctantly, they agreed.

LBJ: I can't honestly say that I've ever been completely relieved of the fact that there might have been international connections.

Cronkite: You mean you still feel that there might have been?

LBJ: Well, I have not completely discounted it.

Cronkite: Well, that would seem to indicate that you don't have full confidence in the Warren Commission report?

LBJ: No, I think that the Warren Commission study—I think first of all it's composed of the ablest and most judicious and bipartisan men in this country. Second, I think that they had only one objective and that was the truth. And third, I think they were competent and did the best they could, but I don't think that they, that they or me or anyone else is always absolutely sure of everything that might have motivated Oswald or others that could have been involved.

Cronkite: What direction does your lingering suspicion lead you . . . to Cuba? Is that the area that you feel might have been involved?

LBJ: Oh, I don't think we ought to discuss the suspicions because there's not any hard evidence that would lead me to the conclusion that Oswald was directed by a foreign government. Or, that his sympathies for other governments could have spurred him on this effort. But he was quite a mysterious fella, and he did have connections that bore examination on the extent of the influence of those connections on him, and I think history will deal with much more than we are able to now.

Cronkite: How would it come out in history?

LBJ: I don't know.

Not a shred of hard evidence has ever been uncovered to support LBJ's suspicion.

CHAPTER 18

A NEW PATH TO PUBLIC SERVICE

Four major new causes: depression, addiction, cancer, and Alzheimer's

During those magical years at CNN, my battles with depression were much more manageable. Over time, my difficult journey to find the right antidepressant by trial and error paid off. I found routines that worked, a medicine that helped, and I became a better man to my family.

My family also learned how they could better assist me.

For example, Edwina determined it was best to give me some space in the mornings, and to make sure I ate something before I really got moving. That type of understanding and love has been so important for keeping my depression under control.

Even though I was managing it better, my depression never completely disappeared.

When Turner was sold to Time Warner, and then again after Time Warner "merged" with AOL, my depression began to reemerge.

AOL's leadership had ousted my champion Ted Turner and had removed him from overseeing everything he had created and built. That was terribly difficult for me to watch.

I not only thought that it was wrong, but that it was a terrible business decision. Nobody else that I've ever met has possessed Ted's brilliance or talent.

It was almost a repeat of years before, when conservative Chandler family members pushed aside Otis Chandler before pushing me out.

Even though I was not ousted at CNN, I knew that after Ted went, I wouldn't be far behind.

The pressures to support the changes from corporate management began to increase. Some of the new people even began to question my news judgment—especially what CNN should consider "breaking news."

One time, I was called into the office of Jamie Kellner, the new CEO of Turner Broadcasting, and questioned by him and the new programming executive, Garth Ancier, about my decision not to do a live broadcast for a particular segment—a situation in Atlanta where a man had climbed atop a crane and was threatening to jump off and kill himself.

I explained that I refused to air it live because I felt it would have been irresponsible. While Jamie and Garth saw it as "compelling viewing," to me it would have been "sensational journalism." That was not my style of news. In the old days, we called it "tabloid journalism."

After that episode and a few others like it, I knew that it was time for me to go. I was not about to be a part of reshaping CNN into a network like Fox News, one more interested in ratings than in providing top-quality information.

One day in my hometown of Macon, about a ninety-minute drive from CNN Center in Atlanta, I sat alone in a restaurant that had paper mats laid out for children to draw on. I picked up a green crayon and started making my list of pros and cons about retirement.

On the "stay" side, there was my love of news, my devotion to the CNN staff, and a generous compensation package.

On the "leave" side, there was my age (sixty), the promise of more time with my family, and the opportunity to finally become the father that I wanted to be. By then Christa also had our first of two granddaughters, Brynn, and the idea of spending more time with her was very exciting.

I shared my crayon-written list with Edwina. We had not discussed my retirement much, but she certainly knew that my work was no longer as fulfilling as it once was.

Not long after, as I walked out of the house one morning, Edwina told me, "You don't look happy today. You've always been happy when you go to work."

She was right, as she so often is.

For the first time since sacking groceries as a kid in Macon, I disliked what I was doing. I decided to retire that very day.

My first resignation call was to AOL Time Warner CEO Jerry Levin. I thanked him for providing absolute support for CNN's editorial integrity on every news issue that had arisen during our years working together.

My second call was to Ted Turner. I thanked him for eleven spectacular years working with him.

My final call was to Turner CEO Jamie Kellner. I thanked him for the wonderful personal friendship that had developed with him and with his terrific wife Julie.

There was no doubt in my mind that it was the right thing to do. But I also knew as I walked out of CNN Center for the last time that I was really going to miss that place. We had done incredible things and, true to Ted's vision, expanded the reach of reliable information across the entire globe.

My staff couldn't believe that I did it, but it was the absolute best thing I could have done for myself, and for my family. While I didn't know it at the time, it enabled me to shift my focus to new purposes: depression, cancer, addiction, and Alzheimer's. I found great satisfaction from that work and a belief that I am doing my part to make the world perhaps a better place.

On the night of my August 2001 retirement party, in front of a large crowd at CNN Center, I decided to answer the question that everyone had been asking me—"Tom, why are you really retiring?" Rather than mentioning the corporate changes, I asked for my granddaughter Brynn to be handed to me on stage.

Holding her up before the audience, I showed them.

"Here's the reason—I'm going to be spending more time with this new granddaughter and my family."

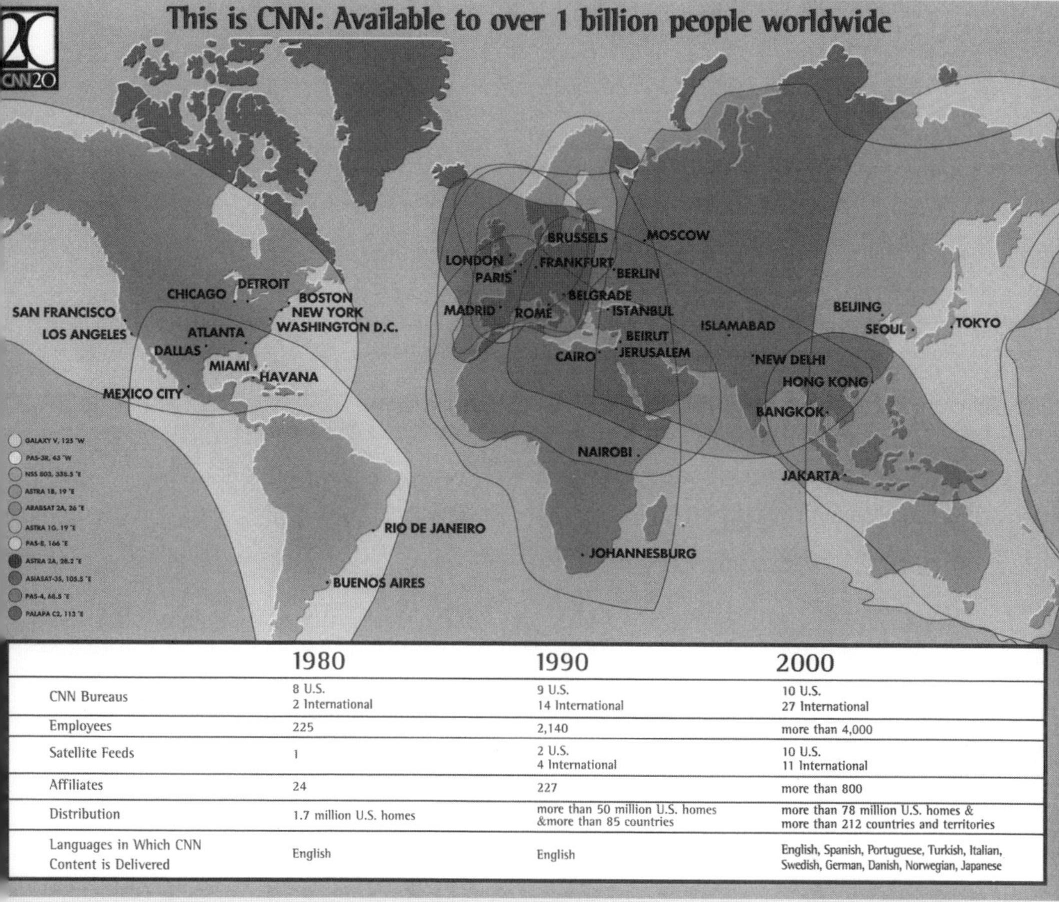

	1980	1990	2000
CNN Bureaus	8 U.S. 2 International	9 U.S. 14 International	10 U.S. 27 International
Employees	225	2,140	more than 4,000
Satellite Feeds	1	2 U.S. 4 International	10 U.S. 11 International
Affiliates	24	227	more than 800
Distribution	1.7 million U.S. homes	more than 50 million U.S. homes &more than 85 countries	more than 78 million U.S. homes & more than 212 countries and territories
Languages in Which CNN Content is Delivered	English	English	English, Spanish, Portuguese, Turkish, Italian, Swedish, German, Danish, Norwegian, Japanese

Expansion of CNN global satellite coverage from 1980 to 2000. Courtesy of CNN.

Tom at 2001 retirement, wearing CNN tie and holding granddaughter Brynn.

My newfound freedom gave me more opportunities to focus on my own mental wellness, spend more time with my loved ones, and begin working on the next chapter of my life—helping other people.

Former president Jimmy Carter had said it best:

"I have one life and one chance to make it count for something. My faith demands that I do whatever I can, wherever I can, whenever I can, for as long as I can with whatever I have to try to make a difference."

Without question, President Carter sure succeeded at making a difference with his time on earth.

Jimmy and Rosalynn became huge influences on me. She was a fierce advocate for mental health and the need for parity between insurance coverage of mental health and physical health.

As a result of managing my own battle with depression, I've long felt strongly that I must throw out a lifeline to those who are in need of help—those who are in their own depths of depression. Retirement is my chance to do more of that.

Left to right: Tom, *Los Angeles Times* leaders Jack Nelson and Dennis Britton, and friends Rosalynn and President Jimmy Carter.

There is an old southern hymn by Edward S. Ufford, written in 1888 called "Throw Out the Lifeline." The lyrics have been a major inspiration for my volunteer work. In fact, almost nothing else has ever compared to the hymn's impact, especially the one that is sung by Ella Fitzgerald, on my drive to be better, and do more to help others.

Throw out the lifeline across the dark wave;
There is a brother whom someone should save;
Somebody's brother! O who then will dare
To throw out the lifeline, his peril to share?
Throw out the lifeline! Throw out the lifeline!
Someone is drifting away;
Throw out the lifeline! Throw out the lifeline!
Someone is sinking today.
Throw out the lifeline with hand quick and strong:

Why do you tarry, why linger so long?
See! He is sinking; oh, hasten today
And out with the life boat! Away, then away!
Throw out the lifeline to danger-fraught men,
Sinking in anguish where you've never been;
Winds of temptation and billows of woe
Will soon hurl them out where the dark waters flow.
Soon will the season of rescue be o'er;
Soon will they drift to eternity's shore;
Haste then, my brother, no time for delay!
But throw out the lifeline and save them today.

I was in my early fifties when I first heard that song during an outdoor church service on Lake Burton in North Georgia.

Growing up, I attended Ebenezer Methodist Church in Macon every Sunday with my mother, and while I have not been a regular churchgoer in my adult life, I've been influenced by some incredible people through different religious communities—especially Reverend Billy Porterfield in Macon, Reverend George Regas in Pasadena, and Rabbi Alvin Sugarman in Atlanta.

That Sunday at Lake Burton, where people came together to sing and to hear a sermon, that particular hymn simply hit me in the profound way that books or films might have an impact on other people. It made me think about how much more I could and should be doing.

Over the years, I became aware of so many people in my life that had battled, or were still battling, depression. In the 1980s, 1990s, and even the early years of the 2000s, mental illness in any form was simply not something that people were comfortable admitting they had.

Right around the time of my retirement from CNN, inspiration came from one of my Atlanta friends, Larry Gellerstedt. Larry was a major business leader in Atlanta, and in 2000 he spoke publicly about his depression in an interview with the *Wall Street Journal*. At the time, it was an extremely courageous act.

In corporate culture, depression was not a topic that people discussed openly. Young professionals feared that knowledge of their "weakness" could prevent future advancements and promotions. Older professionals feared they would no longer be trusted to lead.

When I read Larry's interview, I was motivated to go public myself.

I began to understand that, as a business leader, I could have a positive influence through speaking about depression.

In 2002, following Larry's bold leadership, Atlanta business leader J. B. Fuqua and I agreed that adding our own voices and stories publicly would help diminish the stigma that Larry was working to eliminate.

J.B. was a close friend who battled serious depression for much of his life. He had been hospitalized with it at age thirty. He had even undergone electroshock therapy. Despite that, J.B. had built an enormous conglomerate of financially successful companies, Fuqua Industries. He—like me—understood that suffering from depression does not entirely limit a person's capacity to succeed.

The three of us—J.B., Larry, and I—agreed to sit for an interview about our collective battles with mental health.

We met with a highly respected Atlanta-based reporter named Maria Saporta, who was then working for the *Atlanta Journal-Constitution*. Maria persuaded us to open up about our personal lives and the challenges we experienced.

I described for her some of my darkest times, but I also used the interview as an opportunity to explain how talk therapy and medications had helped me. I wanted my story to give people hope that they can successfully deal with their depression and that there are helpful medications that work.

Sitting with Maria that day and talking openly about my experience was extremely difficult. For many years I had kept my battles with depression hidden from others around me. J.B. had done the same.

As much as we hoped the interview would encourage people to seek treatment, we also hoped to demonstrate that people with depression can still make extraordinary contributions in their professional fields and in their daily lives.

Anxiously we awaited publication of Maria's story.

J.B and I already had achieved enough status in our fields to be shielded, and we knew that publicity about our depression would not harm our careers. We did not know, however, what reactions it might incite from our family and friends.

Fortunately, the article received an amazingly positive reaction. Maria had written it in such a genuine and empathetic way that it generated a flood of emails, letters, and phone calls and received attention across the country. More requests for additional interviews from print and TV followed.

People who knew me well reached out and sent messages of both encouragement and surprise. It wasn't uncommon for me to hear, "Tom, you did a hell of a job hiding your depression for all those years."

Going public with Larry and J.B. was one of the best things I've done in life. It lifted a tremendous weight off my shoulders, and inspired others to share their own stories.

More important, it inspired me to become more deeply involved with other major mental health projects.

In 1980—twenty-two long years before our article with Maria Saporta was published—Atlanta businessman Charles B. West was busy making visionary contributions to the field of mental health. He founded the George West Mental Health Foundation, which helped establish the amazing Atlanta treatment center, Skyland Trail.

Not long after its opening, Skyland Trail benefited tremendously from the generous support of the Fuqua family, even though J.B. had not yet publicized his own struggles with depression.

J.B.'s wife, Dottie, was the one that would get me involved with Skyland Trail, which has been such a pleasure to watch grow. At that time the facility was primarily for adults.

One day Dottie called and said, "Tom, I want to take you to lunch."

Dottie drove me to Skyland Trail, where she and Beth Finnerty, the president of the organization, showed me around. I was introduced to the gardens and to the different methods of therapy they offered, from horticulture to pets, art, and so much more, and I participated in a Q-and-A with the staff.

Immediately, I was hooked. Seeing that wonderful program launched me into a new path of public service in my "later years."

I agreed to become a fully engaged volunteer with the Skyland Trail community, often working as a fundraiser, and helping to publicize its groundbreaking research results with other programs across the country.

Another one of my roles was organizing annual events. The program in April of 2004 remains one of which I'm particularly proud.

Three of my closest professional friends—Art Buchwald, Mike Wallace, and Bill Styron—had also battled severe depression for many years. I knew their stories well. All three men were splendid writers and journalists and were household names across America.

Long before we sat together on that stage, Mike, Bill, Art, and I had all benefited tremendously from one another's help. Art in particular was a real lifeline for those around him. He checked in daily with us to make sure we felt supported.

Two of the most powerful thoughts about depression I had learned from Art and Bill.

Art used to tell me, "The reason not to commit suicide is that you cannot change your mind later on."

Bill called the disease "the shipwreck of the soul."

Bringing this group together in Atlanta was not easy. They had spent so many years hiding their condition that speaking publicly was difficult for them. Bill even went as far as to tell me, "Depression is so overwhelming, it's beyond expression."

Luckily, with Art's help, I convinced the three of them to fly to Atlanta on J. B. Fuqua's beautiful jet for a gathering at Skyland Trail.

With a sense of humor about their serious conditions, Art, Mike, and Bill described themselves as the Blues Brothers. So we named the event just that: "An Evening with the Blues Brothers." Hundreds of people attended.

I moderated a panel discussion that included two of the most influential physicians from the field of mental health at that time—Dr. Charles Nemeroff, now at the Dell Medical School in Austin, and Dr.

Left to right: Psychopharmacologist Dr. Charles Nemeroff, Art Buchwald, and Tom.

William McDonald, now chairman of the Department of Psychiatry at Emory University.

Without Dr. Nemeroff's prior psychiatric help, I might not have been alive to be there that day. He was then, and has remained, my psychiatrist and a good friend.

Many, if not most, of the attendees battled depression themselves or had close friends and relatives who were struggling. Having all those people together in the same room brought a sense of community and a shared experience for the audience.

Our discussion highlighted the reality that so many of us were touched by this misunderstood condition. We also discussed treatments, inequality in healthcare, and the importance of sympathetic community.

Mike, Art, and Bill confessed that their depression had been so serious that all three of them had been hospitalized. However, they also said they had continued their professional work both during and after treatments.

Mike had continued to lead his CBS program *60 Minutes*.

Art continued to write his internationally distributed columns for the *Los Angeles Times* Syndicate.

Bill continued to write Pulitzer-quality books.

What made "An Evening with the Blues Brothers" so historic was its honesty and vulnerability. For two hours those iconic men spoke without reservation, sharing their deepest secrets and fears, and their own journeys with depression.

Mike told the audience how his depression began when two parts of his world collided. Both he and *60 Minutes* were sued by someone I knew well from my days in the LBJ White House: General William Westmoreland. Westmoreland pressed charges against *60 Minutes* for reporting that he had "cooked the books" on Vietnam. He brought an additional suit against Mike as an individual because of the stories he had worked on while covering the Vietnam War.

The trial required Mike to be in court for five painful months. It was during this time that Mike fell into depression as he watched his name and identity as a journalist dragged through the mud.

Mike told the crowd that his doctor had assured him that his dark mood would pass and advised him to keep the condition a secret—especially from the public. Mike's doctor, whom he knew and trusted, said that publicizing his illness would only hurt his television image.

Advice such as that, even from well-intentioned physicians, was not uncommon at that time.

Medical school curricula often lacked classes on mental health, and hardly any doctors were required to have mental health training. The result was that they simply did not know how to help.

If people as wealthy and beloved as Mike Wallace were left on their own to find support during that era, one can only imagine the difficulty for most other people.

We also talked that evening about the role of our families and the indispensable assistance we received from them. To be totally open and honest, we did not shy away from the tremendous hurt we could impose on others.

I shared with the audience that I often had lashed out at Edwina, Christa, and Wyatt when I came home from work. Mike, Bill, and Art shared similar uncomfortable truths about how unpleasant they could be to the people who loved them most.

For years following the "Blues Brothers" event, many people contacted me to talk privately about their own depression. Many were ashamed. Others did not have adequate funds to see a physician, or even know what type of physician to see.

Others did not know what was wrong with them. They simply knew that they "weren't right."

They feared hearing the same words that I had long feared—"Do you know that Tom Johnson has a mental illness?"—not knowing what fallout might come.

Addressing that awful stigma was the essence of the "Blues Brothers" event. We knew that educating the public was the most important thing we could do to encourage mental health treatment for those in need.

Our great friends J.B. and Dottie have both passed away, but along with their son, Rex, and the incredible people at Skyland Trail, great mental health work has flourished here in Atlanta.

Due to the genetic nature of depression, Rex has suffered for many years with mental health challenges of his own. While I would never wish depression on anyone, his personal familiarity with the challenges of mental illness is certainly one of the reasons he is *such* an outstanding supporter for the cause.

Skyland Trail began providing residential treatment for adults in a modest apartment building more than three decades ago. It has since grown to include five campuses focused on adults and adolescents with depression, anxiety, and other mental disorders.

Generous foundations and private donors from around Atlanta came together to make Skyland Trail's growth possible—including, but not limited to, the Woodruff Foundation, the Fuqua family, the West family, the Rollins family, the Glenn family, the Cox family, and many others.

Serving as tri-chair of the campaign that raised $20 million for the Rex Fuqua Adolescent Center at Skyland Trail remains one of the projects of which I'm most proud.

Prior to its opening, many local families found no choice but to send their children to out-of-state mental health centers and to drug treatment programs, many of which were not of high quality. I visited several of them myself.

The J. Rex Fuqua Campus for adolescents fourteen to eighteen years old offers a full continuum of care including residential, day treatment, and education services to help adolescents transition safely back to their families, schools, and communities and equips them to manage their mental illness throughout their lives.

Despite our progress, there is still a long way to go toward producing better research about the mental health issues concerning our children. They need different evaluations, different diagnoses, and different treatments than adults receive.

Other pieces of the fight that Rex Fuqua and I remain hard at work on are insurance challenges, school support, and enabling more people to become mental-health professionals.

We know that so many young students suffer from depression but don't know where to get help, or how to afford the high cost. Our hope is that it becomes more of a group effort, with everyone on staff trained to be looking out for children having a difficult time.

I cannot count how many times I have spoken with schools that have dozens of personnel for their sports programs—which is wonderful—but have limited or nonexistent staffing for student mental health. I often encourage the heads of schools to consider hiring at least one mental health counselor.

In the schools around Atlanta where mental health is made a priority, there has been a tremendous acceptance by students to use provided services. It's wonderful that there appears to be far less stigma with younger generations to seek help and talk openly about mental health with their peers.

School administrators are also reaching out to more experts than ever before. Helping schools put together "tool kits" to help children with mental illness is one of the absolute best things that treatment centers can do for local communities. As a nation, we need to do more in our public schools. Much more.

Unfortunately, not everyone goes to a school with adequate resources or has a job with a well-equipped human resources department.

For those who don't have easy access to professional support, the costs associated with finding help can be a monumental hurdle, if someone can find access at all.

I still spend many hours trying to find psychiatrists to help people, particularly those who do not have financial resources. Money and good insurance do not necessarily mean that someone will have good care. There simply are not enough mental health providers.

It is not uncommon for insurance plans to cover only eight to twenty-one days of mental health assistance each year. This is far too limited for many patients and can add immense stress for someone who is already dealing with depression or anxiety.

J. B. Fuqua and I actually testified before Congress on behalf of the Mental Health Parity and Addiction Equity Act. Fortunately, it passed and was signed into law by President George W. Bush (43). However, too many people still are not covered under their insurance plans for mental health treatment despite federal regulation mandates.

Great centers like Skyland Trail provide millions of dollars each year to care for people who otherwise could not afford it, but that is not a national or global solution.

Private donors like Rex are doing wonderful things to help fund fellowships for young professionals to secure mental health training. It is not a career that enables people to become wealthy, so fellowships and grants at least help reduce the financial burden that these young professionals incur during their training.

Rex and I do this work on behalf of future generations—those of our children and grandchildren—hoping that they do not have to experience depression in the same ways that we have.

Since winning the American Psychiatric Association's Gold Award in 2004, Skyland Trail has been recognized as one of the top models of integrated care in the entire country. Unfortunately, depression itself is not always the only challenge that people with mental illness face.

Another Battle: Addiction

Those suffering with depression also often battle substance use disorders.

Sometimes substance abuse leads to depression, while other times, depressed individuals will self-medicate with drugs and alcohol. This is especially true in an era that has been so deeply impacted by social media and years of the COVID pandemic.

I admit that I was not always so understanding when it came to addiction. In many ways, I once saw it as a personal weakness.

William Cope Moyers, the son of my mentor Bill Moyers, was the one who changed my view.

Cope was working for me at CNN in 1994, and he was, and still is, a brilliant young man with a wonderful family. I had not known about his prior struggles with alcohol and crack cocaine. When he joined CNN, he told me that he had been sober for two years. He became a solid member of our staff.

One night I received a phone call from his parents, Judith and Bill Moyers. Cope had gone AWOL, and we needed to help find him.

Within twenty-four hours I assisted his family to organize Atlanta taxi drivers and retired police officers, who found Cope largely incapacitated in an Atlanta crack house. Taxi drivers often know exactly where crack houses are located in every city.

Rather than returning to CNN, which he was welcome to do, Cope explained to me that his mental capacities couldn't handle the temptations of urban life. He enjoyed work at CNN and loved Atlanta, but he told me he needed to be back in Minnesota where he could live and work with the recovering community at Hazelden Betty Ford.

When Cope explained it in that way, I began to understand addiction as an issue that overlaps in so many ways with depression. It was something he could actively choose to address, but not necessarily control: a feeling I sure could relate to.

Addiction became my next project.

Setting my involvement in motion was a meeting in 2018 with Frank Boykin, retired CFO of Mohawk Industries and a fellow Atlantan.

Frank described his personal story about how he and his wife Karen nearly lost their son to opioid addiction. They said they went to bed many nights not knowing if he would be alive the next morning.

To address the issue of addiction in the community, Frank and I have worked closely with attorney Jack Hardin to bring Hazelden Betty Ford and Emory University together to create the new Addiction Alliance of Georgia led by Dr. Justine Welsh.

William Cope Moyers—now a senior executive at Hazelden Betty Ford—has been instrumental in its founding and development. I strongly recommend William's books, especially *Broken* and his latest one, *Broken Open*.

This program focuses on prevention, education, research, treatment, and recovery. It is already saving many lives. It's come at an opportune time for greater Atlanta, as there has been a sharp increase in opioid-related deaths and suicides there and across the nation.

Raising money for a new Georgia addiction center, the Addiction Center of Georgia (AAG), has been a monumental challenge. It has taken a tremendous amount of time and effort over the past four years. I'm very pleased that there is a particular emphasis at the center on helping the underserved.

Unfortunately, many people are still influenced by bias and the idea that addiction is a moral failure, or impacts communities outside their own. As a result, some would-be donors choose not to help, which is incredibly sad for so many reasons.

At the Addiction Center, we know that addiction cuts across all different racial and ethnic groups and sociodemographic levels. This is a tremendously important part of our work.

Despite what we have accomplished in Georgia on the issues of both depression and addiction, the nation still has a long way to go.

A Daughter's Battle Is a Father's Battle: Alzheimer's

Our daughter Christa Johnson Shaffer was diagnosed with Alzheimer's during the chaos of the COVID-19 pandemic. Hers is a rare form called posterior cortical atrophy that begins in the back of the brain and progresses forward to the front.

By 2024 the disease had progressed to a point where Christa was no longer able to drive, bike, write legibly, dress herself in anything complicated, or even buckle her seat belt.

With the help of MD Anderson, Mayo Clinic, Emory Healthcare, Dr. Sanjay Gupta of CNN, and others, I have searched the world for possible treatments, with a long way yet to go. Two specialists have been the closest version of our own lifelines that we've found: Dr. Allan Levey of Emory Brain Health Center and Dr. David Hafler of Yale University.

Both doctors recommended a major new medication, LEQEMBI, which Christa is receiving by infusion. I urge others to familiarize themselves with this and other new medications. Researchers hope that this medicine will slow and perhaps even halt the progression of this rare form of dementia.

At this point there is no miracle drug for Alzheimer's. Even the smallest victories are tremendous ones. There is nothing to do but keep supporting research and care for our families who have been stricken by this terrible illness.

I pray that the efforts we make now, contributing what we can to doctors and researchers on the leading edge, will help countless others struggling with Alzheimer's down the road.

Although I may not be able to throw out a thousand lifelines, I do know that I can throw out one at a time to people in need. I have been doing that, and I'll continue to do that.

I encourage anyone reading this chapter to think about those around you and ask yourself: "How is he or she doing?"

You never know when something as easy as a phone call, a knock on the door, or a luncheon could really help someone who needs it. Small gestures like that often are so important. I intend to do all I can as long as I can to help.

The poet James Russell Lowell said it best:

Though old the thought and oft exprest,
'Tis his at last who says it best,
I'll try my fortune with the rest.
Life is a leaf of paper white
Whereon each one of us may write
His word or two, and then comes night.
'Lo, time and space enough,' we cry,
'To write an epic!' so we try
Our nibs upon the edge, and die.
Muse not which way the pen to hold,
Luck hates the slow and loves the bold,
Soon come the darkness and the cold.
Greatly begin! though thou have time
But for a line, be that sublime,
Not failure, but low aim, is crime.
Ah, with what lofty hope we came!
But we forget it, dream of fame,
And scrawl, as I do here, a name.

I'm doing everything I can to make my eighth inning in life as strong as I can make it—especially by helping others whose lives are "in the ditch" and in need of a friend who cares. I want to do it privately with no public recognition.

I am still aiming high in the years I have left.

CHAPTER 19

THE LATER YEARS

Still driven in my eighth inning

As I've mentioned throughout this book, the single greatest regret of my now eighty-three years is that I became a workaholic and neglected to be a caring, loving husband to Edwina and father to Wyatt and Christa when they were young.

During my retirement, I committed to becoming a far better husband and father than I had been in my earlier years.

It's an easy message to ignore when you're in the throes of your career, but I really urge young parents not to become workaholics, not to neglect their children in their early years, and to remember "being nice" starts with your spouse and those you love the most.

I'll never forget the day that Christa came up to me after I had missed several of her high school soccer matches and cross-country runs. Looking up with her hands on her hips, she reminded me, "Don't forget that you're a daddy, too."

There is no excuse. I could have done it. But what I did was place becoming a success in my profession ahead of being the success that I should have been as a parent and husband.

However, my retirement from CNN in 2001 enabled me to change much of that.

There was also the new opportunity to be the best grandfather to Brynn—my first granddaughter—and Julene, Brynn's younger sister. Grandparenting Brynn and Julene has been one of the most spectacular experiences I've ever known.

My good friend Larry Temple of Austin is one of the few friends with whom I have shared my deepest feelings over the years. He knew that I had experienced depression and issues with my own children.

It was Larry who told me long before Brynn and Julene were born that I just had to wait—that grandparenting would be an incredible "second chance" and the very best stage of my life, as it was for Larry.

He sure was right.

Edwina and I have traveled with them, and our daughter Christa and her husband Bill, but I hope there will still be more time for us ahead.

Until COVID-19 struck in 2020, Edwina and I never missed an important event in the lives of our two granddaughters. We've had enjoyable family trips to many places.

As Brynn and Julene have gotten older, they've made it a point to come stay with us in Atlanta, and Edwina has taken wonderful "girls' trips" with them, including an Icelandic cruise in 2023, not long after Julene's twenty-first birthday.

Even though I'm a better grandfather than I was a father, the past isn't totally forgotten.

By far the most painful statement that anyone in my family ever made was when Christa told me: "I only wish that I had had a father who was as good to me as my daughters have in you as a wonderful grandfather." Christa sure was justified in telling me that. As a daughter, she always was loving and responsible in every way.

I think it's important for me to write this, although several people have urged me not to. It shows that I have serious human failings, and it's an important part of my story. It's certainly inspired me to try to be better in my older years.

With a great deal of effort and patience from both of us, even Wyatt and I have built a stronger relationship.

Some of my favorite memories are weeks we spent together in his camper. We made a wonderful trip to Alaska, and another to various surf spots along the Pacific coast of Mexico. Wyatt always went for the big waves. It was exhilarating just watching him.

My retirement also has allowed for more time spent with the love of my life, Edwina.

When I left CNN, being a better husband was just as high on my list as being a better father. Edwina had put up with so much for so long, and I owed her more. Much more.

In some ways, I think Edwina knew what she was getting into when she and I first began to date. During my years reporting for the *Red and Black* at the University of Georgia, she would come down to the newspaper office and study while I worked. Other times she would make the weekend drive with me to Macon so I could work at the *Macon Telegraph*. Even then she could see that I was a workaholic.

Still, neither of us knew just how much my battle with depression would impact our relationship. The situation often left Edwina to be both mother and father to our children, which wasn't fair to anyone. Worst of all, sometimes I'd unfairly lash out at her in anger, especially during the darkest phases of my depression. For all these many years, she has been my absolute rock.

At one point I bought Edwina a beautiful diamond necklace. I told her that each stone represented an apology for my failures and a request for forgiveness for all of my transgressions during our marriage. She looked at the necklace and then said with a smile: "I think you better keep on buying." And I have.

In addition to mental health and addiction, there are two new missions that I have taken on: cancer and dementia. All of which have impacted me for very personal reasons.

Edwina was diagnosed with multiple myeloma—bone cancer—in 2017. She has battled it successfully with expert advice and treatments at MD Anderson Cancer Center in Houston and Winship Cancer Institute of Emory University in Atlanta.

When Edwina was diagnosed, I was serving on the Board of Visitors of the MD Anderson Cancer Center. We also had close relationships with the Mayo Clinic as a result of my nine years of service on that board.

On the medical center boards where I've served, there has always been a rule that board members don't jump the line. That is something that Edwina and I have absolutely never wanted to do. However, being able to pick up the phone and talk to expert researchers and scientists has certainly been wonderful.

For her treatment, Edwina chose Dr. Robert Orlowski of MD Anderson and Dr. Sagar Lonial of Emory Winship Cancer Institute. Both doctors are brilliant oncologists with world-class reputations in multiple myeloma research and treatments.

In October 2022 Edwina underwent a successful trial of CAR-T cell treatment at Emory. It involved gathering six million of her CAR-T cells, sending them to be reengineered at Janssen Pharmaceuticals, and returning the reengineered cells into Edwina, where they became "warrior cells" killing the cancer cells.

The results, as of this writing, have been absolutely astounding. What was once a death sentence now is in near-complete remission. It has just been the most spectacular gift, allowing her to keep living a life with family and friends that she loves. She and Julene, now twenty-three, completed a two-week trip to Japan as recently as May 2024.

For me, the news of Edwina's cancer has always been, and remains, of deepest concern, but she has been steady through it all. She simply has the most amazing optimism and positive attitude of anyone I have ever known.

As her condition has improved, Edwina and I have been able to help raise more money and awareness about new cancer breakthroughs. It's wonderful getting to do this together.

In spite of health challenges, Edwina and I have been fortunate to share indelible memories traveling through the years both as a couple and with our closest friends. There have been dozens of unforgettable trips to China, Russia, Mexico, Japan, Thailand, Singapore, Vietnam, Myanmar, Egypt, England, France, Italy, Spain, and Alaska.

One particularly notable trip we enjoyed came after an Atlanta charity auction. Jane Fonda was holding a fundraiser that included many of Atlanta's most influential and wealthy residents to support the Georgia Campaign for Adolescent Pregnancy Prevention (GCAPP).

Among many expensive auction items was three nights on a ship named the *Sea Dream*, which had fifty deluxe staterooms. The Las Vegas auctioneers tried to secure bids on individual rooms, but the crowd just wasn't buying, with only a few having sold. So I suggested, "Why not just auction off the entire ship?"

The idea seemed to appeal to everybody in the audience. After all, it would be an all-expenses-paid trip from St. Thomas to St. Bart's, with stops for champagne and caviar at some of the islands in between.

Looking around the crowd, I saw several millionaires and even a few billionaires. I was confident that the luxurious *Sea Dream* voyage would be a big draw, and I figured the best way to get things moving was for me to open up the bidding with a big number.

I called out $150,000. I expected to quickly hear $200,000. But no other offer came.

Just like that, I had suddenly—and *very* unexpectedly—won all fifty rooms on the ship.

Edwina and I didn't exactly have $150,000 to spare at that time, but it turned out to be one of the greatest trips of our lives. We took friends from all of our years in Boston, Washington, Austin, Dallas, LA, and Atlanta.

Judith and Bill Moyers, Billye and Henry Aaron, Mary Margaret and Jack Valenti, Phyllis George, Marianne Rogers, Jane Fonda and Ted Turner, Barby and Joe Allbritton, and close family members. Lady Bird Johnson's health did not permit her to join us, but her daughters Lynda and Luci did. It was an absolutely magnificent time.

Another unforgettable trip was one to India, where we were introduced to Mother Teresa. There was something about this frail little woman that I never had experienced before, or since. There was an aura about her that can only be described as saintly.

While we love to travel together, we both maintain a few of our own separate passions, and spend time away.

No history of Edwina's life can overlook the Wilderness Warriors, a group founded by Edwina's friend Martha Myers of Dallas more than forty years ago. It's composed of the same eight members who still make annual wilderness trips, and they travel with each other every year. The wonderful trips that these women have organized include mountain climbing, river rafting, ocean kayaking, camping in below-freezing weather, hiking, and more. No man ever has been invited. Every attempt by a husband to participate has been unwelcome and denied.

That group of her very best friends—including Deedie, whom we met alongside Rusty Rose when I was at Harvard Business School—has been especially supportive of Edwina during her recent years battling multiple myeloma. I'm so grateful for that.

A number of our longest-lasting friendships were formed during our years living in Boston. These include Deedie and Rusty Rose; Carol and Bill Wyman; and Bobbie and John Harrell.

Deedie and Rusty, having started their lives with limited financial resources as we did, managed funds successfully. Rusty and I enjoyed many hunting and fishing trips, and we had great husband-wife adventures until, tragically, Rusty took his own life after battling severe depression.

Bill Wyman rose to become chairman of the consulting firm Booz Allen and later owner/partner of Oliver Wyman and Company. His wife Carol, one of the most blunt, outspoken, and wonderful friends of our lives, showed up in our small apartment at Harvard, looked in our tiny refrigerator, and exclaimed, "Edwina, you're going to kill everybody." She saw open cans of peas, tomatoes, and other foods in the fridge. From that day forward, I think every item in our refrigerators has gone immediately from a can into a sealed glass or plastic container.

As can happen with the years, Carol and Bill ended their marriage, but we have remained close with Carol. Bill has been critical in assisting us in our global search to find medical treatments for our daughter, Christa, and her rare form of dementia, posterior cortical atrophy.

John Harrell was one more in our circle with great connections to the Mayo Clinic. He rose to become the chief financial officer of the

Mayo Clinic Foundation in Rochester, Minnesota, during which time Mayo expanded to Jacksonville, Florida, and Scottsdale, Arizona.

In my opinion, Mayo is by far the most outstanding center in the world for comprehensive diagnostic evaluations of complex medical issues. I refer many people with serious illnesses to Mayo when other medical centers have been unsuccessful.

One other deeply important connection that we've kept from our past is with LBJ and Lady Bird's two wonderful daughters Lynda Johnson Robb and Luci Baines Johnson. We have remained a part of each other's families throughout the years, and we have worked on a few remarkable projects together.

As the years have passed, it's our marriage, our children, and our grandchildren that are without question my greatest accomplishments. I have come to absolutely revel in the time I have with my family, and Edwina's Chastain family of Athens. Beyond that, it's been helping people "get out of the ditch."

Tom with his "sisters" Luci Baines Johnson and Lynda Robb.

I hope the work in my later years has been of some small impact. I think it has been. But just as importantly—I've loved the work and enjoy knowing that other people are getting their life back together, just as I did.

I've benefited enormously from my own approach to keep my depression under control: backing away from the stressors, increasing my level of medication when necessary, and spending more time outdoors or getting professional massage. Thanks to my choice to go public, it's also far easier for me to discuss my condition, and talk therapy truly does help.

We must get the toxic stuff out of that canister we all carry around inside us. Clean it out occasionally with somebody you trust. It's also critical that the people who form your support system have people they're able to talk to as well.

By learning to manage my battle with depression, I have enjoyed so much more of what life can offer, and deeply wish to help as many others as I possibly can.

It's not to say that I do not occasionally still have bouts of depression. I do. But I'm now able to manage it well.

For fun, I still love to read and to jet ski. I get out on Lake Nottely in North Georgia where nobody knows me, turn my cap backwards, and twist the throttle wide open. It's those little things that put the years behind me in perspective.

I've often questioned whether I could have enjoyed the professional achievements I did while also being a better husband to Edwina and a better father to my children. The answer is that I truly don't know. For me, it was always about success, and outworking everybody. This meant coming in earlier, staying later, and working harder than others.

Even though I continue to give my best to everything I do, it wears me out faster than when I was younger. But I've come to live with it. Just as the battery in my cell phone needs to be recharged, I take an afternoon nap, recharge my batteries, and I'm ready to hit the road once again.

One time when I was vice chairman of Times Mirror, a senior vice president, Phil Williams, told me, “Tom, you’ve made it. Enjoy it. Don’t push yourself so hard.” That advice wasn’t so different from Bill Moyers telling me decades earlier in the White House, “Stop running!”

I’ve never been able to help it.

It’s just natural for me to go at life full speed. Driven.

CHAPTER 20

TRUMP'S REELECTION

The journalists must unite.

It is very difficult to predict the impact of Trump's reelection on international relations, U.S. domestic policies, and many government programs that existed prior to his inauguration on January 20, 2025. However, one of the areas that almost certainly will be affected is journalism.

During the campaign it was clear that Fox News served as a strong advocate for the Trump side. MSNBC was more supportive of the Kamala Harris liberal agenda. Throughout the campaign, I felt that CNN sought to provide better-balanced coverage than either of those outlets. The epic Biden v. Trump debate on CNN on June 27, 2024, certainly had a negative influence on President Biden's situation that cannot be overstated. More than any other factor, his poor showing in that debate led to his painful decision to step aside.

It is my view that the so-called Big 3 networks (ABC, NBC, CBS) were relatively fair and balanced in their newscasts. The one show that consistently blasted Trump and supported Harris was *The View* on ABC.

In my judgment, the one news organization that did by far the most comprehensive news coverage was the *New York Times*. However, its editorial pages—separate from news coverage—contained significant pro-Harris and anti-Trump content.

It is impossible to know exactly what Trump will do in his second term, but his contempt for journalists who hold truth to power has certainly remained clear. Trump has expressed his determination to punish his media critics, as well as others who opposed him and his candidacy.

Trump's rhetoric has damaged our democratic process, just as it has damaged public attitudes about the press. Both the Gallup and Pew polls show that media rankings are at or near all-time lows.

Based on a lifetime of working with many of the finest news organizations and journalists on the planet, I was hopeful that the best news outlets would not be intimidated. However, less than a year into his second term, I have been disheartened to see that two of the greatest papers—the *Washington Post* and the *Los Angeles Times*—have chosen to bend a knee.

Both billionaire owners of the *LA Times* and *Washington Post*, Dr. Patrick Soon-Shiong and Jeff Bezos, have clearly decided to kiss Trump's butt, just as some world leaders who were forced into tariff negotiations in April 2025 did. Both the *Washington Post* and *LA Times* pulled their endorsements of Kamala Harris only days before they would have been published. While their general news reporting has continued to be strong, their editorial pages have been undermined.

The *New York Times* has stayed fiercely independent, and the Associated Press has continued its role as a definitive, unbiased source of national, international, political, and state coverage. The *Wall Street Journal* continues to provide strong news coverage.

Various other outlets—such as CBS's *60 Minutes*—have come under intense fire from Trump lawsuits. On April 22, 2025, the executive producer of *60 Minutes*, Bill Owens, stepped down after nearly four decades with CBS News because of corporate interference. Owens wrote, "Over the past months, it has also become clear that I would not be allowed to run the show as I have always run it. To make independent decisions based on what was right for *60 Minutes*, right for the audience." This coincides with a moment when Trump is suing CBS for $20 billion dollars.

It has become clear that many billionaire owners are not using their wealth to protect independent journalists.

There is no way to predict what Trump's second presidency will mean for the White House press corps, but the administration's attempts to assert control over who is included in the press pool has already had a significant impact on free and fair reporting being done within the White House. Punishing reporters for coverage the White House does not like is simply reprehensible.

It's crucial for the press corps to remain fiercely independent and provide the nation with truth it deserves. The press is not the enemy of the people as Trump accuses it of being. It's also an important era for reporters to assist one another. One never knows who will be the next reporter banned from Trump's press conferences, so it's critical that reporters support one another against a tyrant who has chosen to seek a war with truth. An example of how this can happen is reporters yielding their own time during press conferences to allow fellow journalists to follow up when Trump evades or belittles important questions.

The best exemplar I can think of is Maggie Haberman of the *New York Times*. I believe she is one of the strongest journalists reporting on Trump at the moment, and I hope more will follow her lead, rise to her level, and support other fearless reporters as much as they can.

In my opinion, the press should cover President Trump's next four years much as they covered him during the campaign, with one major change. Every effort should be made to fact-check presidential statements *immediately*. As soon as a media organization can determine that a statement is false, it should be reported.

Sadly, too many news organizations are in very difficult financial condition, which threatens their capability to report independently. This is especially true in small and medium-sized markets where newspapers have been downsizing or disappearing in recent years as print subscriptions and print advertising have shifted to digital media, especially to the internet. It will be difficult for weakened news organizations to stand up to the awesome power of the Trump administration. Readers and viewers must also choose sources that are known to be devoted to accuracy and actively support these organizations. News is not supposed to be entertainment.

As Richard Tofel wrote on November 2, 2024, in his Substack newsletter *Second Rough Draft*:

> The press itself, despite the anguished hand-wringing of some, did a generally decent job of describing both the stakes and the odds. This time, everyone knew he might win, and what many worry it may ultimately cost us, and he won anyway.
>
> THE TASKS AHEAD
>
> Now the press must do three things, and must do them with determination and skill if we are to give this Republic its best chance to endure.
>
> First, it must continue to do its workaday job of reporting the news, of holding power to account, of describing the changes that are being made and proposed. Most of all it must do this work with restraint and proportion, not saying the sky is falling when the winner of an election fairly won is making choices he is entitled to make.
>
> But at the same time, it must prepare to defend the Constitution that makes its existence as the world's freest and most powerful press possible. Until and unless that Constitution is threatened, it must not claim that it is. But if such a threat eventuates, through extralegal means or a perversion of the law itself, it must step up. I fear that may occur in the next two years (before the voters can weigh in again). If it does, the press must fight, if necessary to the point of being silenced, with a courage, even a physical courage, that it has rarely had to muster in this heretofore blessed country.
>
> In 2017, Marty Baron, then the editor of the *Washington Post*, famously said, "We're not at war; we're at work." This time, we must be at work, but also preparing, if an errant leader chooses so, to be at war.
>
> Finally, the press must display judgment and discernment about the difference between the first two tasks, between what may be merely unwise or even dangerous, noxious or offensive, and that which would threaten our fundamental liberties. Reckless foreign policies, unwise tax legislation, and duly confirmed appointments are firmly in the category of "elections have consequences." Imposing martial law, suspending the Constitution, subordinating the prosecutorial power of the Justice Department to the personal whim of the president, and giving illegal orders to the military are not. They are beyond what the people have

placed in Donald Trump's gift. And those things are true no matter what the Supreme Court holds—judicial supremacy was not the framers' plan. Discerning and drawing this line will require steely prudence and calm determination.

....

OUR JOB NOW

It will be critical, in the days ahead, for the press to look this situation hard in the face. And it will be tempting not to do so, to look away, to find other explanations, from political tactics to surface phenomena to unworthy prejudices. The temptation will be especially great because most journalists are among the winners of the past forty-plus years, among the people against whom the rebellion has been mounted. It was during this same period that journalism went from a working-class to a middle-class profession, that it came to be dominated by people with elite education, that it came in some very important respects (gender and race) to look more like America while in others to look like it far less.

It has been a bitter and disappointing week for me, and I know for many of you as well. Now we have big things to do, with the stakes higher than they ever have been for things we hold dear, perhaps including our very freedom to pursue our craft. Lick your wounds if you must, but indulge in that for just a moment. There is work ahead, maybe the most important of our lives.

CHAPTER 21

JOURNALISM'S DEVASTATING CHANGES

We need the watchdogs.

Domestically, the most important role played by the press is that of watchdog keeping our leaders and our institutions in check. But the institution of the press itself has gone through devastating changes in recent years that threaten its abilities to serve as the major public protector that society needs it to be. These changes have weakened the press as well as undermined the public trust in it. Some of it is the fault of the press, and some of it is not.

For most of American history, newspapers and newspaper reporters have covered city hall, state government, Congress, the courts, and the White House. They have worked to keep America well informed about domestic issues as well as foreign. While I was lucky enough to participate in the "golden age" of journalism, I feel that I am now watching the demise of high-quality news at nearly every level. Even the most prominent organizations, such as the *Washington Post* and *Los Angeles Times,* are losing great journalists at a significant clip, for reasons that are regularly attributed to disappointment with their billionaire ownership.

During my years as a publisher, wealthy families and individuals such as the Chandlers owned news organizations, yes, but there was a collective desire across the nation for good information that newspapers genuinely tried to deliver. So many critical moments depended on it, from coverage of Vietnam and civil rights down to local matters. The second half of the twentieth century was full of change, and journalists took their reporting seriously. Readers and advertisers, in response, showed their appreciation with their subscriptions and financial support. There was also no arguing about the fact that great newspapers produced essential information. If a story ran on the front page of the *New York Times*, there was no doubt that it was important news. If a truthful, yet damning, story ran on the front page of the *Washington Post*, it might mean the downfall of a president.

In his 2023 article "A Powerful Tool for Fighting Corruption Is Going Extinct," Serge Schmemann of the *New York Times* wrote, "Looking back at those papers isn't just the nostalgia of an old newspaperman. They were the building blocks of community, democracy, politics. Their loss is a major reason behind the acute polarization and political confusion we are suffering today."

In the same article, Schmemann quotes journalist and "news desert" expert Penelope Muse Abernathy's own sage wisdom: "Part of the beauty of having many reporters is they showed up at meetings. If there was a bond issue, they reported this is what it was going to cost. What happens is we end up paying more in taxes, there's more corruption, and nobody's minding the store."

In short, good journalists historically have done the necessary digging and "homework" that many Americans fail to do themselves—and that is okay; not everyone has time to be a reporter. However, now in 2025, we seem to have a society that not only wants to ignore their homework but has also lost interest in supporting journalists who are still doing their best to keep the public informed. In the worst instances, reporters have become political targets, as have librarians and schoolteachers. This is not the way that a democracy should function, and we cannot support leaders who turn a blind eye to violence, or who seek to silence great reporters.

It is not enough only to have law enforcement, internal auditors, medical review boards, government accounting offices, ethical standards committees, and audit committees. Most institutions only want to see the positive news written about them, and over time, many do fall victim to corruption or mismanagement. However natural the desire might be to seem like you're always doing a good job, exclusively positive coverage is propaganda, not news. This is where hard-hitting journalism comes in.

The existence of a vigilant, independent press serves as a different type of policeman on the block. Bad things—even if they're simply mistakes—often happen when nobody is watching.

Some ask: "What business is it of the press, anyway? It is not the press's business."

But it *is* the public's business, especially when it comes to our government and our public institutions. Sometimes the press is the best—or THE ONLY—representative of the public. Think of historic moments like Watergate, and the corruption of Richard Nixon. If it hadn't been for Bob Woodward and Carl Bernstein at the *Washington Post*, Nixon's cheating and lying would have never been exposed.

There is a deep irony in the fact that even with the decline of newspapers, the world today has more "information" available than at any time in history. But we need to be more proactive about asking ourselves, "What kind of information is it that we're consuming?" and why have we allowed information to become so construed as entertainment? The primary reason we send children to school is to learn, not to be entertained. The primary reason that adults work is to earn a living, not to have fun. Of course, productivity and happiness can overlap, but the point is that worthwhile endeavors generally take hard work. Making sure that we're informing ourselves with high-quality information is no different. Consuming accurate news responsibly is not always fun, nor does it always coincide with our politics; however, it's both a duty and a privilege. Not every person on this earth has high-quality journalism available, and like many things in life, we have taken its existence for granted.

I don't mean to imply that quality information can never be entertaining, but there must be distinction. For example, sports coverage continues to be very popular in both print and electronic media. The *New York Times* now derives huge readership from crossword puzzles, games, and recipes. I continue to love the Sunday comics in newspapers. It's not that fun and entertainment are inherently bad; it's only when entertaining an audience, amplifying a political agenda, and generating "clicks" become the main reasons that an outlet puts out material that it becomes destructive to our society.

Misinformation is not only rampant because it's designed to be provocative, but in the era of smartphones, it's now in our faces at nearly all hours of the day and night. Through all of our "smart" systems that track and analyze our preferences, the algorithms that shape digital life are able to target our most deeply rooted motives and insecurities. The sheer number of news "sources" adds even further issues: newspapers and cable TV no longer dominate the news cycle; social media has caused a great deal of confusion and reader burnout, and there are almost no regulations that protect consumers from downright lies. Technology is simply moving too fast, and our legislators too slowly.

"Deepfakes" are now rampant and have become so convincing that it's impossible for average consumers to know what is real and what is AI-generated. Prior to the 2024 presidential primaries, New Hampshire residents were spammed with calls featuring Joe Biden's supposed voice, telling them to skip voting in the primary. Similar instances have been influencing elections across the world. This problem will only grow unless and until the public is provided with a trusted way to easily know what is real and what is fake.

With big tech now coming out in full support of Donald Trump's second term, we can safely assume that the government is not going to protect us from these threats, so it's time that we decide to start protecting ourselves and our children. Screen time has become an epidemic of unthinkable proportions that has led in part to the nation's greatest mental health crisis in history, social division, political division, and so much more. No different from deciding to get clean from alcohol, crack, or any other addictive substance, we must decide that consuming all of our news and entertainment through our phones is a habit worth breaking. While print is not as significant as it once was, the information that's gathered and distributed by newsroom-quality reporters and editors remains vital to our society. I believe that we all have a stake in seeing that quality media have the resources to do this essential work.

The downfall of great journalism has a long history—much of which has taken place in our local communities—and it's not simply because readers and advertisers have abandoned print news for electronic/digital forms of distribution in record numbers. Over the past fifty years, media organizations have also participated in their own demise.

Sometimes because of financial hardship, other times because of greed, there has been mass consolidation of local news sources as chains like Gannett and Media News have purchased countless local newspapers across the country. Sinclair Broadcast Group has purchased nearly two hundred TV stations. These consolidations are dangerous because so many people trust their local stations at significantly higher levels than news coming from national outlets. What they may not know is that their local coverage is being dictated by a national owner, such as Sinclair, that often projects a political bias.

Much of the consolidation was driven by owners wanting to improve profitability, not to improve news and editorial quality. Many publishers reduced the size of their news staffs and the percentage of their news content. Overall, the consolidation of newspapers has been absolutely terrible for the industry and our nation.

Schmemann noted in the *New York Times* that from the start of the twentieth century to now, the United States went from roughly 24,000 daily and weekly papers down to about 6,000, and we continue to lose them at a rate of approximately two per week. As one may expect, the largest gaps in local news are in the poorest areas.

One of my hopes to bolster good reporting is that we will enhance public television and National Public Radio so that they can become even more indispensable than they already are. While they are not perfect, I would love for them to have increased public support so they can provide more quality news, documentaries, and long-form journalism such as *Frontline* and *NewsHour*, formerly anchored by Judy Woodruff.

I do not, however, support government funding to rescue our commercial media. Keeping the integrity of the U.S. news media on track is difficult because they must do it themselves, unlike other national news organizations such as the BBC—a wonderful service that maintains its independence despite reporting to a British government review board.

I only wish this BBC model would work for America, but I don't believe it can.

For the era that we're currently living in, I believe most in the foundation model.

For example, in St. Petersburg, Florida, the Poynter Institute owns and operates the *Tampa Bay Times* as an independent newspaper with the highest of standards. Their coverage of the Church of Scientology is an example of high-quality, independent journalism that shed light on something about which it was critical to get information to the public.

The model of a 501(c)(3) foundation owning a newspaper might be the answer in markets where the newspapers are now facing closure. However, it takes a very brave foundation to endure the wrath of local citizens—especially when coverage takes on local sacred cows. Unfortunately, even the largest foundations would have a hard time keeping the largest newsrooms afloat.

At 5 percent, a billion-dollar foundation could spin off fifty million dollars per year. That's an enormous sum, but it is still not enough to subsidize a *Los Angeles Times*–sized newsroom. Foundations could, however, be a tremendous backstop for smaller local news organizations.

In regard to policy options, I once championed the Fairness Doctrine, which required broadcast media outlets to prove that they provided public-service content with their broadcasts and that they offered political balance in their news shows. Until Ronald Reagan chose to abolish it, that doctrine once served the nation well, and I saw the benefits firsthand when I was in charge of completing the applications for FCC license renewal at the LBJ family media properties, KTBC-AM-FM-TV, in Austin. However, I no longer support those measures.

I fear that self-serving appointments to the FCC and FTC, much like what has occurred with the Supreme Court, will give corrupt presidents the control over the media results they want, instead of the results that our democracy needs.

Another worthwhile consideration is the formation of independent boards to monitor news organizations, such as the one that exists at the *Wall Street Journal*. That independent board was established as a condition by the prior owners before they would sell the *Journal* to Rupert Murdoch in 2007. It was a contractual requirement to ensure that the *Journal* would be able to keep its journalistic integrity, and I believe it has had a genuine impact. Some very well respected people in the news business have sat on that board. The *Journal*, unlike

Tom with the *Washington Post*'s publisher, Katharine Graham, and editor, Ben Bradlee.

Murdoch's Fox News, continues to produce high-quality journalism to this day.

While different ideas may work for different media corporations, there is not one silver bullet that can return print media to its former glory. There are, however, a number of lessons from my fifty-year career that I believe are worth sharing as we all navigate the future of news and information.

My suggestions below are not meant to favor any political narrative; they are only meant to support an environment that favors the discovery of truth. I speak as a former news executive who made a living helping to discern fact from fiction, and as someone who learned a great deal of important lessons throughout my career.

The one rule that applies to everyone involved—those who consume the news, those who report the news, and those who own the news—is that the truth matters above all else. Get the facts right, and do it with integrity. The world will be a better place for it.

To Those Who Consume the News:

Gallup's "Confidence in U.S. Institutions" poll from July 5, 2022, showed that while 70 percent of Democrats "trust media," only 14 percent of Republicans and 27 percent of Independents reported feeling the same way. Over the past few years, I'm afraid that those numbers have dropped even further.

With good reason, some of you reading this book are angry with the press. But it's critical not to lose faith. If you continue to demand and support it, truthful news always will be available to you somewhere and in some form.

I am not saying that the major, "most reputable" outlets get the news right 100 percent of the time; they surely do not. But it's important to recognize the outlets that prioritize integrity through making corrections and are willing to report on issues even if they are unpopular with their viewers.

Online outlets are too focused on quantity, not quality. Clicks and views mean dollars, but this model does not lead to educated readers, or a well-informed society. I urge you to avoid these outlets, regardless of their convenience. It's important to remember that there's "no such thing as a free lunch." If information is free, it is not going to be high-quality journalism.

Newsmax, Breitbart, and other right-wing outlets have been cheerleaders for Trump's fabrications and his shouts of "fake news," and so many other harmful stories and conspiracy theories with no evidence. These stories are not truthful, but sadly they are compelling to large audiences.

On cable TV, Fox News seems to have influence among conservatives and others that is unlike anything I ever could have imagined. I even cannot convince many old friends and relatives to switch from Fox News to news outlets that include experts from both sides and who provide factual information. So many viewers have become addicted to Fox News, and it has become the dominant television news channel in ratings, well ahead of CNN and MSNBC. In my personal opinion, Fox News has almost become the propaganda arm of the Trump administration. It's so disappointing for me to see. However, Fox viewers are rightly entitled to believe that left-leaning news organizations are often "unfair" as well. At times, they certainly are. I do not advocate for partisan news of any type. News organizations should do their very best to be independent and nonpolitical.

It's unfortunate that many in mainstream media, including CNN, did not report more thoroughly on President Biden's deteriorating mental and physical condition leading up to the first 2024 presidential debate.

Former *New York Times* media reporter Ben Smith wrote about the January 6, 2021, attack on the Capitol: "There's only one multibillion-dollar media corporation that deliberately and aggressively propagated these untruths. That's the Fox Corporation, and its chairman, Rupert Murdoch; his feckless son Lachlan, who is nominally C.E.O.; and the chief legal officer Viet Dinh, a kind of regent who mostly runs the company day-to-day." (Viet resigned in 2023.)

The 2023 Dominion lawsuit brought against Fox has further exposed Fox's disregard for truth. Fox ended up paying Dominion

$787.5 million and acknowledged that it had broadcast false statements about Dominion. It's the largest known media settlement in U.S. history.

Even though the most powerful people at Fox News knew Trump had lost key states in the 2020 election, and that there was no evidence of fraud, Fox News lied to prevent losing viewers to other right-wing outlets. NPR reported that during Fox's lawsuit with Dominion, one of Dominion's lawyers suggested, "It's not red or blue, it is green." To which Murdoch agreed. To put it another way: Greed is what drives Murdoch's empire, not high-quality news.

After Trump's second inauguration in 2025, the true impact of these lies was realized. In his inaugural address, Trump referred to the January 6 offenders as "hostages." These were people who were responsible for destruction at the U.S. Capitol and the harm of officers standing in defense of our country, and many were convicted by a jury of their peers. After reshaping this history through countless lies, Trump pardoned more than fifteen hundred insurrectionists. Regardless of party, there is no excuse for this, and right-wing media, as well as spineless members of Congress, have a role to play in what happens as a result.

It's this type of agenda-driven rhetoric that is tearing our nation apart. Information shouldn't be solely about politics *or* money. Information should be about the facts and the truth.

Long-form journalism is another medium that society is losing. Perhaps people simply no longer have the attention for it, which is another result of our addiction to screens and social media. While long-form journalism is increasingly rare, it fortunately still exists at organizations like *ProPublica*, the *Atlantic*, and the *New Yorker*.

I encourage everyone to support these outlets, not only to keep them alive, but also for the sake of reader sanity. Sometimes it's important to engross yourself in a long-form piece that makes you think and feel, rather than listening to the talking heads or skimming your phone for fifty headlines, even if they may be well reported. Taking the time to read and learn is good for the mind, and it helps us connect with information rather than simply becoming anxious and over-inundated with depressing news. Information is only as worthwhile as our ability to digest and process it, and long-form journalism is a tremendous way to create the space that is so needed for responsible consumption. We also must leave space and time for action. The right to organize, protest, and express ourselves at the ballot box is critical. News is simply ink on a page if society doesn't do anything with it.

Fortunately, good journalism and good journalists still remain. But you need to look carefully, and support their efforts by paying a fair price for their work. Great journalism is not free, and you should not want it to be. Just as low salaries have discouraged countless people from pursuing other noble professions such as teaching, we must ensure that great minds not only want to be journalists but are paid a fair wage to do their job. It is the only way to ensure that those positions remain viable.

Consumers must ultimately remember that it takes hard work to be a discerning reader and watcher of news. It's important to read multiple sources, to consider dissenting (but informed) opinions, and to keep track of new projects that great journalists are helping to start.

To Those Who Report the News:

In my view, the only way that the world can counter fake news is with accurate news. One key to this fight is to train young journalists on the highest quality standards of journalism.

We need as many strong, highly educated reporters as possible. Leaders must see the importance of responsible media to society, especially to the future of democracy.

There are five things in particular that I would encourage young people interested in journalism to understand, and the old guard to never stray from.

ONE: Be fearlessly independent.

Tell the news how it should be told, rather than how anyone other than your editor expects you to tell it. This might not make you popular, but it will make you reputable.

Back when I was a sports reporter for the *Macon Telegraph*, the local coaches and players loved favorable coverage. They did not like to read anything unfavorable—even when it was accurate, especially if their team lost.

In those early years, I learned my very first and best rule of journalism from Sam Glassman, a crusty old sports editor: "Tommy, get it right—just get it right." That meant that I should be accurate about every aspect of what I was reporting, including the correct spelling of the quarterback's name.

Bill Ott, the editor of the *Telegraph*, taught me another rule of journalism: "The day you write a story to help a friend or to punish an enemy is the day you should quit."

Years later at the *Los Angeles Times* we had a splendid reporter, David Shaw, whose sole job was to report on the media, including on our own paper, and I believe that every news outlet should have their own version of Shaw. He wrote blistering articles about how the *Times* was doing a poor job reporting and covering topics such as the Los Angeles Police Department. He was an in-house ombudsperson, without that title—the most independent media writer I ever have known.

TWO: Local news is critically important.

Readers want to know what is happening in their hometowns, and local coverage should be returned to local journalists who want to report on what's best for their communities. It's terrible that original newsgathering by local organizations has been virtually obliterated in many cities, especially in smaller markets where local news is so badly needed. It's not that owning local news sources should be discouraged, but local media outlets should be journalistically independent. Our society is being seriously harmed by the disappearance of local voices, as well as financial squeezes on trusted organizations that supplement local news, such as the Associated Press.

But the AP cannot shoulder the entire burden of international reporting, and it cannot replace local news.

THREE: Respectful relations between media and officials are important.

I have always advocated for mutually respectful relations between journalists and members of the business community. Not cozy relationships. Professional relationships. I still do.

Reporters should get to know their sources to a point where, if possible, they can respect each other and trust each other. But reporters should *never* protect sources because they have become friends.

There is one approach that I use when mentoring young journalists—as well as my friends in business. The idea is not original to me but I have lived by it: "When you are trying to decide between right and wrong, ask yourself, 'How will my actions, taken in private, look when published on the front page of the newspaper that my mother reads?'"

FOUR: If you're considering working for an online news organization, choose carefully by knowing its reputation and selecting one that's still built on in-person reporting.

Good reporters work primarily in the field, not stuck in an office behind a video screen. If you truly want to *report* the news, then strive to work for an organization that provides you the resources to cover the news aggressively and independently.

FIVE: Some of you may have to decide between a career in media and one in government.

Many people think that "crossing over" from one side to another contaminates journalists by making them partisan forever, but many successful journalists have crossed over: Bill Moyers, David Gergen, George Stephanopoulos, Diane Sawyer, Herb Klein.

I saw my own time in government more as another professional role, rather than a political one.

Yes, LBJ was known to exaggerate, to embellish, and to spin. He once told the White House press corps during a trip that his grandfather died bravely in the Alamo, which of course was untrue. It also was a joke. We press officers should have corrected his statement immediately, and that's a mistake that I acknowledge to this day, even though I considered it pure humor. The unbelievable reality is that I still think back on that incident, and yet I wonder how many untruthful moments Trump's various press secretaries will remember into their eighties. Lying has become the new norm. "Alternative facts," we've been told they're called. If you break from this path, you will have great opportunities as a respected "truth teller" throughout your career.

I never knowingly told a lie to the press. I say that because I often am asked, especially by students: "Did YOU ever lie as a press officer?" Even though we—the LBJ administration—disliked the watchdog role of the press as much as many in government and in business dislike it at times, we respected them.

I do believe that I became a better editor, a better publisher, and a better head of a global news network because of my government experience. I learned to understand the inner workings of government, both the positive and negative aspects of it.

My time in government helped build my list of contacts, and made me comfortable dealing with very high-profile individuals.

But even though I never worked on a political campaign, critics of the *Dallas Times Herald*, the *Los Angeles Times*, and CNN watched me carefully for signs of partisanship.

Republicans and Democrats alike criticized coverage of Presidents George H. W. Bush, Bill Clinton, and George W. Bush by the media organizations I was leading at the time. But critical reporting is not the same as unfair reporting.

Based on my real-world experiences, I can empathize with the feelings of the press as well as those the press covers. I've earned my share of scars as a member of both sides, but the truth is the truth. Society is better off with honest information. There's a reason that corrupt leaders wage wars on truthful reporting—it is the bedrock of democracy.

To Those Who Own the News:

Now, as much as ever—the United States of America needs a strong, independent free press to stand watch over our democratic form of government.

Journalism, as many once knew it, is a profession in peril. So is our democracy. Around the globe, the threat is just as real.

The most important elements of running a great news organization are simple. Report news by supporting well-paid, competent reporters, who have the resources to gather original information from all over the world, and who are guided by unbiased editors. Equally important, do not tell reporters what to report, and do not let reporters include their personal opinions in their work. That is not their job. Opinion pieces should *only* be found in the editorial and op-ed pages.

Excellent newspapers require excellent newspaper staffs, but even the biggest papers are now cutting staff positions.

Across the country, thousands of journalists have been losing their jobs, and other highly respected journalists have simply chosen to resign from their posts. More and more of the "original information gatherers" are gone. They are losing their jobs because of the crushing decline in advertising and circulation. This economic squeeze makes reporters "too expensive."

As a former news executive, I assure you their value is priceless. The loss of these newsgatherers is the single greatest threat to an informed society.

So many great newspapers also had important international bureaus during my career that have since disappeared. At one point the *Baltimore Sun* had twelve of them. ABC, CBS, and NBC—the Big Three networks—all had terrific foreign bureaus. We must work to bring them back, even if it's done in a modern way. It's true that in the era of camera-phones, we can get footage from so many people in so many places, but it's also important to know and trust your sources.

Without vetted international correspondents, how can we learn of mass starvation, brutality, corruption in foreign governments, human rights abuses, nuclear threats, and more? Foreign correspondents are also critical for understanding how other nations are impacted by American actions, and how they perceive us as a nation. Good relations with allies and others abroad depend on us being able to understand one another through the sharing of information and human-interest stories.

It is my firmly held view that it is the owner of a media organization and his or her handpicked editors who determine the quality of journalism in their newspapers, magazines, television channels, radio stations, and other media properties. To that point, it's reasonable for readers to question if billionaires should own news media.

I once was hopeful that billionaire owners such as Jeff Bezos and Dr. Patrick Soon-Shiong, shielded by their immense wealth, would protect their reporters without hesitation and refrain from imposing their own bias on the news coverage that their papers produced, but that has not proved to be the case. Particularly during Trump's second ascent to the presidency, billionaire owners of nearly every major outlet have started to cater to him, either by refusing to endorse Kamala Harris as the only candidate who had not waged a war on journalists, reducing air time and column inches for outspoken Trump critics, or giving MAGA pundits a platform to tell lies as a means of seeming "fair." This is not good, well-balanced coverage, and it is up to editors, publishers, and owners to make responsible decisions.

When Jennifer Rubin, one of the *Washington Post*'s most recognized columnists, resigned in early 2025 to open a new media outlet, the *Contrarian*, she wrote the following: "We've watched as corporate and billionaire owners of media outlets abused their audiences' loyalty and undercut journalism's vital role in a free democracy. . . . Instead of safeguarding democratic values, they have enabled the gravest threats to democracy—Donald Trump and his allies—at the very time when a robust and independent press is most essential. We need an alternative, truly independent outlet that is unafraid of the administration and unwilling to equivocate or bend the knee."

The motto of the *Contrarian* is not insignificant: "Not Owned By Anybody."

Owners and shareholders must understand that accurate news is not a business whose sole purpose is to make money or build political clout. It's important to be financially strong, yes; but it's equally important to produce trusted, accurate news so that people can make their own decisions as part of a functioning democracy.

Some news outlets, such as Fox News, blatantly use their power to influence elections and public policy, advance personal agendas, and stifle competition. While this style of influence certainly has made certain owners vast amounts of money, it has also torn our world apart, subjecting the entire globe to ever increasing levels of misinformation, war, climate issues, and more. I fear now that even the "good" owners are doing it as well, simply in a less egregious way.

My question to an owner like Jeff Bezos at the *Washington Post*—who has an estimated net worth of roughly $250 billion and is expected to become one of the world's first trillionaires over the next decade—would be "Why not simply start a fund that protects the integrity and salary of every single reporter on your staff?" I cannot think of a more worthwhile contribution to society than protecting independent journalism.

Finally, owners must keep their eye on the future.

Regardless of how much money the companies made during the boom time of my career with Times Mirror and CNN, most media executives—myself included—did not do enough to seriously study the impending digital threats that were coming. As a result, we did not invest sufficiently in the future of new media technology. Times Mirror even turned down an opportunity to buy half of Turner Broadcasting and CNN for $300 million.

However, I witnessed smart investments in future technology when I served for nine years as a member of the AP board, which undertook various projects to modernize the AP.

The best news organizations and news owners understand that good journalism is a never-ending pursuit, not a destination. There must be genuine love for digging and telling the truth.

It's my wish that all journalistic outlets remind themselves of, and nurture, the sacred understanding they are meant to work for the truth, not for the pleasure of their audience. News that caters to readers' and viewers' "taste," rather than striving to give them the most accurate news possible, is a disservice to everyone. Honest news creates space for relevant discourse, and it's that discourse that makes our world a better, less divided place—even for the billionaires.

Without a free press and investigative journalism, terrible things inevitably happen. We need the watchdogs, and we must support the ones that are thoughtful, deliberate, and putting themselves on the line to produce great reporting every day. It is a public service, and journalists truly are the fourth pillar of our nation's democracy: *the fourth estate.*

The motto of the *Washington Post*, "Democracy Dies in Darkness," is the best of all the media slogans in this new world.

I will not sleep well if the few good watchdogs we have left disappear. Nor should you!

CHAPTER 22

SPARKLE

The right one

This chapter is a love note to the most wonderful lifetime partner a man could ever hope to find—Edwina Chastain Johnson.

Since we met at the University of Georgia in 1962, life with Edwina has been a never-ending adventure, full of love and support, though not without challenges.

Looking back at our wedding in 1963, I sometimes can't believe that I was able to persuade her to marry me. I don't know where I would be today if she had not.

First, let me explain why I nicknamed Edwina "Sparkle."

There was a Sunday newspaper comic strip that many of us old-timers may remember titled *Dick Tracy*. Sparkle Plenty was the beautiful, smart, hyperenergetic star with an indominable spirit.

Just like Sparkle Plenty, Edwina is the happiest, most positive person that I ever have known. Her mother, Woodlyn Chastain, was also one of the funniest people that I've ever met. Happiness runs in the Chastain family blood.

The joy that Edwina brings to my world has made the good times great for us and for our family, and the bad times manageable.

It's ironic that Edwina chose me as her husband, because my nature has always been far more serious than hers. I suppose we both understood how well we complement each other as a couple.

Professionally, Edwina played a larger role in my success than anyone would ever know. My mentors and colleagues absolutely loved

Edwina Chastain Johnson. Courtesy of Harry Langdon.

her, and so did their spouses. As beautiful as she is on the outside, she is even more beautiful on the inside. Edwina was never just a pretty face. Many of our greatest relationships were built because of her magnetic personality, and her wisdom helped us make the most important decisions of our lives.

Personally, Edwina's support cannot be overstated. She got me through my darkest days of depression, sometimes helping with a soft hand, other times with a very firm one. Had Edwina not forcefully demanded it of me—threatening to walk away—I would not have received the psychological support that saved my life. I respect her judgment enormously.

When I had regained my emotional balance, once again it was Edwina who encouraged me to speak publicly about my depression.

"Tom," she told me, "if you always try to keep your depression a secret, you will never be a free person."

Her guidance led me to the significant depression and addiction work with which we are involved actively here in Atlanta. Supporting Skyland Trail has become one of the most important causes of our lives. Working to help others provides me an extraordinary sense of purpose.

Edwina deserves so much credit for all of it.

Her strong support did not stop with my depression. Through the highs and lows, she has always managed our family with solid judgment.

Of course, Edwina can light up a room like no one else when there are highs to celebrate with friends and family, like the births of our wonderful granddaughters Brynn and Julene.

When times are bad, as they were when we both lost our parents, and when Edwina was battling her bone cancer, multiple myeloma, she has always been the steady captain, guiding our family through the storm.

We've been fortunate to call some of the most magnificent cities in America home, but one of the best things that ever happened to us was returning to Georgia, our birthplace, in 1990, while both of our mothers were still alive.

To this day, there is nothing better than breathing the clean Georgia air as we spend time together at our Lake Nottely home, or sit at a card table and enjoy playing the game of Rummikub with family and friends. Edwina regularly wins.

Edwina's close travel companion, and one of our most treasured friends in life, Mrs. Lyndon Johnson, has captured so many of Edwina's wonderful qualities over the years in letters to us that sing out in a way that only Lady Bird could write.

> Dear Edwina:
>
> You have been very much in my heart (even more than usual!) these past days. You were so dear to take in this avid traveler, and to make me feel so especially comfortable and at home. I enjoyed being with you enormously.
>
> Your lovely house emanates warmth, liveliness and a happy life full of work and satisfactions.
>
> Edwina, I am so in awe of your talents—running the house so efficiently and gracefully, in between taking a six-mile jogging stint, raising a growing family and having such fascinating guests as the three Chandlers, Phyllis George and Irving Stone for lunch. You make it all seem effortless, and I applaud, *applaud!*
>
> Thank you—very deeply felt indeed—for your welcome, your hospitality, and all your kindness.
>
> Thank you for being you.
>
> Love, Lady Bird

Even though Edwina's spirit is far too large for anyone, even Lady Bird, ever to capture in words, it's for those same reasons and more that I—along with Wyatt, Christa, our grandchildren, and a truly countless number of family and friends—love her so deeply.

So many phases of our lives simply would not have been possible without her, and she's never lost the positive balance that has gotten us through so many situations over the years. Even over the course of writing this book, she has humored me with her usual grace.

"I'll tell you what—I'm so ready for this book to be over," she told me one day. "I've never seen anyone so stressed. Either you'll like the book or you won't like the book, but stop stressing over it. I don't want to hear about it anymore!"

For more than sixty years, that's been our wonderful marriage: full of life and always looking forward to better days ahead.

Edwina, thank you for everything. You are the one who has made it all worthwhile.

All of my love,
Tommy

CHAPTER 23

LESSONS LIFE HAS TAUGHT ME

1. Do your *personal best* at all you undertake. Nobody can ask for more.
2. Work hard. It pays off. You will get out of life an amount roughly equal to what you put into it. Laziness does not work.
3. Do right. Integrity is so badly needed. When in doubt about "doing the right thing," ask yourself how your actions—taken in private—will look when published on the front page of the newspaper your parents, your children, or even your best friends read.
4. Praise works; criticism does not work.
5. Humility and selflessness work; arrogance and selfishness do not work.
6. Giving credit to others works; taking credit for others' work does not work.
7. Working together as a team works; being alone, a one-person band usually does not work. (There are major exceptions to this one: artists, writers, scientists, singers, musicians.)
8. Openness works; closed minds and closed meetings do not work.
9. Trust works; distrust does not work.
10. Loyalty works; disloyalty does not work.
11. Truth works; lying does not work.
12. Humor works, at times; silliness never works.
13. Excellence works; mediocrity never works for long.

14. Treat others the way you wish to be treated. Being mean or "tough" on others does not work.
15. Listen more. You never learn when you are talking.
16. Do not try to build yourself up by cutting down others.
17. Expect failures and defeats in life. But remember: "Life is 99 rounds." You can get yourself back up and go on to other rounds of success and happiness.
18. Do not define your self-worth solely by a job. A job can be taken away from you. If you have defined yourself solely by your job, what do you have left when it's taken away? (I was devastated when I was removed as publisher of the *Los Angeles Times* in 1989.)
19. Do not become a workaholic. Have fun. Develop hobbies outside of your career. Workaholics have an illness, an addiction. I know. I was one. We don't know what to do with ourselves when we are not working. "Do not work so hard at making a living that you do not have time to make a life!"
20. Take time for family and friends. At the end of life's way, they will mean more to you than fame, fortune, and titles.
21. Do not become blindly loyal to a company. Companies will not necessarily be loyal to you. But NEVER be disloyal to a company, a friend, a family member. Resign from the company before you become disloyal to it.
22. Always measure your "psychic income." It will mean more to you than your financial income. Ask yourself occasionally: "Am I happy?" If not, go do something that will make you happy. But do not resign from one company before you have identified a new opportunity. Being out of work without income is NOT a good move. Where practicable, stick with your current employment until you find a new job.
23. Have a dog. It will love you unconditionally. It will love you no matter what your wife, girlfriend, boyfriend, mother, father, lifetime partner, or any combination of the above thinks of you or does to you.

24. Make a list of exciting things you most want to do in life before you "check out" or before you get too old.
25. Take care of yourself. Always!
26. Believe in yourself. Always!
27. Never give up on your dreams. Never!
28. Don't marry the wrong spouse. It's tough enough living with the right one. I know. I have been married to the "right one" for more than sixty years. To marry or not is one of the biggest decisions you'll make. To have children is an even bigger decision. Your children always are your responsibility—all your life. You always will be their parent.
29. Do not neglect your inner self, the spiritual side of your life. By this, I do not mean solely religion.
30. Be generous to others. Stop thinking so much of yourself. Help others who need help.
31. Remember this quote, seen in a cemetery: "It isn't how you die, it's how you live. It isn't what you take from life, it's what you give."
32. Ruth Chris got it right with her words: Do what you love, and love what you do.
33. Never make any decision while you are angry (except a decision to cool down before making any other decision).
34. Be nice. Though it is nice to be important, it is more important to be nice.
35. Be thankful for your blessings, especially your family, your friends, and your health.
36. If you want to feel rich, just count the things you have that money can't buy (your family, your friends, your health, your reputation, your education, your good memories).
37. If sitting beside or talking with somebody you do not know, get a conversation going by saying, "Tell me about yourself," not "What do you do?"

Many of these "lessons" are original. Some are borrowed from quotes, expressions, and notes I have collected during the past sixty years. To the original authors, whose identities I have long ago forgotten, I give full credit and thanks.

CHAPTER 24

BEST PRACTICES FOR JOURNALISTS

1. Get it right! (My first editor at the *Macon Telegraph*, sports editor Sam Glassman)
2. Tell the truth. (Helen Thomas, UPI, on my first day as a White House press officer)
3. Demand excellence in yourself and those who work with you. (Otis Chandler, publisher of the *Los Angeles Times*)
4. Be fair! (Ted Turner)
5. Never compromise on your principles! Integrity is critically needed in all professions! (Bill Moyers)
6. Having two or more sources does not mean you have the truth. (Lesson of Cardinal Bernardin story, Operation Tailwind story, Richard Jewell/Olympic Park bomber story—all false)
7. Admit mistakes. Take responsibility! Publish the correction as visibly as the initial mistake, not in a corrections box on the bottom of page 3.
8. Never use your power as a journalist irresponsibly. The day you protect a family member or a friend from truthful reporting is the day you should resign. Be a watchdog, not an attack dog or a lap dog.

INDEX

Page numbers in italics refer to illustrations.